'*Darlingest*'

MILVERTON IN THE WAR

Colin & Lindsey,

Best wishes,

Elizabeth Leworthy

Front cover designed by Bev Blackmore. It includes a sample of Nellie Clemens' handwriting.

The silhouette photo of Milverton church was kindly provided by Lindsay Fortune.

The Milverton in the War logo was designed by Bev Blackmore for the exhibition in 2005, and re-used throughout.

The back cover, designed by Bev Blackmore, includes the photograph of Milverton's wartime fund raising target board. Photograph kindly provided by Nigel Woods.

'Darlingest'
Milverton in the War

Written by

Elizabeth McDowell

Jane Woodland

with contributions from the community

Edited by Chris Lent

Cover design and graphics by Bev Blackmore

Milverton Books

Copyright © Elizabeth McDowell 2016

First published in 2016 by Milverton Books, 5, Woodbarton, Milverton, Taunton, TA4 1LU
Contributions by Jane Woodland, and Julian Dakowski. Editor, Christ Lent
Cover and graphics © Bev Blackmore

The right of Elizabeth McDowell to be identified as the author of the work has been asserted herein in accordance with the Copyright, Designs and Patents Act 1988.

All rights reserved. This book is sold subject to the condition that it shall not, by way of trade or otherwise, be lent, resold, hired out or otherwise circulated without the publisher's prior consent in any form of binding or cover other than that in which it is published and without a similar condition including this condition being imposed on the subsequent purchaser.

British Library Cataloguing in Publication Data
A catalogue record for this book is available from the British Library

ISBN 978-0-9955169-0-8

Typeset by Amolibros, Milverton, Somerset
www.amolibros.com
This book production has been managed by Amolibros
Printed and bound by T J International Ltd, Padstow, Cornwall, UK

ABOUT THE AUTHOR

Elizabeth McDowell was born in Gloucester during the war. She was educated at Girls Grammar Schools in both Chichester and Winchester before moving to Surrey. She worked in advertising and PR before joining BBC Television where she had a long career during which time she gained an Open University Degree. On retirement she moved to Milverton and undertook voluntary work. With a keen interest in history she was unable to resist the temptation to research and reveal the story of Milverton in the war that lay behind Nellie Clemens' letters. Having done that she continues to research her Ulster and Scots family history.

CONTENTS

List of Illustrations	ix
Introduction	xiii
Timeline	xviii
Nellie Clemens	xxi
Helen Amy, née Clemens	xxiv
Acknowledgements	xviii

PART ONE

Milverton village in 1939	1
Nellie's Letters 1940	9
Nellie's letters 1941	53

PART TWO

1.	Preparing for the Worst	89
2.	Sup Up and Clear the Cellars – War Declared	96
3.	Defending Milverton – Home Guard	101
4.	Doing Your Bit – What did you do in the War, Granny?	109
5.	Military Invasion	126
6.	Gone to the Country – Evacuation	143
7.	Doubling Up – Education	160
8.	Raising a Laugh – Entertainment	178
9.	Feeding the Nation	188
10.	On the Fields	199

11.	Dig for Victory		210
12.	For Medicinal Purposes		217
13.	Waste Not Want Not		222
14.	Make Do and Mend		231
15.	Over Here – Just a Bit of Tin		240
16.	Party Today, Worry Tomorrow		261
17.	Silver Linings and Dark Clouds		268

APPENDICES

1.	In Memoriam	275
2.	Milverton's Civil Defence Volunteers	278
3.	The 2nd Battalion, The Middlesex Regiment – British Expeditionary Force (B.E.F.)	281
4.	3892 Qtr. Truck Company And The Battle Of The Bulge	288
5.	US Quartermaster Corps	300

Sources   305

List of people named by first mention   309

LIST OF ILLUSTRATIONS

1. Map of Milverton.   4
2. Telegram reached Muswell Hill 17.6.40.   9
3. Helen's letter. 'Sunday, Dear Daddy'…   31
4. Stirrup pump.   92
5. Emergency Powers, *Somerset Gazette*, 1941.   110
6. *Daily Express*, 26th June, 1942.   115
7. 8th Corps Exercise, showing Milverton in relation to Sidi Barani (Watchet) on the Egyptian coast. National Archives.   137
8. 'Operation Instructions 1, for 4th Bn Green Howards, 8th Corps exercise.   138
9. *Somerset Gazette* 15th June, 1940.   147
10. *Somerset Gazette*, 1st November, 1941.   156
11. 'Milverton, Free film show', *Somerset Gazette*, 18th October, 1941.   182
12. *Daily Mirror*, 4th September, 1939.   183
13. Mrs. Vickery's bill for supplying food and laundry   189
14. Food Facts.   193
15. *Daily Mail*, 3rd August, 1944.   206
16. 'Victory diggers', *Sunday Times*, 28th September, 1943.   212
17 – 'Grow beans', *Reynolds News*, 12th April, 1942.   214
18. 'Thank you.' *Daily Express*, 13th August, 1940.   223
19. This is Nellie's receipt, with her initials, 'MRC' at the top.   227
20. Spitfire Nine times repaired.   229
21. Sun Suit, *Sunday Sun*, 23rd July, 1944.   235

22. Utility mark. 238
23. Map of Furnes, showing position of 'C' Coy. 286

Facing page 96

1. Nellie Clemens.
2. Nellie with her daughter Helen, in the garden at April Cottage.
3. Wilfred Clemens wearing his ARP uniform (family archive).
4. Mr. and Mrs. William Deacon.
5. Cardscroft, second house, next to white house. Home of Mr. and Mrs. Deacon.
6. Mrs. Vickery.
7. Miss Gertrude Vickery in the garden of April Cottage.
8. Captain Eric Muffett of the 86th Light AA Regiment. Miss Vickery's friend.
9. Sand Street, with April Cottage, three doors from right – with three windows. Milverton Stores in shadow at top left-hand side.
10. The Lodge, the home of Mrs. Bedford, where Nellie and Helen and Miss Rattenbury stayed before moving to April Cottage.
11. Milverton Home Guard photographed at Milverton School.
12. Soldiers of the Pioneer 1942-44 in charge of the QF decoy at Luckham Farm, Milverton.
13. Thomas and Daisy Ling on their wedding day, married 23rd September, 1939.
14. Ted became a truck driver supplying ammunition and petrol to the RAF. His story is told in 'Military Invasion'.
15. Ted Perry joined the RAF after a short spell in the ARP.
16. Evacuees – the Watkiss family, with back row, Mr. Watkiss, their father, a sub-conductor with R.O.A.C. (Royal Army Ordnance Corps) next to Bruce. Front row – Robin, Jean, Audrey and Shirley. They are mentioned in 'Gone to the Country'.

Colour photographs facing page 160

17. Brendons in North Street, where the WI made their jam and preserved fruit.
18. Poster.
19. Milverton's War Funds Board, found in cellar of Carlton House now in Milverton Archives.
20. Poster designed by Bruce Watkiss when an evacuee schoolboy, redrawn from memory as an adult.
21. Mural above fireplace in St. Michael's Rooms.
22. Dog Tag found by Julian Dakowski.
23. Selene and Shona Withers holding the photographs of Vincent Tuminello they had taken to Milverton School, without realising the significance or what his story would reveal. They are sitting on the gate to Doltons Field, where many of the American soldiers lived in tents.
24. Menu for a Thanksgiving meal given to people in Milverton.
25. Victory certificate given to Erica Tucker when she was a schoolgirl.
26. Photograph taken at the Victoria Rooms, after the 'Telling the Story of Milverton in the War' event as part of the 60th Anniversary of VE Day, in 2005.

Facing page 224

27. Milverton School pre-1914.
28. The actress Eleanor Summerfield. Her parents took over The Globe during the war whilst Eleanor worked at Hestercombe and at the Norton Fitzwarren supply Depot.
29. Milverton Stores in 1930s.
30. Beattie and Lionel Hayes on their wedding day.
31. Amy McGrath, neé Mason. She was a Land Girl at Cormiston in Preston Bowyer.
32. Olive Yesford, Land Girl, (mother of Jacqye Keates) worked at Preston

Darlingest

Farm from 1945 and was billeted with Mrs. Mearn, Preston Bowyer. Before her demob, she asked to return to Somerset as she had met Hubert Cornish – the man she was to marry. She remained in the area.

33. Barbara Williams was a Land Girl who worked with Amy Mason at Cormiston. Here, she relaxes on newly cut hay.
34. Private First Class John Kiacz Jnr.
35. PFC John Kiacz Jnr. With truck somewhere in Germany.
36. John Kiacz, 2nd row, middle with his group from 3892 Qtr. Truck company in Germany.
37. Mrs. Stone with her daughter, Shirley, wearing her 'Victory' dress.
38. Corporal Vincent 'Jim' Tuminello in photograph sent to Mrs. Stone.
39. Writing on back of photograph above. He wrote this caption when back in US but date is wrong.
40. Vincent Tuminello in jeep.
41. Writing on back of photo sent to Mrs. Stone in 1945.
42. Milverton Station.

INTRODUCTION

Sometime in 2003, a neighbour of Helen Amy, delivered to friends in Milverton, type-written extracts of letters written by Helen's mother, an evacuated teacher – Nellie Clemens. The letters, written daily to her husband – who remained in London – described life in Milverton from June 1940 to December 1941, when she was recalled to London. Nellie was an avid writer, using any piece of paper, she could find at a time when paper was in short supply. Her original letters are held at the Imperial War Museum, where they have been expensively and painstakingly bound into three large red-leatherette volumes – every letter, every envelope (often re-used), and – real jewels for me as a researcher – the receipts and other letters she used as scraps of paper to continue the story of Milverton life unfolding around her.

Helen had hoped that the letters might be published, having been passed around various people, Geoffrey Godbert saw their potential and passed them to me. What a joy and treasure they were!

'Rare' is how they are described by the archivists at the Imperial War Museum: an intimate sharing of thoughts and feelings intended for one reader. The letters are an historical resource more valuable than even diaries, which are sometimes written to be read by others. Many books films and TV programmes document the often harrowing experiences of people continuing everyday life in towns and cities during World War Two. But here was a tale about one village tucked away in sleepy Somerset too good to ignore. I set about researching the stories behind Nellie's letters and to see how the war impacted on a small village, having to host evacuees and soldiers, and what it did for the war effort.

Darlingest

In 2005, the 60th Anniversary of VE Day was looming and the Home Front Recall campaign supported by the Big Lottery and the Heritage Fund wished to involve local communities in the celebrations and at the same time the BBC through its People's War campaign urged the population to collect as many memories as it could. Here was a chance to reveal Milverton's role in the war to the people living there today before the wartime generation disappeared altogether. With the help of my dear friend Bridget Goldsmith, then chair of the Milverton and Fitzhead Society, we applied for and were awarded a grant of £3,000 – the society agreeing to be our umbrella for this project.

Until a few years ago, the May Day Street Fair was the highlight of a two week festival, for which all the village societies organised events to be enjoyed by the village and visitors. Our plan was to draw together the efforts of these different societies to give their events a wartime theme for which they would benefit from the grant money. Bev and Shelagh Blackmore went to the London Library to listen to old BBC recordings of *Workers Playtime* from which they devised a script for Milverton's own *Workers Playtime*. The audience came in a variety of work clothes; ate a wartime meal and laughed themselves silly with the cavorting of the Milverton Amateur Dramatic Society. There was a WW2 Poetry and Prose evening; a 'Dig for Victory' talk organised by the then Horticultural Society, and a dance, with some wearing WW2 uniforms featuring a band organised by Bob Hutchins. The Milverton and Fitzhead Society presented an illustrated talk from David Hunt, an expert on the Taunton Stop Line – the region's main defence against German invasion. The Twinning Association together with the committee of the Victoria Rooms screened the film *In Which We Serve*. 'Sgt' Chris Greenhow meanwhile organised a presentation at the Victoria Rooms on 'Telling the Story of Milverton in the War' which featured contributions and memories from former Land Girl Amy McGrath, Helen Amy herself, reading some extracts of her mother's letters, and Bruce Watkiss, a former evacuee. The then head of Milverton School, Mrs. Jill Gray, read from the School logs and Lavinia Davis, read an account of her mother's experiences as

Deputy Billeting Officer from transcripts of the interview with her we recorded before her death. Col. Tony McMahon related the experiences of the soldiers billeted in the village. And, of course, not to be side lined – the WI thespians performed dramatized versions of a few of their wartime meetings – to huge acclaim.

All these events were wrapped around a two-day exhibition in the then St. Michael's Rooms. A large team of Milverton folk had, over months, recorded interviews with those who had lived here during the war, and had researched a wide range of archive material, records and logs. The call had gone out to find artefacts to display. Bev Blackmore devised the graphics for the exhibition, including the logo featured on the cover of this book. He, Lindsay Fortune and Chris Mann, all turned up early on the Saturday morning of 7th May with Stanley knives, staplers and other equipment to help me put up the display, whilst others set about displaying the artefacts. An amazing amount of material came out of suitcases, from attics and under the stairs; and although organiser Jane Brett had made lists of what we had been promised, needless to say items turned up on the day.

But the most important of Milverton's artefacts was discovered not in an attic, but in the cellar of Carlton House, the home of Mike and Jane Brett. Here was found the major part of a painted billboard used to encourage people to donate to whatever was the Government's current Savings drive – War Weapons Week or Save for a Spitfire. This board, now in Milverton Archives, is reprinted on the back cover. We don't know who painted it, but the broken tree in the centre clearly recalls memories of the devastation of World War One.

Very early on, Bill Horner – a senior Archivist in Exeter, had lent me 69 facsimile wartime newspapers. As historians know all too well, it is not just the story you are looking for, but what is printed around it – whether it be an advertisement or a little comment tucked away – that can trigger a 'eureka!' moment. Here was the *Daily Express* front page picture of local man, Michael Wight-Boycott's success in the early hours of 17/18th January, 1943, when he downed three enemy aircraft and attacked another. In another newspaper, describing the North African campaign in Tunisia, a small item mentioned that a legless airman had been captured – Douglas Bader. Some of these articles were on display at the exhibition relating to the experiences of soldiers past and present who had at some point been here in Milverton.

On the day of the 2005 Street Fair, Emma and Russell Jenkins put on a display of wartime advertisements in Milverton Stores alongside products still available today and set out a week's rations on a table outside. The reality of rationing hit Emma, at 4 p.m. when she had to dispose of the butter, cheese and bacon that had been on display – one person's ration for an entire week!

Coincidence came to play a part in finding those who had memories of their time in the village. Over the years former evacuees had turned up revisiting their childhood home and made themselves known to local people or left their addresses in the church visitors' book. I made contact and asked them to note down their memories. Some villagers already had letters form former evacuees and passed them to me. In the Post Office I overheard a couple of visitors asking Keith Gibbons for directions to the farm where their neighbour, Barbara Williams, had been a Land Girl. Barbara had died by the time of the exhibition but her daughter had given me the name of the other Land Girl she had worked with, Amy Mason. Then, a friend of Lavinia Davis mentioned a talk given at her Hampshire WI by Amy McGrath, another Land Girl. McGrath and Mason turned out to be one and the same.

It was truly a community affair and the Festival and Exhibition were both so successful that I was asked to produce a book. This is the result. I have reproduced all the extracts of Nellie's Clemens' letters as originally delivered to the village in 2003 alongside a fuller story, as told by those who lived in Milverton during the war. I won't have everything right and sorting out the chronology of the recorded testimony of interviewees well into their 80s, has not been easy. Milverton is no different than other rural villages, all of which have their own stories. We are fortunate that Nellie Clemens arrived here, observed and told her tale.

Publication was originally planned to celebrate the 70th Anniversary of VE Day, in 2015. Through reasons beyond my control that got put back. The delay has resulted in a more powerful story. During the late summer of 2015 whilst pursuing his archaeological hobby, Julian Dakowski, discovered an artefact which has revealed Milverton's role in one of the most important military enterprises ever undertaken – D-Day.

TIMELINE

January 1933	Hitler becomes Chancellor of Germany	
September 1938	Munich Agreement	
March 1939	Czechoslovakia annexed by Hitler	Civil Defence in place
1st September 1939	Invasion of Poland	
3rd September 1939	War Declared	National Registration – Identity Cards
September 1939	BEF sent to France to defend Maginot Line	
	Phoney War	Food rationing commenced January
9th April 1940	Hitler invades Denmark and Norway	
10th May	Hitler invades Holland and Belgium	LDV (Home Guard) started to recruit and train

27th May – 4th June 1940	Operation Dynamo – evacuation from Dunkirk	Capt. Bazalgette and C Coy 2nd Bn Middx Regiment evacuate 1st June
16/17th June	Operation Pied Piper	Nellie arrives in Milverton
Summer 1940	8th Corps set up-Pyrland/Hestercombe	'C' Coy 2nd Bn Middx arrive
December 1941		Nellie Clemens returns to London
16th January, 1941		2nd Bn Middlesex Regiment leave Milverton
3rd February 1941		'C' Coy 2nd Bn the Cheshires arrive Milverton
7th December, 1941	Japanese bomb Pearl harbour	US declare war the next day
Spring 1942	North African Campaign	
11th November 1942	Battle of El Alamein	
Early 1942	1st US troops arrive	

Darlingest

23rd October 1943	8392 Truck arrives	John Kiazc and Vincent Tuminello arrive
6th June, 1944	D-Day	John and Vincent arrive on Omaha Beach
9th June 1944		Ted Perry arrives on Gold Beach
16th December 1944	Battle of the Bulge	
8th May, 1945	VE Day	

MRS. NELLIE CLEMENS and 'Darlingest' WILFRED CLEMENS

NELLIE BROWNLESS was born on 14th July, 1907 in Liverpool. Her father died young leaving her mother to bring up four daughters on her own. Life was a struggle and a great contrast to that of her future husband. However her mother, who was a teacher, made sure that all four of her girls had a good education – two of them became nurses and one became a personal secretary with a large company in Liverpool.

Nellie attended a teacher training college in Darlington. She was an accomplished painter, and we still have some of her watercolours in the family.

She met Wilfred Clemens – born in Redruth, Cornwall in 1902 – whilst on holiday in Newquay staying with her mother's friend.

He had been educated at what was then a new County School. In his last year, studied electricity and magnetism and machine drawing, considering a career in the Cable and Wireless Service, but had to abandon that idea because of poor sight. In the end he did his training in 1919 as an Articled Clerk with a company in based both in St. Ives and Penzance – completing his articles in 1925. He then worked as an Accountant in Newquay.

Nellie and he were married at St Barnabas Church in Liverpool on Wednesday, 6th September, 1933. The bride was given away by her mother and the bridegroom's father played organ music which he had composed.

They set up home in their own house and even a car and their daughter, Helen was born in 1934. But late that year everything changed due to Wilfred's bad health. Life was tough from then on, and they moved temporarily to live with his parents in Redruth, and then to Nellie's family in Liverpool. In 1937 the family went to London to find work where Wilfred found employment with a Trust company. That failed after a few months, and he ended up working for the Receiver and from there became cashier for a firm of solicitors until 1939 when he became a full time Air Raid Warden.

Nellie was teaching at Noel Park School at Wood Green, and then applied for war work but in June 1940 found herself in charge of escorting children from North Harringay School to Milverton and her letters begin.

Meanwhile, in 1941, Wilfred, was appointed Chief Clerk in the Wood Green Main Report and Control Centre, remaining with the Civil Defence Service until December 1945 as an Operations Officer, as well as acting as training organiser, assistant ARP officer, Acting ARP officer and then Deputy controller during which time he attended many Civil defence training sessions.

In 1946 Wilfred was back in his old profession as senior audit clerk as a firm of chartered accounts in the city of London, where he remained for many years.

Nellie mentioned in her last letters that she did not know to which school she would be returning. She worked on a supply basis at several schools in Wood Green, and eventually went back to teaching at Rhodes Avenue where her daughters had been.

The family attended a Methodist church in London, though Nellie does mention going to St. Michael's Anglican church in Milverton on occasions.

Nellie died young in 1965 and Wilfred carried on alone, with both daughters living overseas. Shortly after the war Wilfred took up genealogy and pursued his interest in politics becoming speaker of the Muswell Hill parliament. Sadly his eyesight deteriorated and after a fall in the early 80s when he broke his hip he went into a home, where his health improved and he was comforted with his radio, his tape-recorder, 'talking books' and many visitors. He died in 1991.

Linda Yerrill

HELEN AMY – Née CLEMENS

HELEN ROSAMUNDE CLEMENS was born in Newquay on 3rd June 1934. Her first three years were spent at Redruth in Cornwall, in Liverpool near her mother's family before finally settling in London in 1937. By August 1939, even before the war began, her grandparents holidaying in London, took her back to Redruth away from possible air raids. It was the time of 'the phoney war' and by Christmas she was back in the family home at Muswell Hill, North London, where later she started school at Rhodes Avenue School. As the war situation deteriorated she was evacuated to an aunt in Kent but, after the fall of the Netherlands and Belgium in April and May 1940, it was considered too dangerous and she returned home to London. A few weeks later she was evacuated to Milverton as part of 'Operation Pied Piper' the government organised mass evacuation of children from London.

Helen spoke of her memories of Milverton and her progress and activities are well documented in her mother's letters, which formed part of the basis of Milverton at War in 2005. Helen found the letters randomly bagged up by her father, she retyped them, fitted them together, few were dated, usually something like 'Sunday evening'. They were often written on the backs of bills or miscellaneous paper, writing paper being in short supply. She teased out the pure gold from this ore and wove a golden story. The letters are deposited in the Imperial War Museum archives who gladly accepted them as interesting examples of an adult evacuee's life. Most remaining letters were from children.

She joined the Brownies in 1941 and used to go to meetings after-school. About that time she was taught in the Old Cricket Pavilion and she remembered being disappointed when her teacher, Miss Morris, left to join the ATS. Too cold in winter, her school moved to the Methodist Chapel Rooms where she was taught by Miss Mills. It was there that her bad eyesight was discovered as, being asked to read the time, she could not even see the clock, although she could read perfectly well, and had been an avid reader. With her new spectacles she was able to see things as they really were, and remembers the thrill of reading the names of shops across the road for the first time.

Her mother, Nellie, returned to London around Christmas 1941, Linda, Helen's sister was born in 1942. Helen remained in Milverton for six months or so with evacuee hosts, the Vickerys, for safety. Her mother and sister visited when they could. Back in London, Helen remembered having to do sums while in the air raid shelter in the basement while other children played until the all clear. When the V1s, known as buzz bombs became a serious threat they returned to Milverton but by then Mrs Vickery was looking after a badly injured son, Nellie and her girls went to Liverpool, though they might by then have been safer back in London. Even with her early education being so badly interrupted, Helen, nevertheless passed her 11+ in 1945 and went Minchenden Grammar School in Southgate.

Helen greatly enjoyed Sunday School, and was a keen Brownie achieving her First Class badge before she was 10. Later on she was a Kingfisher in the 4th Muswell Hill, Girl Guides, becoming a Queen's Guide. Later in the 1950s, she became a Sea Ranger, and then Captain of the 4th Muswell Hill, Girl Guides (the 4TH MHGG) until she married in 1956 and moved away.

Throughout her childhood the family revisited Milverton and Helen remembers holidays where she would help out on the Post Office manual telephone exchange.

Until about 16 she had intended to take up nursing but, having passed her Matric, decided to be a librarian, no doubt because she helped at Muswell Hill Library on Saturday mornings. She chose French, Spanish and English as her A level subjects which led in 1952 to her being awarded a State scholarship to Bedford's College London to study English. However, at the same time she heard that she had come second in the whole country in a Foreign Office exam. Despite the wishes of her parents, particularly her father, she did not take up the scholarship, but joined the Foreign Office in 1952 and worked in London. In late 1953, she met Dennis Amy, who had just completed his National Service in the Royal Marines and was returning to the Foreign Office. They were married at Easter 1956. Under the rules of that time, the Foreign Office did not employ married women, so Helen had to resign her post and took a part-time job with British Road Services. They stayed in London for two years where their son, Robin, was born in October 1957. Their first overseas posting was to the British Embassy in Athens in 1958, where their daughter Bryony was born. Moscow was next, 1961 to 64, during heightened tension between the Soviet Union and the West, the Cuban missile crisis, and especially with the UK, the espionage trial of Greville Wynne. More happily the signing of the Nuclear Test Ban Treaty.

Returning from Moscow, Dennis worked in the Foreign Office before moving to the High Commission in Canberra, Australia in 1966, followed by the Deputy High Commission in Ibadan in Nigeria in 1971. They then had a spell serving at home until 1978, before going to the Embassy in Santiago, Chile, where they lived throughout the Falklands war. The Chileans were particularly well disposed towards the British. They were charged with the task of restoring diplomatic relations at ambassadorial level, which they achieved after several months, returning in 1983 to work in London again. In 1986 they moved to France, where her husband became HM Consul General in Bordeaux. Their final posting in 1990, was as HM Ambassador to Madagascar. Dennis retired in 1992.

As with some other professions, the wife's role was an important part of the "package" and Helen always played a full part in their diplomatic life, a career which she had sought herself. She was always there to advise and be part of the decision-making process. She was able to help in many aspects of work, welcoming, representing the UK, influencing local people, particularly women, building up networks, entertaining giving advice on and getting involved in the aid programme as well is much local welfare work. She was able to find the best targets for Aid Programme projects, to follow them up to ensure they were effective and the money properly spent. But she also took part in private welfare work. In Chile for example, she worked closely with Salvation Army, as well as the Girl Guides, (she was a local Guide Captain) and an orphan village. She also did much the local welfare work in Nigeria and Madagascar. She spoke good Spanish and French which was of great benefit, particularly in Chile, France Madagascar.

Sadly, Helen died in June 2005. She had an inherited kidney disease. She had a kidney transplant from her sister, Linda, which probably prolonged her life by 10 years. But, she lived long enough to visit the Milverton in the War Exhibition celebrating the 60th anniversary of VE Day in 2005, when she was able to take part in an evening of memories held in the Victoria Rooms where her mother taught. It was her last hurrah and there is nowhere else she would rather have made it than her beloved Milverton.

Dennis Amy

ACKNOWLEDGEMENTS

Where do I start? This is a community book and the community has contributed in so many ways. Starting with research for the exhibition in 2005 I owe my thanks to

Geoffrey Godbert, Jenny Fry, the late David Adam, Lavinia Davis who recorded interviews; David Hawkings, and Joan Killip helped me to write notes from School logs and WI Minutes. Shirley Adam and Chris Greenhow collected memories from former evacuees and those who had lived here during the war as did the late Shelagh Blackmore. Mike and Jane Brett, Andrew and Mary Chalmers, Bob and Yvonne Hutchins, Lorna and Lindsay Fortune, Chris and Jane Greenhow helped organise the display artefacts as did Chris Mann. Tony McMahon took away a copy of a hand-drawn map I had discovered in the National Archives, and deciphered it as being a major military exercise on Exmoor for the North African Campaign. It is included in this book, along with the narrative found some weeks later in another file at the National Archives. My dear friend, Bridget Goldsmith, then chair of the Milverton and Fitzhead Society, encouraged me and helped me through the morass of paperwork to get the grant to fund it and Tod Dalton for looking after the pennies once they arrived. Bev Blackmore produced wonderful posters and graphics, the logo of which is used in the book.

It was Shelagh Blackmore who wanted a book. It is sad that she did not live to see it, but her contribution is acknowledged here, as is that of her cohort in helping to stage the 'Worker's Playtime' evening – the late Margaret Kennedy. WI members also made a valuable contribution, as did Mrs. Gill Gray, the headmistress at Milverton School.

For the book, I am indebted, first of all to Nellie's daughter Linda Yerrill and son-in-law Dennis Amy, who over the years, have encouraged me and provided information and to those locally, who have helped in so many ways by solving problems or finding new material. Jackye Keates did some 'sleuthing' by locating people I wanted to talk to and the Rev. Helene Stainer, has enthusiastically encouraged and helped me with church records. David Hawkings continued to check records at the Somerset Heritage Centre and Stephen Richardson, updated the information in 'For Medicinal Purposes'. Jeffrey Wilson, who wrote a book about the Somerset Home Guard, has been very helpful. After only a brief discussion, Bev Blackmore sent me his stunning design for the cover within a couple of hours. We were missing a silhouette of the village to go at the bottom. Lindsay Fortune came to the rescue with a photograph. Nigel Wood supplied the photograph of the Milverton Wartime fundraising target board for the back cover. This board has now been conserved and stabilised ready to display again. I thank my nephew, Stephen McDowell for writing the information on the back cover, my brother James, for drawing the map for those who do not know their way around and my cousin, Andrea Cramp, for conforming and checking the texts and Geoffrey Godbert, for proof reading.

At the eleventh hour, Julian Dakowski discovered the dog tag that changed the whole format of the chapter on Milverton's American invasion. His enthusiasm, knows no bounds and his support has greatly encouraged me. Bruce Kiacz, son of John, who had lost the dog tag in 1944, has supplied an extraordinary amount of research as has Joe Tuminello, the son of Vincent (Jim) Tuminello. The time zones may be different, but emails zooming back and fro between little Milverton, San Francisco and Toledo, Ohio have continually helped me fill in missing pieces of the jigsaw. And without Jenny Hoyle's responding to my request to identify 'Mrs. Stone', we would not have linked Vincent Tuminello to John Kiacz in the first place. I am grateful to Mrs. Shirley Davies, daughter of 'Mrs. Stone' who explained why she had the photographs of Vincent Tuminello her grand-daughters had taken to school. She also supplied contact details without which the story would have remained unfinished. Ben Major, as Julian has mentioned, has also been very helpful to me, as was Dr. Luc Vanderweyer at the Belgium National Archives, who researched an incident involving John Kiasc, during the Battle of the Bulge. He also added information about the 2nd Bn. Middlesex Regiment. at Louvain, before evacuation at Dunkirk. But, all this input and research is nothing unless published. True to the community spirit of this project I discovered, tucked away in Preston Bowyer, Jane Tatam of Amolibros. She took on my book without reading any text. Her expert guidance and support has been invaluable and has given me the confidence to complete the project. The bonus is that we have become friends.

My scrubbing of floors and washing of mouldy walls in his house in France in no way pays the debt I owe to my former colleague and dear friend, Chris Lent, who whilst busy making television programmes has found time to edit this book. Without his expertise and critical support it would not exist. I owe a debt also to Jane Woodland who helped me by writing two chapters. She and Chris, being of a younger generation have found the stories fascinating. Not least, I thank my family, especially my beloved nephew Stephen and his friends, for urging me on.

I may have not got everything right for which I take responsibility. There are some spaces to be filled, so please come forward with information to add to the archive. In the last weeks before submitting the manuscript I have been overwhelmed by the help offered and interest shown by so many people in Milverton. I hope that having read this book, they are not disappointed.

COPYRIGHT ACKNOWLEDGEMENTS

Extracts of Nellie Clemens letters held in Imperial War Museum, copyright Linda Yerrill. Photographs 1-3 Amy family archive; 4 By kind permission of *Somerset Gazette*: 5-10, 19, 21, 27, 29, 42 Milverton Archives; 6-8 Nicola Forgan/Amy archive; 11 Jeffrey Wilson; 12 & 24, provided Mrs. Frances Pryor*; 13 John Ling; 14 & 15 Clive Perry; 16 & 20 Bruce Watkiss; 17 & 22 Julian Dakowski; 18 Imperial War Museum; 23 Peter Withers; 25 Erica Tucker; 26 Bridget Goldsmith; 28 Trinity Mirror/Mirrorpix/Alamy; 30 Beattie Hayes*; 31 Amy McGrath*; 32 Jacquie Keates; 33 Mrs. W. Lennox*; 34-36 Bruce Kiacz; 37-41 Mrs. Shirley Davies.

*denotes donor of photographs for exhibition who have either since died or moved away and for whom I have no contact details for next of kin.

7 & 8 p.137-138 Map referring to Exercise on Exmoor and Exercise Instructions, National Archives
23 Map in Appendix 3 p286

MILVERTON IN 1939

Thought of as a small village, Milverton – three and a half miles from Wellington and eight miles from Taunton – was much more self-contained than now. The number of people registered to vote was approximately 800 – (number of children unknown). Its elegant houses reflect the rich past of a medieval wool market town. Its ancient history is well documented in Frank Farley and Don Ekless's excellent book – *A History of Milverton*, published in 1986. Today the Milverton website keeps abreast of the latest historical research.

But in 1939 it is Kelly's Directory that people would have opened for up-to-date information of the amenities available. Milverton was then in the parliamentary division of Taunton, the petty sessional division of Wiveliscombe; the county court district of Taunton and under the administration of Wellington Rural District Council. It had its own Police Station in Fore Street, and a rudimentary fire engine stowed away in Sand Street.

Its streets and houses were mainly lit by gas, provided by the Taunton and District Gas Company in Houndsmoor, and though there was some electricity – Land Girl, Amy Mason and Nellie Clemens had to read and write by candle light in their rooms. Water was supplied from underground springs at Spring Grove.

The village boasted a 300-seat public concert hall – the Victoria Rooms and St Michael's Rooms, a 100-seat meeting room.

There was a railway station and regular buses (some of which were later converted to run on gas). There was a motor car mechanic; two blacksmiths one on the Taunton Road and another at Houndsmoor; two bicycle dealers and for those going on foot, two establishments would repair your boots and shoes.

The housewife, could buy her groceries from either County Stores, or from Tucker's – situated on the corner of what is now Woodbarton and Mrs. O'Connor sold groceries at Houndsmoor. Very few people would have had a refrigerator, so meat was bought daily from the two butchers and fresh fish from a fishmonger. Three bakers provided bread and for those with a sweet tooth, Mr. Sweetland ran a confectionary business in Sand Street.

Tucker's Farm based at Woodbarton and at Baghay delivered milk to your door. If you wanted something stronger, then you could buy from Mr. Shattock the cider merchant or visit The Globe, The White Hart or The George. If you needed somewhere to stay, Mrs. Gamlin had a boarding house in Sand Street.

Twenty farmers are listed in the immediate area, plus a fruit farmer and poultry breeder. There were five builders and decorators; two wood merchants and one coal merchant; a haulier, two newsagents, two stationers and a Post Office. Whilst there was a hairdresser, there seems not to have been a draper, though Sylvia Perry said haberdashery was available at the back of the County Stores.

You could have your furniture re-upholstered and buy tools at the ironmonger. And, you were advised, Thursday was early closing day.

Healthcare was in the hands of Dr. T. A. F. Tyrell at St. Mildred's – where the late Dr. David Watson later practised – and Dr. William Randolph,[1] held a couple of evening surgeries a week, from premises in Fore Street. Ethel Jennings also mentions a female Dr. Alexander, who practised from Carlton House in North Street and Mrs. Deacon a Dr. Byram Blackford, who lived at North Close. Dental care was provided by a visiting dentist, Mr. W. G. Elsmere (Thursday 5.30 – 7 p.m.) Mr. Crichton MacGaffey was a local pathologist who allowed his premises to be used by Milverton's WI to sell their produce. There was an undertaker to look after you when you died.

Children went to the local primary and elementary school in Sand Street, where they were educated until leaving at age 14.

Spiritual matters were taken care of by the Rev. Preb. Henry Maynard of St. Michael's church: the Rev. W. F. Glover at the Congregational Chapel and Mr. Ellis, the Minister at the Methodist Chapel.

Sadly, Rev. Maynard died very suddenly in late April 1940 having had the living since 1920. He was eventually replaced by the Rev. Thomas Palmer who caused a stir amongst some parishioners by his efforts to persuade people to make their confessions to him. Nellie Clemens (see below) reports Mrs. Vickery coming back from a service on 23rd January, 1941 exclaiming, 'I've worshipped in this church for 50 years and nothing has ever happened like it before!'

And so it was to this village Nellie, her daughter and children from North Harringay School found themselves welcomed one morning on 18th June. They were followed almost immediately by soldiers. The story that unfolds tells how Milverton folk coped with the departure of its young men called up to fight, and the invasion of strangers of all ages – some in uniform – whilst quietly keeping abreast of wartime regulations and 'doing their bit' for the war effort.

---

1. Dr. Randolph had lived and practised at St. Michael's House. It became Shaftesbury House School during the war years. See 'Gone to the Country' and 'Education'.

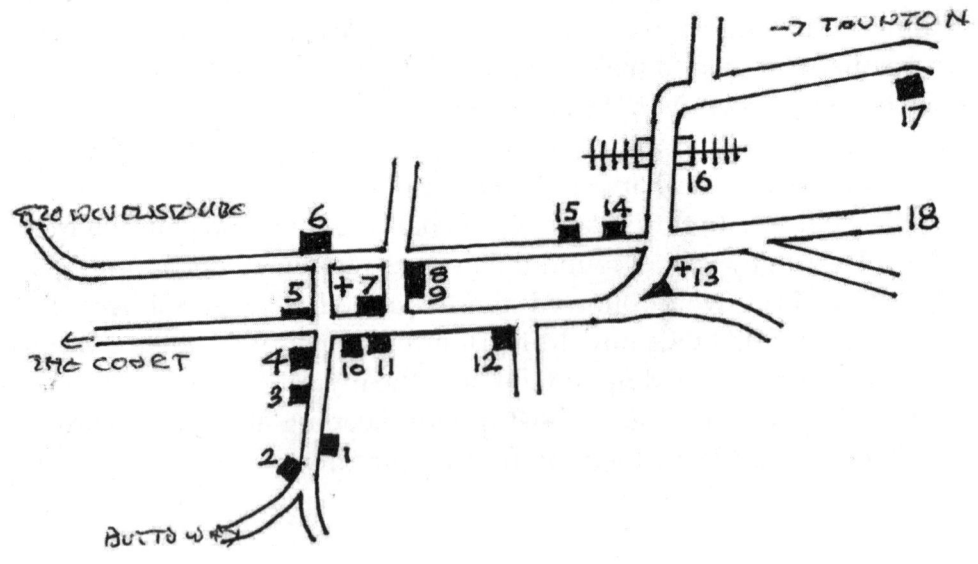

1. Map of Milverton.

1. April Cottage
2. School
3. Tucker's farm and shop
4. County Stores
5. St. Michael's House (Shaftesbury House School)
6. The Lodge
7. The Fort
8. St. Michael's Rooms
9. Parsonage
10. The George
11. The White Hart
12. Victoria Rooms
13. The Globe
14. Cardscroft (Mr & Mrs Deacon)
15. Brendons (Jam Centre)
16. Station
17. Cormiston (where Amy McGrath worked as Land Girl)
18. Turnpike leading to Doltons Field

Part One

'Darlingest'

Dedicated to

Linda Yerrill
and to the memory of Dennis Amy

The following extracts have been copied from Helen Amy's transcripts of her mother's letters, sent to Milverton.

Please note that the spelling of North Harringay School differs from North Haringey Council. North Harringay School, still exists at Falkland Rd, London N8 0NU. Throughout the book 'Harringay' refers to the school.

MILVERTON LETTERS 1940

Milverton in the War

2. *Telegram reached Muswell Hill 17.6.40.*
ARRIVED MILVERTON SOMT LETTER FOLLOWS LOVE NELLEN
(16.6) Train 10.20

Darling

I don't know if I <u>can</u> write but I thought I'd try.

Things <u>never</u> happen quite as we hope do they? We are going to <u>Wellington</u> in Somerset!!! And all because we were at the station half an hour too soon. The organisation really was wonderful. Comfortable room in the bus and nurses and others on duty at Paddington. We were all put in carriages in order. I have 8 of them in my carriage and they are all eating as hard as they can! We arrive at 2.30 we think. The train was filled up and off we went at 10.10 and how my heart ached to see your dear face. But it just can't be helped. I've brought 3

Darlingest

maps with me – all useless so will you put one that shows Wellington in for me please? I believe the nearest seaside place is Exmouth. Have just seen an encampment in the middle of a lovely wheat field, all complete with guns pointing to the sky.

11.50 P.M. SAME DAY!

Too dog-tired to say much tonight except that I love you and to tell you that we are sleeping in the most marvellous house – the home of the Director of Education for Somerset! I'll go on from there in the morning. How I long for you!

MONDAY AFTERNOON

I really don't know where to start. Yesterday really was an appalling day and all the good organisation ended too swiftly. For we had no business to be put into the wrong train and when we arrived at Wellington there was a lengthy pow-wow when it was finally arranged that they should put us in some wool-mills for the night and they went to a great deal of trouble putting out great thick layers of wool for all the children to sleep on. In the middle of all this waiting about we heard that all these arrangements were cancelled and that we had to stay here after all, some L.C.C. schools had to take our arrangements and sleep on the wool. Wilfred it really was ghastly – the dreadful hanging about and waiting for hours. After a cursory medical exam we had to take all the kiddies to this village of Milverton and arrived here at 9 o'clock, 113 of us including 30 infants. The poor souls. Then the fun of billeting began. The people here – nice in their way and <u>very</u> posh – made careful plans for an entirely different set of children and there were heartrending scenes when brothers and sisters had to be parted – especially one little boy of 10 who screamed out 'I must not depart from my sister!' A little thing of 5 and both lovely children. There they were clasping each other in their arms and sobbing wildly. In the end they were fixed together, but there were several of us in tears. The whole thing was dreadful. Helen of course had to stay last because of me and finally at 11.30 we were taken off by a charming red-haired girl who calmly informed me that she was the wife of the Director of Education for Somerset — a man called Deacon, so look him up in Whittaker. The house is charming and everything is so posh and full of taste. We are staying here until we get fixed up somewhere and we'll probably live with Miss Rattenbury. There is a lovely little cottage to let for 10/- a week but we are going to think first.

Mrs. Deacon has three children — very county! Two girls of 6 and 5 Anthea and Rosalind and a boy of 6 weeks — Crispin. (Helen's) in her element and has spent the whole morning with them. She was a bit 'uppish' at lunch time but I think she was thoroughly over-tired and seems better after a good sleep this afternoon. Bless her! When she woke at 7 this morning she said 'I want to go home to Daddy!' Am afraid I had a poor night. There's a lot of heavy military traffic going northwards and we are on a main road.

We had to straighten up affairs this morning and it seems pretty definite that we will have to stay here. You know how disappointed I am, but I must make the best of it and the country really is beautiful — so quiet and peaceful and miles from anywhere. One good thing is that it will be nearer for you to come to me and cheaper. But I cannot see myself getting down to Cornwall much, though I will sometimes if I can.

The staff was going to stay till tomorrow, but they've all gone back to London this afternoon, they may be more urgently needed there. I will finish off after tea.

LATER

We've been trying to fix up permanent lodgings and are going

to see about it this evening. A perfect peaceful evening and I am just going to dine with the D of E.
I do wish you could share all this peaceful country. Am not sure of where to send my luggage so will you address it
c/o School House,
Milverton, Near Taunton
Somerset
And as soon as I know a definite address I'll let you know. Though you could address any letters to this address:-
Cardscroft, Milverton, Somerset.

(18/6) AT THE LODGE, MILVERTON, SOMERSET. TUESDAY

My darlingest,

We had dinner in the garden last night with the D of E. He's very nice and I enjoyed it. Strawberries out of the garden if you please! Afterwards I went with Miss R to see our new home. It's a very grand place, the address at the top of this letter. We are definitely at the servants end and apart from a bit of trouble over which of the bathrooms we must use I think it will be alright. She's an old snob I must say. She has given us a piece of the garden and the sitting room is an L shape leading into the garden. I'll have two beds in my room and Miss R will be next door. We move in there this evening I think.
I went to bed fairly early last night and slept much better, though I'm still sleepy! Mrs. Deacon gave me a cot for Helen as she didn't think we were comfortable sleeping together!

(That cot passed to Gertie Vickery, and eventually to us, our children both slept in it, and it finally bit the dust when it developed woodworm. A very splendid, large affair from Heals, but I didn't think much of having to sleep in it at the age of 6!) – comment by Helen Amy.)

We had a meeting of the school this morning and then played with the children in a field! We are having them every morning from 9 till 12 until we can get school settled.

10.40 P.M.

Well, here I am installed in The Lodge after a hectic time. We went off to Taunton this afternoon – everybody except Mr. Cann, and we had a look round and a nice cup of tea. Then I came home at 5 and came round here to see about fixing things up with this dame Bedford. They were rather unpleasant to me because we had been rather vague about deciding. However here we are now. After supper we went for a walk and met Mr. Warren who had cycled over from another village and then we brought Miss Barker here. The news is dreadful. I still can't realise it and how terrified I am for your sake. Oh, my darling <u>do</u> take care of yourself. Shall I ever see you again? I love you so.

I have written out a list of things I want in the tea chest and I'd like my machine please, so do your best to get them off as soon as possible. Also put in anything at all which you think I'd like or that you feel would be safer down here.

(20/6/40)

I am wondering what has happened about Mrs. Dunphy as I haven't heard any more. I have made friends with a girl at the Post Office who ... seems very willing to do all she can. Houses seem almost impossible to get. There was a sale at a big one today, which will probably be sold for £1000! There is an orchard which brings in £500 a year. Shall we turn to apple growers? It's a lovely house.

Yesterday afternoon we had a staff meeting and fixed up our classes. I have Junior 2 – the bigger juniors, 24 of them so that's not bad. Helen ... seems very anxious to come home. poor bairn, though she's very happy and is eating splendidly – better than her mummy! She has a camp bed in my room, with a Vi-spring mattress – pointed out to me by the daughter of the house! How snobby they are! Mrs. Bedford's war work is to have her dinner in the middle of the day to give her cook less work!! Would you believe it?

Our room is long and narrow and as I lie in bed I see the church tower and hear the quarters chime. I can't read in bed very well as my bed is far away from the light but we have to be very careful of the light – 9d a unit!!

(20/6/40)

After our supper we went for such a lovely walk through the lanes, planning Nature Study lessons and were told we were trespassing. I did enjoy it. The view was marvellous. We must be high because we can see for miles.
This morning I took my class for a long walk – it seemed miles and we got over 30 kinds of wild flowers.

(21/6)

The local schoolmaster *is* a character. A Welshman named Morris and keen as mustard on singing, as you'd imagine. He's having some of our Seniors for singing and Miss R is going to play. Last night we all went to the school to get some stock to start our work with and we just couldn't get away for his talk. In the end Miss R and I didn't get our books and we have to go again tonight.

It's rather a dull morning and cooler too. Do you know I don't feel nearly as safe here as I do in London. Not much ARP or anything. They are dropping a new kind of delayed incendiary bomb to ruin crops. They've already got a specimen dropped at Taunton!

(22/6/40) Saturday

Have just heard your voice. 12 minutes of heaven. Oh! How I love you.

Dearest

Economy!!
 I was getting quite alarmed about our cases and this evening I called on Mrs. Deacon with some sweets for the chrn [children] and she told me she'd seen it at the station, so she lent me an old pram and we collected. Helen was so pleased to get it! She wanted her sandals and another frock. There are several things I still want apart from the box so I'll make a list and put it separately.

(23/6/40)

The P.O. girl has been so charming and her mother came home specifically to look after Mrs. Dunphy so I feel rather awkward about it. Her name is Mrs. Vickery. Everywhere is getting so full up here.
 I found out that the fare to London is <u>28/5</u>. You must have looked up an old ABC. And it's 28/11 to Redruth. So I'll have to go carefully with my money and go there as soon as possible.

(Mrs. Phyllis Dunphy lived in flat below Nellie at 82 Alexandra Park Road. From an extract, not included here, it appears that Mrs. Dunphy may have been to stay in April Cottage.)

I had a wire from Rosa phoned through this morning. They are passing through Taunton at 4 o'clock tomorrow so I am going in to meet her and Miss Rat. is taking my class for me. Don't know whether it will be worth it, but it will be nice to see her. And we are entertaining two masters in the evening! Mr Lamb and Mr. Warren who is coming in from the next village. He's in a lovely place and seems happy enough but he likes a bit of London! Mr. Lamb has gone home for the weekend and is most likely bringing his car back. If you can't manage to stay in this house, he has said you can sleep at his place, but I can't bear the thought of sleeping away from you, and you so near.

My innards haven't settled down to the change properly yet and I can't say my appetite is huge but we get nice food, and are happier in this place that we thought we'd be thank goodness. The maids are nice and friendly and the old dame isn't a bad old stick, but a horrible snob. I suppose we could do worse. This morning we went to the little chapel with 6 of the children. It *is* a tiny place, and there were 26 people there ... it was an old superannuated bloke who bleated – umpteen miserable hymns and prayers and not a word for the children. Am afraid I was bored and we've been arguing church v chapel. Miss R. is very sniffy about all the posh respectable folk who go to church.

You should have seen me taking them all for singing yesterday morning *and* singing too! Miss R. was playing and I had slight help from Mr Cann who is a lazy devil. We are going to learn There'll Always be an England properly. You've no idea how stirring the words really are. Tomorrow we start school as properly as we can. Trestle tables, pencils etc! I shall have 27 of the Standard 4 and 5 children – none of my old ones.

Yesterday morning I discovered that two boys had dropped their gas masks in the river so I went to the ARP post but a woman cleaning the post said there was nobody on duty and she didn't know when they *were* on duty!! (Rosa, long time friend who lived in Plymouth)

(25.6.40)

I saw Miss Vickery on Monday and explained to her about it.

She asked us if we would care to go there, but don't think her mother could do a great deal for us and we haven't time to cook. But she's very nice and I'm sure it would be more matey than it is here.

School started in earnest yesterday morning. We are working under great difficulties, though I suppose we are lucky to have it as good as it is. I have 28 – 14 boys and 14 girls – two years older than the others I had at London. At present we have very little equipment and it makes it even harder, but the children seem glad to be back at work. We have a bit of a rush at dinner time as we don't have lunch till 1 o'clock and have to be back at 1.30. Did I tell you that Helen's school is the pavilion of the Recreation Ground, rather a long way from school but not so far from here. She seems very happy and likes her teacher, Miss Mills. But every day she says she wants to go home!

I was off early yesterday and went into Taunton by train to meet Rosa. I had to wait 35 minutes for (her) train. The station was _packed_ with soldiers and I saw a train of French sailors and soldiers going out. I had about 10 minutes with Rosa. She was just the same. (French soldiers would have been evacuated here after Dunkirk.)

(1/7/40)

Dearest, I'm dying to see you. Among other things you are going to use your most charming far-back manner on all these snobs! Though I cannot include the Deacons whom you _must_ meet. Saturday was eventful, but as you are coming so soon I'm going to leave the whole story till I see you. And yesterday the weather was perfect. I didn't go to church in the morning but in the afternoon we went to the Congregational Sunday School anniversary – the tiniest place and about 30 children – one or two of ours performed in various ways (and I hope you don't think anything low-down!!) We put Helen to bed and then went for a gorgeous walk. There are heaps of lovely walks round here, the country is so hilly and interesting. We were out about two hours and arrived home really weary.

(2/7/40)

How long do you hope to stay? You <u>are</u> trying, you know! You just mention in passing that you hope to come and don't say <u>when</u> or anything! You see accommodation has to be found and I'm very much afraid you can't sleep here. I was going to suggest that we asked Mrs. Vickery to give us a double room and that I slept down there with you and that you had all your meals up here! I haven't said anything to Mrs. Bedford – though I'd wait until I heard definitely – so could you let me know <u>by return</u> (or ring up tomorrow evening).

(8/7/40)

Have just had the rottenest disappointment. They won't let us change! Isn't it the last word? I just don't know what to think. Miss R is out so she doesn't know the sad news. I have seen Miss Vickery who was perfectly sweet about it but isn't it awfully bothering for them. It seems they are tightening up the billeting business very much and we haven't got a legitimate excuse! Miss Vickery's brother in law knows the chief Billeting Officer very well so he is going to see what he can do about it and perhaps it will be managed in a few weeks. What a blessing that we didn't tell Mrs. Bedford.

We have decided to brave the lion in his lair or whatever you do and get this question if visitors and one or two other points straightened out. I'm trying not to feel scared.

(11/7/40)

Fancy tea rationed! It's plenty for our own needs actually, but you may find it a job as it takes almost as much tea to make it for one as for two.

We are still fed up about not being allowed to move. Mrs. Vickery suggests that we keep quiet for a day or two and then she'll see what she can do. She has really been most kind about it. I wish I could settle though. I don't want to go on thinking about being down there if we really can't move and shan't mind so very much if the matter is dropped for the time.

Mrs. Bedford took off 5/- for me being out over the weekend and said I might have mentioned it to her as she'd ordered the food (which of course I might!) But it wasn't bad of the old soul. We are going to tell her as soon as poss when we are having our holidays and then she could use our rooms for her visitors if she wanted to.

A boy has broken his wrist very badly and is in hospital! We had such a lovely noisy time yesterday afternoon – 50 of them in the hall for indoor games.

If you know anyone who is collecting aluminium you could give them the little egg pan in the bottom right hand cupboard and that little coffee pot you bought for me. It's up on the top of the sink cupboard.

Several of our children have their medical exam for Canada. Don't know how soon they'll be sent away.

Miss Rattenbury's young brother called this afternoon on his way to Plymouth. He had cycled from London and said how difficult it was without signposts.

(14/7/40)

We heard from Miss Vickery today that it is most likely that the Billeting Officer will change his mind in a few weeks' time. Last night we watched a mother bird on the bird table feed her big baby bird – it was a fascinating sight – such a greedy baby and such a tiny mother.

Our stock arrived yesterday so we'll be able to get to work in

Darlingest

good earnest next week. Wish we could have a decent blackboard.

(16/7/40)

Would you be <u>very</u> disappointed if I took Helen to see Gulliver's Travels? It is on at Taunton this week, and it would be nice for her to see it. If you really don't want her to go, write straight away, and I won't go on Saturday.

  I haven't told her of course.

  Miss R discovered a golf course at Taunton so I may ask Jean to send our clubs down here. What about it? It's only 1/- a round.

  Quote from a letter from Jean, enclosed with this letter

I wonder if anything else has happened about you moving your billets? It seems rather silly to me when there is room somewhere else and you are not satisfied that you are not allowed to move about. After all, it can't make any difference to a person with a large house like the one you are in.
(Jean – Nellie's sister)

(17/7/40)

Darling

Well, you can go ahead and make preparations for buying the bed and sending down sheets etc, because we've been turned out!! Only before you actually do buy it you'd better wait for further confirmation from me. Mrs. Bedford came to me while I was busy washing clothes tonight and told me she'd been to Miss Andrews to ask her to make other arrangements for us, as <u>she</u> wanted to make other plans and besides there'd be fires etc later on! I wonder what Miss Andrews said, and if she held her tongue. So we are supposed to be going a week on Sunday, but what happens if Miss Andrews can't get permission I don't know. Since starting this we have been down to tell the Vickerys and are seeing Miss Andrews tomorrow. Shall be able to give you all details when I see you soon, D.V.!

I have just been looking out of the window at the loveliest view – a full moon behind light clouds and the strong tower of the church. Over Taunton way there's a brilliant searchlight.

I keep wanting to tell you Bedford gossip but I'll leave it till I see you, it isn't urgent. I had to pay 1/6 for the chest. You see, I gave the bloke 1/- which at first he thought was a tip and then he discovered on his form that I had to pay 8d anyway, and was rather sniffy, so I had to give him another 6d! Quite expensive.

We went into The Fort this afternoon – the sale is on today and tomorrow. A fascinating place full of the loveliest things, but I always feel sad in a house where there is a sale! I saw a topping old oak chest, so Miss Vickery is going to bid for it in the morning and I'll have it, <u>if</u> I can get it for 30-!! Sure I shan't!

(18/7/40)

The Vickerys seem very glad about it, but I think Mrs. V is anxious to know one way or another quite definitely soon as there seem to be lots of mothers coming down and she could put them up if we weren't there. We are wondering if it's going to be a bit dear as she is taking our billeting money and Helen's for rooms – that's 20/6 and then we're paying her another 15/- between us for gas and attendance. Then I'll have to pay for all Helen's food and mine <u>and</u> give the government 9/- a week. Here I am only paying 25/- a week and nothing more for Helen, except the few extras we buy. If I pay 9/- out of the 15/- for my share, that means that our food must only cost us 16/- a week – that is for Helen and me and I'm sure it will be more. Hope you can understand all this rigmarole! We are thinking of suggesting that she buys for our dinner and we pay her but that we don't pay for Helen's dinner – that would make it a bit better – but I'm not very good at that sort of discussion!

Darlingest

The oak chest was sold for £6·10·0 so I <u>didn't</u> get it! Four of those funny stone mushrooms in the garden were sold at a guinea each! Things seem to have fetched very high prices.

Our school windows are being protected with wire netting in frames and are having cellophane strips on as well. What a messy business it seems, sticking it on with some peculiar mixture!

Bye bye my dearest. Write soon. It's rather a hoot about being turned out, but would be most awkward if we had nowhere to go! I decided not to say anything about visitors etc, so we haven't had any arguments.

We were in the village this evening when one of the boys told us there was a parcel for each of us at the station, so off we sped. I wondered how to get mine home and Miss R's was fairly heavy. Luckily there was a boy at the station who seems to have got very pally with the Ticket Collector-porter-signalman, so he brought it along on one of the truck affairs – such a clanking noise.

Miss Andrews didn't have much news. She hasn't got definite permission yet, but I gathered there wouldn't be much trouble over it now. And I think she was wondering how <u>we</u> would feel about getting permission when Mrs. Bedford asked but not when <u>we</u> asked!

Helen isn't at all pleased about leaving. She has got so pally with the maids and I've really seen very little of her lately.

(19/7/40)

We had an air raid practice this morning. I've 20 girls in a small room and just enough space to lie on the floor, so it's going to be lively. The windows have double wire netting on the inside, but there won't be any chance of getting any distance away from the windows.

(20/7/40)

Incidentally, we've heard no definite news <u>yet</u> about permission and dare not take it for granted this time.

Awkward, isn't it?

We mentioned to Mrs. Bedford yesterday morning about going out for the day and asked if we might have sandwiches, and you never heard such a fuss as there was this morning – a thousand questions asked about what we could have and how difficult it was to shop in Milverton etc: The cook got them ready for us and we caught the 11 o'clock bus into Taunton.

It was horribly hot in the bus and I had started the day with a slight headache and by the time we reached Norton I decided that the safest thing for <u>me</u> to do was to get out! So out I got as quickly as possible and left Miss R with Helen. I walked the nasty sick feeling off and by the time I reached Taunton felt much better – about two miles I think. They came back to meet me and Helen had already eaten an ice. We walked straight through to the Park and had our lunch while several Platoons (30 men?) marched past to the tune of Roll out the Barrel. Helen had a good game of jumping off the back of the seat, then we went to inspect the golf course. The pro is evidently a funny old geyser. 9d an hour in the a.m. 2/6 per hour for a lesson, the usual isn't it? Sheep roam the course and a stream borders it! From then we strolled on to an ice cream shop, participated thereof and sent off a tin of cream to...

And then came the crowning event, a dash to the cinema to join the end of the queue and we were <u>installed</u> (Ha ha!) a few minutes after Gulliver had started. How I wish you could have shared the delight of watching your daughter's face and hearing her say 'how quickly the pictures change' in the most astonished voice. She did love it. The Mr Moto film was good and daft but she got awfully tired and floppy. Luckily we saw the Princesses in the news so she liked that and then we stayed on to see part of Gulliver again, at which she was <u>very</u> pleased, but in the end asked if we might go. And so ended her first visit to the cinema. A great event. We had a nice tea at Della's (my treat) and then after doing a spot of shopping, tried to get a bus – hundreds (almost) of people doing the same thing. In the end I managed to get on one and poor Helen got very squashed. Mr and Mrs. Cann were also on and many of our children. Miss R was left behind, but got a bus to Halse and walked from there and loved it.

(21/7/40)

I was horrified to hear that over 300 people have been killed in air raids this month! But it's also awful to know over <u>400</u> were killed on the roads. They are ghastly totals.

Could you find out what Parliamentary division we are in and who is our MP? I suppose Whittaker would have it.

The old lady who died, who owned The Fort was called Mrs. Earnest Swanwick – and was quite a big bug – being some relation of Disraeli – she was quite an accomplished artist and a great collector of old treasures all over the house! One of the Lascelles tried to buy an old clock at the sale for £300 but the niece who now owns the place wouldn't sell!

(22/7/40) IN BED 22.45

Well we've got permission! Called Miss Andrews this evening just as she was putting down the receiver after telling Mrs Bedford (who has not mentioned it to us!) so we went to tell Mrs Vickery and have arranged to move some of our things on Friday evening and the rest on Saturday morning, so we will be there for dinner on Saturday. Am rather worried that it is going to work out more expensive than it is here but shall have to see. In a way I shall be sorry to leave the comfort of this house but am sure we will be happier.

Miss Hopkins called as we were having supper to tell us that she had arranged to give all our children a picnic in our orchard on Saturday! She doesn't know what she has let herself in for, I'm afraid. She stayed a long time and it was nice to have someone else to talk to.

(24/7/40)

No, am afraid you are going to be disappointed about Mrs. B and her East Enders. She isn't having anybody else, so she says. I only wish some official would come and find out the amount of room there is here.

(25/7/40)

Have just popped out of bed as there seemed to be some disturbance with men shouting, but I can't hear what it is, unless it's 'Cow!' The search lights are brilliant, we can see them from such a distance here – I was glad I got out of bed. I was surprised that you didn't recognise my chair! I've seen photos of them. It is like an armchair on its back and swivels round so that a man can lie in it and switch himself round to watch the skies.

(26/7/40)

Life has been fairly quiet lately. We had a chat to an ARP warden last night – there seem to be no air raid arrangements at all here and he seems rather worried. He says Jerry goes over every night now. It takes them 12 minutes from Lyme Regis to Bristol! Last night the wardens were out all night and I actually heard the planes at 11! But nothing happened. We've fixed up to use a central passage for our safe place – hope we don't have to use it.

Last night we were both rather fed up! We were both hungry and supper was late – then it was a sort of spicy spaghetti which Miss R loathed and which I could just about manage. So I was very daring and went to the cook and said we were hungry, and she said they hadn't another thing in the house! We were miserable. So we went out to try and find Mr Lamb to make us laugh but he wasn't in. However this morning he knew all about two ladies calling on him. Village gossip!

(28/7/40)

Well, we've arrived! You should have seen the stuff we collected on Friday night – we might have been here for years. We asked two boys to help us and they got a sort of handcart from Mrs. Vickery and it took them three journeys! I just unpacked my frocks and then after supper – the best supper since we had been at the Lodge – we went for a walk down by the river – it was a lovely evening.

Yesterday we were quite busy doing odds and ends in the morning, and I paid Miss Mills an early morning call to tell her that I'd heard from a boy in my class that he and his little sister were going home again (They were the two who must not depart from each other!) their mother and father are staying here in this house and they *are* taking the children home – a great pity!

We had a cup of tea at the Lodge and looked at all the rooms. Mother and daughter had motored to Wells for the day. Then off we set and you never saw such a funny sight! Laden with all sorts of oddments and we just rolled along laughing.

Mrs. Vickery had everything very nicely ready for us, but we are finding it rather cramped after our palatial quarters. However, I dare say we'll soon get used to it. We went shopping after dinner. I'm afraid it *is* going to be more expensive here than at the Lodge and it's awfully awkward to divide the cost of everything between us and Miss R so that I do not know exactly how we'll get on. Still I think it will be fairly fair.

We had a hectic time at the party. I discovered that one or two infants were going so I took Helen as well, and she had a great time making my class do as they were told and being generally rather bossy. There were 73 children there and Miss Hopkins had a colossal tea ready for them. I've never seen children eat so much, greedy little pigs a lot of them were too. They had competition games with prizes of chocolate, and it was after 7.30 before they went home. I think a good time was certainly had by all. Miss Hopkins is very quiet and retiring and some of the children didn't know who it was who gave the party until cheers were called for her!

Here we are relaxing in the courtyard while Helen is at Sunday School. It's a perfectly gorgeous day and the sky is a brilliant blue, it looks quite Italian in this yard, with the cream walls and green tubs. Miss R sets off for her holiday in the morning about 9 and then the fun begins. I've heard that we have to do ordinary work for another week – so I've 36 children of all ages to deal with. Some fun! There are a good many rearrangements for next term, but I'll be able to tell you about those when we meet a <u>week</u> on Friday D.V.

(29/7/40) MONDAY

c/o Mrs. Vickery
Sand Street,
Milverton

Dearest heart,

I've had my lonely supper and my breath smells beautifully of one of Mrs V's spring onions! The evenings <u>are</u> drawing in, upon my word, for it's just 9.35 – sorry 21.35! – and here I am with the gas hissing and the brown rubbery curtains drawn. Did I tell you that we've got a solid kitchen table instead of that spindly one and it's quite handsome stained brown? The curtain has been taken off the shelves and they have been stained and house our books etc and against the wall by the door there is a cupboard for our china and food. They have put brown lino on the floor and it doesn't look at all bad – but you'll be seeing it all soon I pray. I am going to hang my picture up in this room and may remove one of the fawns if I like! Ditto anything else we don't want! One of the main disadvantages of this room is the way every sound about can be heard – it's really awful and you may remember how the lavatory is situated! 'Nuff said! Most embarrassing or embarassing or embarrasing.

Now what news have I got for you? Am afraid my late habit of writing in bed at night must be discontinued – I don't find the candlelight very good, but as I'll be alone for the next fortnight it will be easy in the evenings.

Mrs. Bedford sent a message to say that if it was a question of the Austin children not being able to stay in their present billets, she would have them!! Can't understand it. Anyway the children were safely on their way to London by then.

(30/7/40)

We had the most exciting find today. The children all rushed at me on the way to school with a creature in a box and I could not believe it was real – an immense fat caterpillar – about 4 inches long and pale yellowy green with bright blue spots on! Nobody had ever seen such a thing. After several enquiries I've got as far as discovering that it is probably the caterpillar of a death's head moth and quite rare! So when we go into Taunton on Saturday morning I'm going to take it to the museum and see if I can find out all about it. The death's head moth takes about 2 years to form! We have christened him 'Percy'! It has made quite a lot of excitement and I'm almost tired of watching the uncanny creature.

I didn't tell you that Miss Andrews isn't sure that she can give me permission to take Helen away! What are you going to say about that I wonder!

(3/8/40) (1/8 – A POSTCARD)

Thursday evening. I have just heard that Helen has been taken off the scheme where 10/6 is paid for her, and from last Saturday she counts as an 'accompanied child' and the government pays 3/- a week for her, so we no longer have to pay back 9/- a week. There seems to be no written word of this arrangement – only what the Billeting Officer tells me, but it is correct according to the forms the Vickerys have been given. The fact that I am a teacher seems to make it very complicated!

My machine has arrived – <u>broken!</u> Isn't it awful? I can use it, but the case is badly smashed and several things have happened to it. I got word yesterday that it was at The Lodge and collected last night. Freda signed for it and of course didn't examine it and it was all so beautifully packed but it must have had a terrible blow. I am sending the label back, because it didn't come by train – Freda didn't know what the van was. Probably we sent it at our own risk but perhaps you'd get into touch with Brocklehursts straight away and see what you can do. I went into the Singer shop in Taunton today and asked about quoting for repairs if necessary, but I won't send the machine away until I hear from you about it.

I took Percy to the Museum – and he <u>is</u> a death's head moth – the Curator doesn't think he's looking too healthy. He wouldn't keep him, as they are short staffed! But I know what to do with him so we may be able to hatch him out ourselves. It's a lovely old world place, we must go there together sometime. Saw the hall where Judge Jeffreys held his Bloody Assize.

Helen is much better this morning, thank goodness. I gave her breakfast in bed and now she has gone up to The Lodge to see the new kitten and puppy they have got there. I went up on Friday evening to find out about the machine and heard that after we left on Saturday the police came to count the rooms and she _is_ having soldiers! Freda said it was worth 5/- to see her face. Isn't it a scream?

Percy is dead! I don't know what I'm going to tell the children. It's really very disappointing.

(6/8/40)

A lovely warm day. Tomorrow afternoon we are taking all the infants to the bathing place and having our tea there. King's Hams it's called. They are cutting corn everywhere and the children have caught hundreds of rabbits. Did I tell you I _have_ got permission to take Helen?

(12/8/40)

At Exeter we discovered we were at the wrong end of the train and had to get into a _very_ crowded part and stand until we got to Newton Abbot. Then I luckily got a corner seat and all was well. In our carriage were two soldiers - one a grand D'Artagnan of a fellow with a too long tongue. Neither of them thought much of the army, but said the Navy and Air Force was wonderful.

(28/8/40)

Tonight I've been busy gardening! You'll be able to occupy yourself in the garden splendidly! I lifted a lot of onions and dug the whole bed over - really strenuous work, but I loved it.

(31/8/40)

Mrs. Vickery had heated my dinner hot so I enjoyed it when I came in. She _is_ thoughtful. Today Ursula (Rattenbury) went into Taunton and said she would have her dinner there - but there were a few veg left over, so she heated those for her tonight and Ursula was jolly glad as she hadn't been able to get a proper meal.

(4/9/40)

<u>NB</u> Ask Mrs. Dunphy if she could get a bit of butter and sugar to bring with you. It's such a nuisance to get a temporary card here but <u>bring your ration book as well, because of the meat</u>.

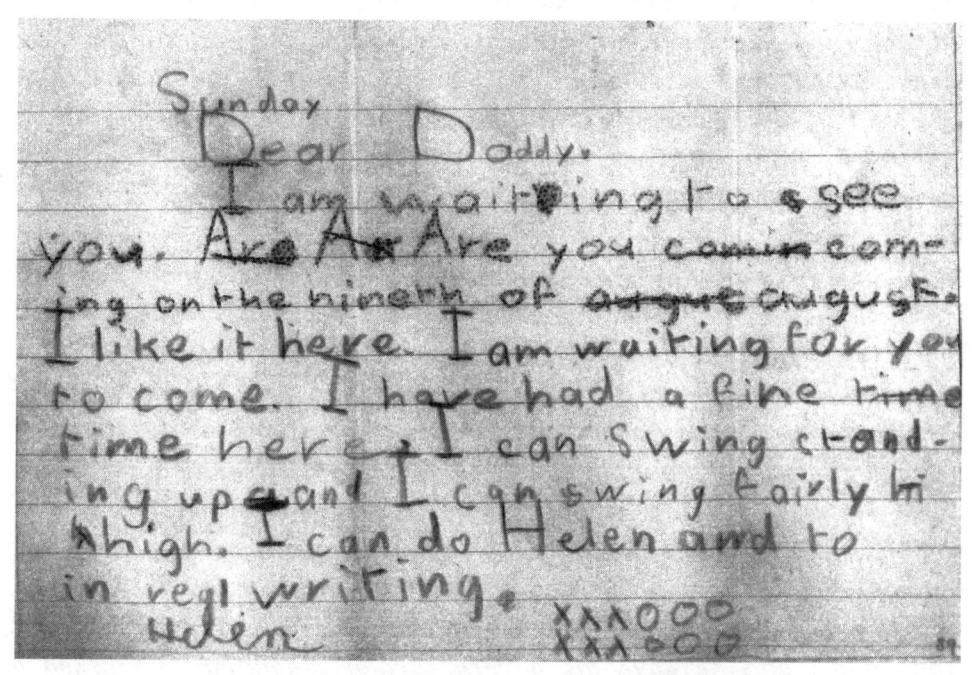

> Sunday
> Dear Daddy,
> I am waiting to see you. Are Are Are you coming coming on the ninth of august august. I like it here. I am waiting for you to come. I have had a fine time time here. I can swing standing up and I can swing fairly hi high. I can do Helen and to in real writing.
> Helen xxxooo xxxooo

3. Helen's letter. 'Sunday, Dear Daddy'…

(11/9/40)

I've been drowning my sorrows at the dance! I hadn't really thought about it, but Mrs V persuaded us to go with Miss V. so we went about 8 o'clock. I put that red and white frock on and tied a red ribbon in my hair and felt quite well dressed. All the girls wore short frocks. What a strange mixture of a night it has been. First and foremost, you were in my thoughts all the time, and in imagination I danced with you always. I sat out a good deal was only natural. At first not many soldiers were in, *but they had a whip round, produced 35/- and went to collect more soldiers – rather like going into the highways and byways! The soldiers were quite a decent lot but look horribly small by my huge height. I took a violent dislike to one toothy tall bloke who crooned into the mike and danced as the manner born. Imagine my surprise when he came and asked me for a dance! He bellowed the words of the song You Will Live to Love Again! In the end he announced that I was getting into the way of it and didn't ask me to dance again. I talked to several of the men. What tales they have to tell. One fellow saw his brother of 19 blown to pieces in Belgium. Another saw umpteen men mowed to death in a trench by machine gun. Several of them had had their homes bombed and haven't heard from wives etc. They all say they are a bloodthirsty lot with no pity for anyone. What a dreadful state! Their CO is a charming man and I heard several of them say they'd follow him anywhere. I talked to his batman who couldn't say enough about him – he just seemed to adore him. He has a quiet manner, dark good humoured eyes and a gentle voice. They say he's wealthy too, but cares nothing for money and is only an Active Service soldier – not really keen on war. What a man he must be! I sat and chatted to him for some time and he gave me a very cordial 'goodnight'. I asked a shy tall soldier for the last Ladies' dance and was sorry I hadn't asked the CO because I heard afterwards that he did dance. Miss Vickery had a good time and was brought home by a strange man, the best dressed fellow there! So I teased her about it. It's the first dance she has been to since her father died and she upset herself rather thinking of the way he used to welcome her home.*

The village children have a holiday today as the school is being used for folk who are being billeted. They have come from Bexhill, poor souls, and do look tired. They say thousands are in Taunton from Hastings. Really, my throat feels as if it had a continual lump in it. I do feel sorry for them.

(12/9/40)

We heard today that that boy Clegg who was sent to Wellington tried to escape to London as was caught at Taunton. Poor boy! He must have been very unhappy. Miss Vickery says there is a terrible delay in telegrams and <u>no</u> trunk calls, so goodness only knows when I'll hear from you.

(14/9/40)

We hear that Mrs. Bedford has some quite respectable folk billeted with her and seems to have missed the soldiers after all! Shame.

15/9/40

Helen went on to The Lodge as arranged. Freda is leaving next Friday so we are going up to say Cheerio to her one night. I believe there are some very respectable people at The Lodge!

(16/9/40)

Tonight we walked down to the mill to get a rabbit for Mrs Vickery. The scene was a perfect Walpole. A youth disappeared into a big dark kitchen calling his mother and then we saw his sister leaning against the door. I had met her at the dance - 21 - rather petulant looking and married with thick wavy hair parted in the middle and hanging loosely over her face and she stood with her hands on her hips and red nails gleaming. Her mother bustled out - a short stocky figure and asked after Helen. I have talked to her before. In the fading light the place had a strange look and I could imagine anything happening - passions rising - a push under that mill-wheel - lovers in the twilight - anger - yes and laughter too. A flickering candle in a big bare kitchen can be an eerie thing. Anyway, we got our rabbit - ready skinned for 10d and walked home again.

Darlingest

(17/9/40)

Mrs. Vickery went to Taunton this afternoon and made me feel so homesick tonight – I could have cried, in fact I very nearly did. It reminded me so much of the old days when mother would suddenly go off shopping and bring all sorts of odds and ends and show them all when she came in. That's what Mrs. Vickery did – talked about them and showed them to me, and I could have burst. I wanted your nice comforting arm round me and your shoulder to put my head on.

It's been a windy blustery day today with fitful warm sunshine. News of the gales is comforting news isn't it? I wonder what your opinion of then invasion is now? We listened to Lord Haw Haw tonight – the nasty sneering man.

(18/9/40)

My thoughts were with you a quarter of an hour ago – downstairs, I was chatting to Mrs. Vickery. She, poor soul, is worried today. Her son and his family living in Exeter have had to leave their home because of unexploded bombs and they are waiting for the whole place to go up. She _is_ in a way, poor dear. I _am_ sorry for her. And when she talks about it she says she shouldn't worry me because I have my own worries about you! Bless her!

We have been up to The Lodge this evening to say goodbye to Freda. There's a family living in our room – evacuees from Bexhill – and she's being even meaner than she was to us – the old devil. Really you'd hardly believe that a woman could behave as she does.

I went to the concert with the Vickerys tonight. My word, what a crowd! The hall packed to overflowing. On the whole it was disappointing. A marvellous dance band with an accordion leader, but too loud and blaring and very little variety of talent. One attractive artist, Bailey by name, who draws for Punch, sketched 5 members of the audience and they were topping. But they all worked hard and everybody seemed very happy and fell again for a big fair haired lad who played a Chopin waltz and Mozart's Sonata in C most tenderly! Lots of people talked which rather spoilt it. I saw my CO but did not speak to him and Helen has not won the doll. It was called Amelia. We hear that the soldiers are getting up some sort of entertainment every Thursday night, so Milverton will be quite gay and a very expensive place to live in.

(19/9/40)

Mrs. V (dear soul) brought me your letter, a card from Jean and a cup of tea at 7.30 this a.m. and she *did* look pleased to see your writing.

(26/9/40)

Miss Vickery had more tales about Mrs. Bedford and how awful she is. She says the people can have a bath if they pay 1/- for it!!! Did you ever hear of anything so awful. Other bits of news about her which were just as bad too. How I wish someone would show her up!

The children were sent home very rapidly at dinner time and we discovered that Taunton had a air raid warning with bombs at Norton and they say the All Clear could be heard here, but I didn't.

(28/9/40)

After a late tea I changed my frock and Mr. Vickery took me to a Whist Drive run by the soldiers. I thoroughly enjoyed myself and was fairly near the top. There were 20 tables and I only played with one woman who was *too* eager. I had one farmer partner who said to me 'That be unlucky for we!' I wish I could describe them all to you. The C.O. Bazalgette* his name is gave out the prizes and said Goodnight to me most cordially and after I went into the canteen with Mr. Vickery and had a sandwich. Quite a gay day.

This morning we were late getting up and just about got to Chapel – Harvest Festival and a very nice service. The minister, Mr. Ellis, preached – a gentle calm manner with a few new ideas. You'd have liked him. Wonder if you went to Muswell Hill. This afternoon there's a show by the Wiveliscombe Sunday School so we are going to that.

(29/9/40)

We went to such a nice Harvest Festival Service this afternoon. Everybody worked so hard. One of the ladies in the congregation said she couldn't understand what the children said as they were evacuees!

(1/10/40)

We had a little scare tonight about 7.30. Heard a funny sounding aeroplane overhead and I remarked that it was earlier than usual, when we heard a bomb drop (or a gun!) so I thought I'd have Helen down here. The aeroplane sounded as if it was hovering rather near. We heard several more bangs as I was bringing her down and soldiers who had come for their weekly tub were arguing about whether they were guns or bombs, but agreed that some of them were bombs alright.

Mrs. Vickery expected two soldiers for baths and three rolled up, so the bathroom has been on the go for nearly 3 hours. I think she got a bit fed up with it.

The new vicar came into school this morning and seems a very amiable man. He told me the school history of 3 nephews and nieces living at Potter's Bar in about 3 minutes and gave Miss R and myself a hearty invitation to tea any time!

(3/10/40)

I've had an invitation to go cocktailing tomorrow night! Miss Vickery came in from Mrs. Brooke the policeman's wife with the message, at first, I refused – said I didn't drink cocktails – but Miss V seemed so disappointed that I said I'd come and not drink anything. It's on the way to the Dance you see. Yes! Another dance – for the Cricket Club this time. Mrs. Vickery is Secretary responsible for the refreshments and the poor soul is in such a way because she can't get all they generally have. She's been in by the hour talking to us. I'm sure she'll be thankful when it's all over. I'm not very keen on Mrs. Brooke. She's a dressed up looking young thing, but quite pretty and seems quite quiet and harmless. It's stupid of me to take a dislike to her. The policeman is young and keen on his job and not a bit popular after an easy-going old stager and he knows it.

(4/10/40)
Friday 1hrs

Just a few words tonight. Am just in from the dance. I helped Mrs V a bit to clear up after the refreshments. Poor soul. She's tired and goes to such a lot of trouble over everything. Am afraid I was rather disappointed in the dance. Friday is a bad night as far as the soldiers are concerned. They've been paid and such a lot of them were tipsy – even the officers – and it wasn't a bit nice. I think I must be old fashioned. I love to see people happy as you know, but the sight of two soldiers, their tunics unbuttoned, careering round the middle of the hall together running with sweat just sickened me. Actually I had quite a nice lot of partners, including officers, but my C.O. has gone down in my estimation, alas! I had a homely chat with a smart young mother who is living near Milverton and I thought I liked her till I saw and her friend carrying on with the sergeant. We _do_ see life.

Goodnight precious, or is it good morning?

Darlingest

Saturday night 2200 (hrs)

I felt quite ashamed of my outburst about tipsy soldiers this morning when Mrs. V said she was glad they'd enjoyed themselves anyway, perhaps for the first time since they'd been back from ???? What beautiful simplicity!

(5/10/40)

At 3 however, I changed her frock and made her look slightly presentable and then took her for a walk. It was a lovely autumn afternoon, sunny and misty and delightful. We went a new way, and stole two apples from a too-easily-get-at-able orchard. Delicious they were too! We walked miles and finally found ourselves on the Wellington Road – half way there, so we set off along it and I said we'd stop the first thing and ask for a lift. To Helen's delight, it was a horse and cart driven by a real old character. So up we hopped when he said he was going to Milverton and I wish you could have seen Helen. The old man – 76 come December – asked how old she was and said 'She be a bright little maid!' The ride was certainly a good lift. I'm sure we walked over 3 miles which was good for Helen. And she was a real little companion too. I thoroughly enjoyed it all. We collected some good things too for the Nature Study Box we are sending to London. Tea was ready when we got home and then I went for our bit of shopping. At the County Stores I asked for jam which was all dear, so I suddenly thought of syrup- and asked if he had any. Mr. Jones looked at me and then said 'It's no use, I can't resist your smile!' He dived under the counter for a pound jar!! What _do_ you think of that?

(6/10/40)

On the way home we saw the Army led by the C.O. and very smart he looked too, with a young officer behind him, looking straight ahead. Very different from Friday night!

I did go to Communion this morning, but Mrs. V wasn't in time. I woke at 20 to 8, she brought me a cup of tea and I was in church before 8 o'clock which was quick going. The church looked beautiful, the altar floodlit and looking so lovely and well-cared for. I don't know who the bloke was, but he was a curious mixture. He read so slowly and made everything sound as if he really meant it, but he was clumsy in his movements and banged round rather. It's the Induction of the new vicar this afternoon.

At 'our time' tonight I was running home from the Whist Drive and here I am drinking cocoa in front of the fire, all alone, with you in my thoughts. The Whist Drive was quite good fun and I was fairly high up, but not high enough. There were more people than last time – 100 played, I think. I was chatting to the lady where Mr Cann is billeted and she seems very disgusted with some of the females who have arrived here. Dragging Milverton down, she calls it! And I must say, some of the specimens are pretty awful. I suppose it's always the way when there are soldiers. I met one _very_ nice soldier but I wouldn't know him again if I fell over him! He had a nice voice and well cared for hands. He had an awkward seat (Ha! Ha!) and didn't know I was his partner at first and played his Ace on my King – a singleton too! The poor fellow was horrified when he discovered! We were down and in the next hand I had to play a King on my partner's Ace! Strange, wasn't it?

(11/10/40)

It was a Great Day in school this afternoon. We all assembled at the Victoria Room and there was a semi-circle of nobility on the platform. The Miss Mills, the new Vicar, his wife, the delicate aristocrat who lives in that big house, the gates of which are across the corner near here. Helen made her first public appearance and presented Mrs. Broadmead (OBE, JP) with a spray of red carnations!!

I also had a very nice letter from Miss Barker, who seemed <u>really</u> pleased about the Nature Study things, which arrived very quickly in London. So I'm pleased too.

By the way, bombs fell 6 or 7 miles away the other night – windows smashed etc, but no casualties. A Queer affair.

CUTTING FROM THE LOCAL PAPER

PRESENTATION OF SPORTS PRIZES

On Friday afternoon the 11th inst, at the Victoria Rooms, Mrs. Broadmead presented the prizes to winners of athletic events held in the Recreation Ground on Saturday, September 28th. The competitors were children from the Milverton Council School and evacuated children from North Harringay (Hornsey) and Denmark-Street (West Ham) Schools, London. Others present included Miss Mills, the Rev. A. Palmer (vicar) and Mrs. Palmer, the Rev. W.F. and Mrs. Glover, Mr. J. Totterdell, Mr.Pragnell (Bexhill), Mrs. W. Cann, Mrs. Belcher, and Mrs. A. Wimbush. The visitors were welcomed by Mr. W. I. Cann (Headmaster of North Harringay School) and singing which took place was conducted by Mr. J. Emlyn Morris (Headmaster of Milverton School). Mrs. Broadmead was presented with a spray of carnations by Helen Clemens, of Harringay. The following were the recipients of prizes: Boys – I. Hutchings, R Cording, J. Neale, C. Rich, R. Spitzer and R. Tomasi. Girls – J. Buckland, C. Redwood, B. Chappell, S. and R. Summers, I. Ilsesly, N. Jennings, M. Smith and D. Wetherell. Thanks were expressed to Mrs. Broadmead for presenting the prizes by Miss Mills and the Rev. A. Palmer. Mr. Pragnell, of Bexhill, a member of the London Polytechnic Athletic Club, who helped to judge the sports and gave some useful hints to youthful athletes, was thanked for his assistance.

(13/10/40)

We haven't heard the news all day, but did hear Princess Elizabeth and were all charmed with her, especially the bit at the end 'Come on Margaret'. I could imagine Mums having a little weep over her.

Mr. V has 3 nice soldiers in tonight but there hasn't been a game of cards and I'm glad as I didn't feel much like it.

(19/10/40)

I went to the social, after all, chiefly because of our kiddies who were taking part. There were _thousands_ of people there – well at least 250! It was a crush. Fortunately the kiddies turns came early and people listened very quietly to their rather sweet little song. But after them, Mr Jones of the County Stores sang. He has the strangest falsetto – curious to listen to isn't it? Folk at the back did _not_ listen – very rude of them I thought. I spent most of the evening surveying the landscape from a form with Mr and Mrs Cann. It was impossible to dance, there were so many. It was amusing to watch. I wish you could have looked on with me. One or two of the soldiers got a bit lively and one was turned out by a young officer. I was fascinated by the firm way he was shown the door! Mr Vickery was again disappointed. Too many people for him to run the thing the way he wanted to.

I took her out again this afternoon. We went along the Wellington road again nearly reached the village where we were last week and went to see some saw mills and came back along the same road. Our friend of the cart passed us when we were nearly home and he smiled at Helen. Helen wanted me to ask him for another lift, but I really thought we were too near home. It was a wonderful afternoon, so warm and sunny and the colours were brilliant. In the distance there was a blue soft mist over everywhere and the clouds were high and fleecy. I felt happy, somehow, going along the lane with Helen, taking her hand, and watched her delight and interest in everything she saw. We are going to take you the same way next weekend. The country _is_ lovely here, isn't it? I think it's all the little valleys and rises which make it so interesting and now with changing trees and brown ploughed fields and the shadows and lights it is beautiful. It made my heart ache and how I would love to paint it all. How can there be war? And yet, as we were sitting resting on a log of wood listening to your delightful old ducks, an aeroplane zoomed low over our heads and the realisation of war was brought back to me.

(20/10/40)

Mr Vickery is home on holiday for a fortnight so we'll have quite a lively time.

There's been some fun today because an officer who has taken a great fancy to Miss Vickery came to tea and there were great preparations and borrowings of silver and china! We've been teasing her about it no end, so you'll have to put a word in too. He is quite nice – his name is Muffett.

(21/10/40)

Mr Cann has asked me to do a bit of supervision next week and is going to tell the office so that I shall get paid for it. It's really very decent of him and I don't mind because it's only a case of looking into the Victoria Rooms a bit, as the children are going to be allowed there, if they are not wanted in their billets.

(24/10/40)

That telegram was a comfort as well as a disappointment. Mrs. V brought it with my cup of tea and biscuits and held the candle while I read it.

(25/10/40)

From what Mr Cann said today I gathered that he expects me to go to the Victoria Rooms a lot next week, which I'm not anxious to do but it's a blessing from the money point of view, isn't it?

(26/10/40)

This morning I wandered down to the schoolroom, but thank goodness no children turned up, it was such a lovely morning. So I collected Helen and we went for a good walk. Up the hill to the Halse road and then turned right and down a hill onto the Taunton road. We must take you that way one day. When we got back I went and did a spot of gardening with the boys. They've got a plot of ground belonging to Miss Hopkins all divided up into allotments.

Sunday 0.30 hrs!

The saddest part of a dance here is coming home alone and putting myself to bed! Here am I tucked in bed with a hot water bottle and a glass of milk and I'm not a bit sleepy. The dance was <u>very</u> nice and I'm glad too because Mr V worked so hard over it. I had several partners but oh! How I longed for you. I think everybody heard about my husband in London hurt with two broken ribs!

Sunday after dinner

We had a real 'character' at chapel this morning – he had a shock of curly iron-grey hair, a dark grey walrus moustache and gold rimmed glasses. His voice, deep Devon, would have filled the Albert Hall, so you can imagine how strange it sounded when he apologised for a bad cold and said he hoped we'd all hear. Helen was fascinated. I wish you could have watched her face as she sat gazing at him. <u>His</u> favourite Old Testament character was Nehemiah and we all sang fervently. Darling, how I wish you could be with me, sharing all these little things with me. I wanted you to be sitting by my side in the little chapel, listening to his ardent prayers and looking at our small daughter's face.

I went to Church this morning with Mrs. Vickery. I asked her to call me, but I was so beautifully fast asleep when she brought me my tea at 7.10. I'm glad I went. I can't help it, but I think I find more of what I need in a quiet and lovely building. The soft light on the altar was beautiful and the pattern that the minister made as he moved calmly through the service had a comfort about it that I can't feel in chapel.

(28/10/40)

I had spent the evening with the Vickerys. The officer was there at first but had to meet a new officer so left early and I quite enjoyed myself listening to Mr. Vickery playing all sorts of things on the piano. I had supper in there too. They don't like you to feel lonely. Mr. Vickery said yesterday how very different his mother was since we came, much happier and brighter and how she had said she couldn't settle here after we left! I gathered that they think Miss R is rather a queer stick, but I don't say much about her. (Mr. Vickery, Mrs. Vickery's son.)

Mr Vickery was telling us about the Officers' Mess and the drink that goes down. I was astonished at the stories which he told. You'll be hearing about it when you come down. Mr V didn't arrive home from the dance till after 4 in the morning!

(29/10/40)

I've had a messy morning. This 'on duty' business is awkward. I feel certain nobody will go to the Victoria Rooms yet I feel I must earn my money somehow. So I've wandered about talking to any of the children I meet, but I really can't do much.

By the way, there are umpteen planes about, with their wings sloping backward. Whose are they? We have just heard the news about Greece and Italy. I suppose it won't be many minutes before Greece gives in and we'll be in more of a mess. There'll be another National anthem to play on Sunday nights!

(30/10/40)

It was wet and I thought I'd better get me to the Victoria Rooms in good time. It was as well that I did because I had quite a mob there. They were there all morning as well. What a din there was! I'm hoping it's not going to be as cold and wet tomorrow. It's too much like work! Yesterday I trotted there and back several times but no children appeared.

(31/10/40)

It's been cold and miserable again today. I have been down at the Victoria Rooms with some children.

Your wife, clever thing that she is, came home with a prize from the Whist Drive tonight! 2/6 for the <u>lowest</u> score in the first half! I only missed the booby by 3. What do you think of that? I have a 2/6 voucher to be spent anywhere in Milverton and I don't know what to do with it!

I've had quite a day today. This morning we had to have the children in the small room because they were preparing for a Jumble Sale in the big room. One of the boys left his mac and cap there, and he found them on the table marked 9d and 3d!

(1/11/40)

It's a perfectly lovely morning and I've been on the prowl a bit. The kiddies are bored stiff and will all be delighted to be back at school again on Monday. They have nothing at all to do with themselves. I heard from Mr Cann this morning that we are to be turned out of the village school next week and all have to squash in the Victoria – rooms again – a great disappointment and our early closing at 3.45 will cease! The village school is getting so crowded. Helen will be down at the chapel – a longer walk for her – <u>and</u> for Miss Mills. What a lot of messing about there is! We don't get much chance to settle down, do we?

(13/11/40)

Nothing special happened yesterday afternoon except that we had cold games at the Rec and six bombers and 2 fighters came over our heads, to everybody's delight. By the way, we have decided that we did <u>not</u> see a German plane on Saturday! We have seen two planes just like it since, so it may have been American or something. What do you think?

(16/11/40)

The soldiers are on the move again! They think they are going to be sent abroad. We shall have new ones here. When Miss Vickery told Helen, I hear she was really sad to think that Mr Muffett was going and she knelt down and said a prayer for peace! What <u>will</u> that child do next?

(17/11/40)

Sunday dinner time.
   A lovely smell of roast pork and I'm hungry. It's a piece from one of the Post office pigs. Hitler or Gobbles! [sic]

(30/11/40)

Poor Mrs. Vickery had a nasty turn this afternoon. It's been <u>bitterly</u> cold today and she feels it terribly. This afternoon she went cutting Brussels sprouts in the garden and when she came in she nearly fainted with the pain under fingernails. She looked in agony. It was terrible. I was so sorry for her. I couldn't help crying a bit. I don't think she has really recovered yet. It must have been terrible.

(2/12/40)

We have started to think about exams so life during the next three weeks is going to be distinctly hectic, what with these exams, the concert, parties for the children, carol singing and what not! We won't have time to breathe.

The soldiers are definitely going next Sunday, so the dance on Saturday will be decidedly hectic. I shall <u>not</u> be there! Miss V is feeling very sad about Eric. I can't even guess how the affair has progressed, but I don't think he is in love with her. There's a mixed lot of Irish and Scotch coming, so they say, so there'll be some fun!

I've such a lot of odd things to gossip about. The new Vicar or his services and how he's making everything very 'high'.

(5/12/40)

Mrs. Deacon called to ask if Helen might be an angel in a Nativity tableaux affair that the vicar is producing at xmas time! Mrs. Deacon is to be the Angel Gabriel. So tomorrow she is going to have her clothes tried on! We are moving with the elite of the village this time.

We went to the vicar's place at 5 to see about clothes and Helen is thrilled stiff. She'll look a little picture too. A golden halo and a long yellowy orange dress. I haven't seen the wings but I hear they are huge. It really ought to look lovely. It's on the weekend before Xmas.

If you can get any chocolate or sweets will you do so please? Buy a good bit - but don't be extravagant. We can't get <u>any</u> sweets of <u>any</u> kind in Taunton!

(8/12/40)

Miss Vickery has another heavy cold. She does seem to get them a lot. She went to the Dance last night, the nicest that they've had, she said. I decided against it, but they are having another next Saturday – only 1/6 so I may go. The soldiers haven't gone yet and don't know when they are going.

(9/12/40)

It's going to be a barracks place on the south coast – no wives or women!

(11/12/40)

Wednesday Bed 21.34!

Life is going to be hectic for the next fortnight! We have been busy marking exams and painting programmes for the concert tonight. Things are really livening up in connection with that affair at last! Then there was a rehearsal for Helen's nativity play after school, and we weren't home till 6.30. You'll be able to see it I hope. Helen has been chosen for an extra scene, leading Mary and Joseph to the Inn. She holds a little lantern and looks a darling. There was a whispered confab about who should be chosen and I heard 'she has a splendid sense of acting' and Helen was picked out. Pride of her parent is enormous! But I _am_ pleased. I've been asked to dress the kids and keep them quiet, but shall get out of it when I know you are coming definitely. There are to be several rehearsals next week – one or two of them late I'm afraid. Their wings are beautifully made of crepe paper.

   The parents of one big boy sent for him yesterday – he had to go to London for the holidays. He was in tears, and didn't want to go. Aren't parents idiots!

(13/12/40)

We've been rehearsing today and the concert seems rotten. It may be better tomorrow.

There's a dance on Xmas Eve, so do bring your shoes. Also, do bring some butter, if possible, and your sugar ration. It doesn't matter about tea or meat. I suppose I'll only be writing about once more before I see you! Cheers!

(14/12/40)

We have a proper rehearsal of the Tableux tonight so Helen will be up late.

(15/12/40)

We were at the rehearsal till a quarter to 8 chiefly because I took Mary's part for them as the girl who was Mary didn't turn up. She sent a message to say she had visitors and couldn't come and the folk who are doing it were rather ratty! I was the only free female so I offered to do it, so that the others could have their rehearsal. I had on one of Mr. Palmer's precious capes for my robes and it wasn't bad. Helen was very much impressed! The little angels look sweet and I think the whole thing ought to be quite good.

I went to chapel this afternoon and <u>what</u> a service! The Sunday School kiddies were on the front two rows and there were 5 of us including me and Miss R at the organ. The old geyser was fifteen minutes late and a funny old stick he looked when he did arrive, but he was nicer than he looked. The children go out fairly soon so you can imagine what the singing of several unknown hymns was like, with me in the congregation!

I've been making fairies' wings all evening. The concert is getting blinking well near now, and I am afraid it's not up to much.

MILVERTON LETTERS 1941

(5/1/41)

Mr. Muffett is going on a course and the soldiers will have left before he has finished, so there is great sadness here. I think Gertie is really feeling very bad about him. And Mrs. Vickery too. She's very fond of him.

(8/1/41)

Do you remember a girl called Winnie chatting to you last week? I said she was very good at Composition and she was keen on her tummy? Her father has a job in the North of England somewhere and wants to take his two girls. So they have to go next week. Great distress. My class is fast disappearing – two in one week. I hope I don't lose my job too soon.

(9/1/41)

Have you heard this story about a man who was asked if he lived in a safe area? Oh, yes, perfectly safe, said he, no women or children, no hospitals, churches, shops or old buildings! Perfectly safe!

(12/1/41)

Mr. Muffett is going on leave on Wednesday and Miss Vickery really does think he won't be back again. Yes, I'm sorry for her, because I'm sure she has fallen for him and he certainly doesn't look as if he is going to do anything about it – yet, anyway.
We had quite a scare tonight. Heard a plane horribly low, then a whistling sound and were sure something was happening, but discovered it was Eric imitating a bomb when he heard the plane! The wretch. Actually a good number of incendiaries <u>were</u> dropped the other night – actual damage one haystack destroyed. They didn't land on houses.

(14/1/41)

Poor Mrs. Vickery is <u>very</u> upset about Mr. Muffett going. He has a week's leave and then has to go on to the new place. But he may come here for his leave at Easter! She really can't bear to think of the soldiers going, she's got so fond of those she knows and I think she's worrying about what lies before them – poor devils.

(15/1/41)

Mr. Cann has had a strange, not too pleasant experience. Plastered all over the village this morning were little notices, with nasty things about him on them! One said he was a spy. All very mysterious. He has decided it must be one of the soldiers. You see, one morning this week, he was caning a boy and a soldier who happened to come in, interfered in a very rude way and of course Mr. Cann was furious and reported him to the Major. It happened that this particular soldier has defended the boy before. One night Mr. Cann turned the boy out of the canteen and this soldier turned on him. All very peculiar. Dirty deeds in a village!

    We have had heavy snow this afternoon but it has stopped again. The roads are like glass and I'm sure I'll never get to school.

(23/1/41)

The highlight of the evening was Mrs. Vickery's outburst about the Vicar and his Roman-ish ways!! It seems he is taking kids for confirmation classes and insisting on <u>Confession!</u> Horror upon horrors!! She can imagine nothing worse. Her eyes flashed and she breathed fast and was altogether furious. The Vicar certainly seems to be putting both feet into it – a pity in a peaceful old place like this. 'I've worshipped in this church for <u>50</u> years and nothing has ever happened like it before.' I'm most interested to know what will happen.

We have a Cheshire regiment here now – a quiet lot so they seem. There will probably be a dance a week on Saturday. I hear they don't like it here and nobody seems to be doing much for them. I asked one fellow if there were any Liverpool men and he said there were a few, so I <u>may</u> find somebody I know! Our boys have had strict orders from Mr. Cann to keep away from the soldiers, but I don't think it will make much difference.

(24/1/41) BED 2320! FRIDAY

Sweetheart,
I've been out on the razzle tonight – to a Whist Drive. I wasn't quite bad enough to be at the bottom, but was far from good. It was a nice quiet, friendly affair and I was glad I went. There is to be one next week, to try and buy <u>one stretcher</u> for Milverton! Several soldiers were there, so I asked some of them if they came from Liverpool – one or two did. I hear that it's in an awful mess – The Adelphi badly smashed and Wavertree and Edge have had a bad time. It was good to hear the North Country (if you can call it that!) voices. They seem a more respectable lot than the Middlesex men, but perhaps that is just prejudice. (Can I spell it?)

(25/1/41)

Mr. Cann tells me that the boys who are being confirmed have been told to write to their parents about confession, so you really can't put much blame on Mr. Palmer. At some women's meeting Mr. Palmer ended in tears and said he'd never been in such a place as this!! Poor man! He is a bit daft, I think, all the same.

(2/2/41)

Helen and I had a fine game in the snow this afternoon and made quite a presentable snowman. I did enjoy it. Mr. Vickery threw a snowball at me and in <u>trying</u> to hit him back I aimed a beauty right down poor Mrs V's neck while she was standing at the sink! We all had a real good laugh about it. (There was an outside sink where Mrs. Vickery cleaned vegetables.)

(5/2/41)

It's been bitterly cold here today, with more snow, but this evening it has been raining so it must be warmer. Somehow I didn't expect this kind of weather in this part of the world. Helen went to a Lantern lecture after tea today, given by Church Army sisters. She was all thrilled and filled with a feeling of adventure, I think, going all alone after tea to a meeting! She had 1d and came back with a Testament - Matthew. She was most surprised to find it was the same as the Bible! Bless her little heart. I told you I'm having her to sleep with me for the time? Nothing else much of interest.

There's some fire watching scheme, about watching the school building at night - not more than 48 hours a month, but it sounds rather useless for our part of the world. What do you think. I feel it's unnecessary here, yet, anyway. I've put my name down as a volunteer, anyway. Also there's a refresher course for 3 days in April to be held in Taunton. If I get paid as usual I will go - not unless!

(6/2/41)

The highlight of the evening was Mrs. Vickery's outburst about the vicar and his Roman-ish ways! It seems he is taking kids for confirmation classes and insisting on <u>Confession</u>! Horror upon horrors! She can imagine nothing worse. Her eyes flashed and she breathed fast and was altogether furious. The Vicar certainly seems to be putting both feet into it - a pity in a peaceful old place like this. 'I've worshipped in this church for <u>50</u> years and nothing has ever happened like it before!' I'm most interested to know what will happen.

(10/2/41)

Three more cases of chicken pox in school, so our numbers are still very low.

(11/2/41)

Last night Miss Mills was able to tell me a lot of odd bits about the Vicar. The pew doors are being put back – he's had to admit he was wrong to do it!

(12/2/41)

Mrs. Vickery's son and daughter-in-law from Exeter are coming for the weekend so there will be a houseful. Specially as Eric is coming and it's Reg's weekend home too. I would like to go out for the day on Sunday or even away for the weekend. I'd better come to London!

    About 80 soldiers have come just for tonight – off on some stunt tomorrow, and they are sleeping in the Victoria Rooms! So we had a grand clearance tonight. The Sergeants are having the doubtful privilege of sleeping in the cloakrooms! Poor men! I ran down to the Post Office with a letter for Mrs. V this evening and there they were strolling about in the rain. Now I wish I could have invited the whole gang to spent the evening in my home!

(13.2.41)

It is getting lovely here now, the children are finding snowdrops already and heaps of catkins. It is glorious to think that spring is really on its way.

    Thousands of troops pave passed through here today. The lorries etc have only just stopped now and there has been one long continuous stream since 9 o'clock this morning. Everybody has a different tale, but there's some big stunt on Exmoor, I believe.

(14/2/41)

Eric has arrived for 48 hours leave, so great cluckings in the nest! Mrs. V fussing round with food and asking me in to see him (much to poor Miss R's dismay!) Miss V looking charming and hanging onto his every word. I do wish he would hurry up and propose. Mrs. V's son and family from Exeter are coming for the weekend, and she is so pleased that he'll meet the family! She's a dear, so pleased and excited about it all. She insists privately that poor Eric is looking very thin – reminding me rather of Miss Bassett and your neck!

(16/2/41)

I went to the dance and didn't come home till midnight so felt I wouldn't do the letter justice. Didn't have a terribly thrilling time. The Vickery family from Exeter came. They are nice and the wife, Kathleen, is charming with an interesting good-looking face. There weren't many men there, so a fine collection of wallflowers there were. I danced several dances but sat talking to Kathleen for quite a time and didn't stay till the end. There were two of our kids from school there – so I put a spoke in their enjoyment. It's a hectic weekend here, with Eric arriving on Friday evening, Reg on Saturday dinnertime and the others at tea time. He brought Helen a jigsaw, too hard for her, but we've managed to do it. A pictorial map of Scott at the South Pole – you'd be interested in it, I know.

(17/2/41)

I bought one of the new 2/6 stamps for Helen's Savings stamp book. Some strolling players are coming to the village at the end of the month just for schoolchildren, but the plays seem awfully old.

(18/2/41) Bed Tuesday 22.20

The Cheshires still can do no right and I am still defending them! We were talking about it in school today – the Vickery opinion seems to be the opinion of the whole village but both Mr. Cann and Mr. Lamb are convinced that these are the better men – better discipline etc! They certainly aren't doing much for the poor fellows this time in the way of entertaining them. It all seems quite different but I don't suppose they care much – they are going in two or three weeks' time.

(19/2/41)

There's a wretched plane buzzing about – more than one, in fact. I did a wicked thing too. I lit the candle and went downstairs with my bottle. Miss R discovered that my blind was half way up and I had no idea! Helen must have pulled it up. Miss V heard somebody yell 'Put that light out!' but had no idea it was here! I might have been fined £1!

(23/2/41)

Mrs Vickery and I went to communion this morning. It was so lovely out. Really one misses the best part of the morning, staying in bed! It was the First communion of the children who have just been confirmed so it was rather a special occasion. I found the service very satisfying.

(27/2/41)

Mr. Muffett has been moved to Marlsea (could be Nailsea) near Bristol. It is definitely settled now that those actors shall do the Merchant of Venice next Friday.

(1/3/41)

Mrs. Vickery's mother has come home with a very bad cold and is staying here. I don't know how long for. Mrs. V is rather

Darlingest

peculiar about her poor old mother.

(2/3/41)

All the soldiers have gone off on a stunt – there wasn't one in the village and it looked so quiet.

(5/3/41)

Miss Vickery had a bad 'do' with her heart in the night so stayed at home today and I had to deliver the message at the Post Office. This evening I was in a shop and Mrs. Burston (of the Post Office) was there. The old lady is is still in bed and Mrs. V is nearly off her head.

(8/3/41)

Don't build <u>too</u> much on next weekend. Miss R is going out for the day on the Saturday, early I the morning too, and I'm not at all sure that I ought to leave Helen with Mrs. V as things are at the moment. But I'll find out about trains <u>this</u> weekend and let you know in plenty of time – letters take so long to reach you. If I ought not to come I'll come as soon as ever I can – that is as soon as the old lady goes back, I suppose. Miss R didn't think but she only arranged to go out this week and it would be less work for Mrs. V if she were here to give her her (Helen) meals. Blow – but you never know, it may be OK.

We had a great time with the Travelling Theatre yesterday, but I haven't time now to tell you about it.

I got right in to the middle of things yesterday, much to my delight. The company consisted of seven women of all ages, they did all their scenery – chiefly curtains – put up lights – had their lunch changed etc inside one hour! I don't think all the children appreciated it, but I thoroughly enjoyed it. Helen was thrilled and has a <u>fair</u> idea of the story. But she thought Gobbo's blind old father was his <u>grandmother!</u> Indeed it looked more like a woman.

It was a wretched afternoon – cold rain and snow. After the show we gave them snatched cups of tea and helped them a bit etc. Miss R and I – the men did nowt. I took one of the younger girls shopping! Think, dear, I've walked and talked with a real live actress! I felt as proud as punch. <u>What</u> a life though – far removed from being all beer and skittles! The company has been going for 12 years. I hope we have them again. That Shaftesbury School was invited but didn't come because of germs!!

(9/3/41)

Mrs. Vickery came in to tell us she has to put the cost of our dinners up to 1/3 a day, a difference of 1/9 a week. It's fair enough, I suppose, and she doesn't try to 'do' us. She said she didn't like telling us. She's brightened up considerably again, so things are better, though the old lady is still upstairs.

(21/3/41)

Today the two little Watkiss children were playing in here and Mrs. Vickery came in and found them playing with the clock and wasn't a bit pleased, so I'll have to forbid them from playing here before we come home. I can't say I'm thrilled at finding them in here – all making a noise. Mrs. V's mother has gone a bit off her head so there is even more trouble now. They are having a time. We had a Nature Study lesson in the orchard today and the children found 23 different kinds of things growing there! I didn't think there would be nearly so many.

(25/4/41)

Helen came in about 7.15 absolutely thrilled with her Sunshine Corner and looking a little picture with her pink cheeks and shining eyes. She went out to the front twice with other children to sing and she sang two lines alone – Miss R said one of them was actually in tune. Tomorrow night they are going round the village singing and Helen is so excited at the thought of it, that I haven't the heart to say she mustn't go. She'll just have to be late.

(26/3/41)

Mrs. Spiller, Mrs. V's mother, has gone peculiar again and Mrs. V has had to go there for the night. She is determined to have the doctor this time and I do hope she doesn't change her mind. Poor old soul – she seems a regular devil.

Helen has gone out singing with her sunshine corner. She could hardly eat her tea for excitement!

We watched the children go past singing – Helen's face all glowing. I had told her to leave them and come home early, but I said to Miss V that I didn't think she would. However, just then, in she popped, which I thought was splendid of her, because she was enjoying herself so much., it was a very showery evening, so I don't think as many children turned up tonight as last night – there were 70 last night.

(27/3/41)

Helen has done such a nice kettle holder in weaving, brought it home at dinner time and promptly gave it to Mrs. Vickery, much to my disappointment! But I'm just going to keep it myself, because it is so nice.

I should think the whole of the army went through our village last night. Our own men went out at 4 o'clock and from then till 8 o'clock there was a continuous stream of streaking motor bikes and great heavy tanks. The children were out cheering them all.

Helen is going to the Sunshine Corner again tonight, but I have told her she can't go tomorrow. It's really a bit too much for her.

Helen enjoyed her Service again, but I am not letting her go tomorrow night. It's too much, every night. They are having a surprise night one night, though, and I know she'd be awfully disappointed if she missed it. She told me she sang again by herself!

(28/3/41)

Friday after tea

It has just started to rain so heavily for the first time today and Helen is just setting off for her Sunshine Corner. I said she wasn't to go tonight but she has heard that it is a surprise night so I've let her go. She's rather tired and touchy, so I'll be glad to let her have an early night tomorrow.

We got a <u>pound of marmalade</u> today!! Our ration for this month. We were thrilled to see it. We were also lucky enough to get some cheese, so we are well away.

Milverton and district (as part of the Wellington district) is having a War Weapons Week just after Easter. The whole Wellington District aims at £775,000 and our share is £5,000. Wonder if we will get it. Miss Vickery doubts it, but nobody ever seems to get less than they aim for. Taunton more than doubled their aim of £250,000, but most people agreed that that was too low an aim.

Helen is going to pick primroses with Miss R's class. They have had permission to pick them on the Wimbush farm – that big place on the Wiveliscombe Road.

(30/3/41)

Now, where was I? Oh yes, in Sunshine Corner. Not as many children went last night, being bath night but they made a hell of a din and I can't say I was delighted with it. The whole idea just doesn't appeal to me. However the children were happy, but I've an idea they just gloried in the chance to be able to shout at the tops of their voices. It was nearly 7.30 by the time we got home. Tonight Helen is having a bath and bed in <u>very</u> good time! It's the last night of this Mission on Monday. Miss Mills will be glad when it's over, says the children have been very temperamental crying etc, but I don't think there's much in what she says, as only three of her infants have gone at all!

Mrs. Bedford is still being an old devil up at The Lodge, in various ways, and she is getting away with it. I really cannot understand why she is not made to give up more of her rooms. It really is most unfair.

(31/3/41)

Helen thoroughly enjoyed the last night of Sunshine Corner, sang a verse alone and was given a big text-card. I believe she has done quite a bit of singing alone but she must have felt shy on Saturday.

APRIL 41

Written on the backs of bills and letters, and a notice from the Ministry of Health, dated April 1941

> TO PARENTS
>
> For the sake of your children's safety, do not bring them home for the Easter holidays. They would be running great risks in the Danger areas; and while they were away, their billets might be filled, and then they would be unable to go back. The Education Authorities and School Governors have been asked to keep the school premises and playgrounds open in the holidays so that the children may be kept happily occupied. <u>Leave them where they are until the government says it is safe for them to return.</u>
> KEEP THE CHILDREN AWAY FROM THE DANGER AREAS

(1/4/41)

Mrs. Vickery made all arrangements for the doctor to see her mother tonight and then he forgot to go. She was fed up when she came in. She's very tired with running backwards and forwards. Her mother lives right at the other end of the village. (Silver Street)

A Sunshine Corner is a sort of happy-go-lucky meeting for children. The Missioner told them stories, but most of the time they were yelling hymns of a revivalist nature 'I'll meet you on the other side of Jordan' etc! yes, I believe Helen can sometimes sing in tune now, but I don't think tune matters very much at a service like that. I think even I could sing alone!!

One of the little infants, Gerald, is very seriously ill with pneumonia, poor little fellow! And this village doctor is a damned fool.

(2/4/41)

Mrs. Vickery has had the doctor (another one) for her mother and there's nothing really wrong with her. She's very relieved.

(5/4/41)

We are without the Vickery's tonight. There has been more fuss and trouble about the old lady and Mrs. V is sitting up all night, so Miss V went to keep her company. It is all very sad and pitiful. I really don't know what will happen. Of course the simplest solution would be for the old soul to die, but she seems determined not to do that yet!

(6/4/41)

I didn't go to chapel this morning. Instead, helped to cook the dinner as Mrs. V went to bed when she came back. The old lady seems much better again!!

Darlingest

(7/4/41)

Mrs. V has gone off to spend the night with her mother. Am afraid she's getting quite done in and I don't know what will happen. It's upsetting for her – <u>and</u> in a way for us, after everything going so smoothly here.

(8/4/41)

Mrs. V is near to bursting point about her mother. I really don't know what will happen. She slept there last night and I got up early and did this room – first bit of housework for ages! I'm very glad we are going away and it's a pity Miss R isn't as well. It would give her a break.

(21/4/41)

Everywhere here has been spring cleaned and looks nice and fresh and there's a lovely country smell that I had forgotten. The Vickerys are still having trouble with the old lady. And so our holiday is over and we start school tomorrow! Can't realise it – we've had a good long break.

(22/4/41)

I told you it's our War Weapons Week? Aim for this village and the hamlets around is £5,000 and we have reached £3,500 already. Helen collected 9/1 on her holiday so we went along with great pride to buy stamps. So now we have enough for another certificate and a few over so I'll make it up to another one – that will be 5 she'll have in her book. It will be useful someday.

(24/4/41)

We have also had a further bit of excitement for War Weapons week – a march past, with Admiral Acland taking the salute. <u>Do</u> look him up and tell me all about him – a local big-wig with 2 rows of medals and a hooked nose. All the village was out – a real piece of entertainment. But the sight of the soldiers made my eyes fill with tears and the Home Guard always make me feel sad too. Helen was ready for bed, but she leant out of the window and had a grand stand view of the proceedings. (Rear Admiral Edward Dyke Acland, C.B., M.V.O) Thorne House/Pencraig, High Street.)

Our village total is now £6,500, well past the £5,000 mark. Wonder much it will be by Saturday night? I finished off Helen's certificate for her, so she has 5 now. I can't manage any more. Our Cheshire Regiment is off to Egypt on Friday and an R.A. Regiment is coming in. The Advance Party has created a favourable impression! I believe they are coming up from Cornwall.

(28/4/41)

We all went to chapel this morning. There were 3 soldiers there – none of the last lot came to chapel at all. Miss R said it made her quite nervous when she played the organ!

Lots of camouflaged buses full of soldiers in tin hats passed through the village during the morning – off on some stunt, I suppose. We have heard that the Cheshires are off East in a fortnight's time. What do you know about the Cheshire Regiment?

Could you find out from Harry Andrews about the workings of a parish? How much say the parishioners should have in the affairs of the church –what is the difference between a <u>Parish</u> church council and <u>Parochial</u> C.C. How the voice of the parishioner can be heard? If there's a yearly general meeting of those whose names are on the list of Church members? Who has the final choice of a vicar for any particular parish? Am most curious to know exactly what right Mr. Palmer has to go the way he is going. And is there a plain simple book about the government of the C of E? Hope he doesn't mind answering these questions. You can tell him a bit of what is happening here, by way of explanation if you like.

Darlingest

(30/4/41)

I stood at the window in the dark and thought how I'd have liked you with me, to drink in the peace of the quiet village. The sky is overcast, but there's a comfort in the outline of houses against the sky and the trees in the Olands grounds made a beautiful silhouette. The wind has dropped and is just a warm breeze now. A nice day tomorrow perhaps. Good night beloved. God bless you.

(1/5/41)

It is definite that we are starting school next week at 9.30 [sic] and probably go on like that all through the summer and we are all very fed up about it. I shall try to get up early, I think. We have a week's holiday at Whit!

We are having wire netting put on the Hall windows. All the cellophane is being pulled off. What a waste of money!

(2/5/41)

The Cheshires are coming back again! No room for them in Greece now!

(3/5/41)

It's been a <u>lovely</u> day today. Beautifully sunny and really spring like. I did so long for you to be out with us this afternoon. We set out about 2.45, Miss R, Helen and I went up past the Rec. Actually Helen had gone to the Rec first to have a swing. We went along that road and turned down a lane to the left and found a marvellous farmhouse which we had never seen before. I know it would appeal very much to you. It looked as if someone with plenty of money had rebuilt the whole place – added hard tennis court, planted new trees etc. Perhaps its position is rather too low-lying, but it was sheltered and sunny. From there we wandered over a field and found a lovely long winding lane where we looked unsuccessfully for birds' nests. In the end we came to a boggy field which Helen did <u>not</u> like! It was a delightful walk and one which I shall take you when you come at Whit.

(4/5/41)

No wonder we liked the farmhouse we saw yesterday. It belongs to Coates, one of the cotton millionaires! Own swimming pool and a very super place. They have umpteen evacuees living there. Miss Vickery says there are 60 people living in the house. (John Balfour Symington Coates there is a comment that they may have had 60 evacuee children there.)

(5/5/41)

Poor old Helen broke a cup during her clearing away operations and was dreadfully upset about it. Cried like anything. China is rather difficult to replace too.

(9/5/41)

Do you get a free pass to visit us as a Civil Defence Worker? I had a disappointment today, because we claimed for our return fares to London and only discovered afterwards that we are only allowed 2 return affairs a year and we have already claimed that. So I am 30/- worse off! Of course we really did know but we just forgot – all of us.

We've had a nice walk this morning – a lovely morning, and I have at last seen a thrush's nest with five little blue eggs in it. I was delighted. It was a new and <u>very</u> enjoyable walk.

(26/5/41)

We've got a peculiar lot of kids, but my own six aren't too bad. It makes the school seem much larger and so crowded, but we mustn't grumble. I've got 22 now.

(27/5/41)

Mrs. Spiller has been up to her tricks, letting part of her house to two women this morning and turning them out tonight!!! Poor Mrs. V is in a way.
It was my dinner duty and pretty hellish. Such a lot stay now with all the Bristol children and it was too wet to go out. They had a tear gas test in Taunton. Miss V was the only one in the bus who didn't wear her mask! She wanted to see what it was like and didn't feel anything. Evidently it didn't get inside the bus.

(28/5/41)

We have been round Olands garden this evening. It was open to the public. Very lovely too. You would have liked the peeps in the house – reminded me very much of Kenwood but much smaller of course. They have a marvellous view for miles and a most unexpected peep of the church through the trees.
   Mr. Wimbush sent a message asking us to go and look at the apple blossom, so we went off straight after tea and didn't get back till 8. Helen had a fine time here with Kathleen and couldn't believe her good fortune at being up at such a late hour, though I _had_ told her to put herself to bed! Too much to expect. As a matter of fact the apple blossom wasn't much of a show, being nearly over, but we had a topping walk there – a new way and we also saw the garden at rivers – it really is a glorious place. On our way we passed a converted farmhouse which greatly took my fancy. I've never noticed it much before. The owner has let it and lives in the lofts over the stables, most cunningly converted and the whole place was so attractive and I know you'd have loved it.
   On our way home we watched an old man splitting hazel sticks for thatching. He's been at it all his life and we had quite a little lesson about it. Then at the Mill the boy there was

telling us how he shoots trout and gave an interesting lecture on fish and their habits, so it was quite an eventful walk wasn't it?

Several of the Bristol children have already gone back and today the parents of the nicest little girl in my class came for her! I was so sorry to see her go. But Mr. Cann thinks they've sent us all the criminals. The reports of the children that he has received are appalling.

(31/5/41)

We had an Alert in Taunton while I was in – also a good many bombs very near last night. One at Fitzhead killed some sheep! But I didn't hear a thing. With the moon it will be worse again I'm afraid.

(1/6/41)

Sudden shock this rationing is! I really don't think it's because of how it will affect me, but because of what it implies.

(3/6/41)

One of the boys from Bristol has run away today. The Police are after him and it really is most interesting – the way they trace them. The boy has left a younger brother in my class here, and <u>he</u> says he's going to run away next weekend! Most of the Bristol children have gone back – we are not sorry.

(4/6/41)

Fancy old Kaiser Bill dead today! How little his death means now!

Well, Helen has been to her first Brownie meeting and was delighted. She won't be able to go to Sunshine Corner as well, as she doesn't get home till 5.30 and S Corner starts at 6.

Darlingest

(6/6/41)

Miss R and I had a few hectic words at dinner time about superstitions. She <u>does</u> get furious. Mrs. V was terribly upset because she brought some hawthorn blossom into the house and it's supposed to be so unlucky, I know. Miss R went off the deep end about Paganism etc and said she'd stood it long enough, because she thinks it's all so silly, so I must be careful not to mention the word 'superstition' again!

The boy who ran away has been found, but I don't know if we are having him back. He is already on probation for stealing £20!

Miss Mills brought us a pound of sugar from London. Wasn't that sweet of her?

(9/6/41)

Helen had blocks of chocolate and a card from Eric today. Wasn't it nice of him?

Reg has been moved from Dulverton and is doing relief work, He has had to give his bungalow up and has brought his furniture here. He has some lovely things including some real antiques. One small folding table of very old dark oak is a lovely thing. (Reg, *was Mrs. Vickery's son and worked for the railway.*)

(11/6/41)

Joan Vickery, my bête noir, is going back to London Saturday. Mr. Lamb said the Lord does answer prayers sometimes! I am delighted and am praying that nothing happens to change the plans.

(12/6/41)

Have just been having a stroll in the garden. It's a picture, with everything bursting into life and every inch of the ground growing vegetables.

(13/6/41)

This morning we went for a walk and saw such a difference in the hedges and trees. And this afternoon we had games up at the Rec, a nice change. Also my two free periods I spent in the orchard, so I've had a real open air day.

Have just heard the good news about cheese and jam and the bad news about butter! Lots of ups and downs, but we are very lucky.

(15/6/41)

There's great goings on here. Reg brought the rest of his furniture home yesterday and there was a lot of shifting round. I knew Mrs. V was doing a lot, but didn't help until I heard her helping with a big double bed and then I took a turn, feeling very guilty about not doing it sooner. They are letting one of their cottages furnished, using Reg's furniture to do it – a good way to store it, as he us going on relief work for the summer. He had a presentation of £24 before he came away, so we had to read the names and letter he received.

We've had a disappointment this week, because all the arrangements had been for Joan Vickery to go home and she isn't going after all! I do detest her too and it would have been lovely to be without her.

(16.6.41)

This afternoon I suddenly plucked up courage, after the concert, to give a little speech! I told the children that we didn't often have a chance to thank Mr and Mrs Cann for the care they have taken of us (meaning the children) and thought they might like to do so now! Whereupon they all clapped good and hearty and one of the senior girls called for three cheers for the staff, which rounded the little incident off nicely. After all, I _do_ think Mr. Cann has been good to the kids.

Darlingest

(29/6/41)

Bombs fell horribly near here on Friday night and we saw the ruins of cottages and a school less than 5 miles beyond Taunton. They say it was a beastly night there, but no trouble in this village.

(30/6/41)

Mrs. V has had a hectic time in various ways. They heard last weekend that the military were going to take over the cottage so there was a grand rush to get the furniture in, and the new tenant helped and is very satisfactory.

I told you about seeing the bombed out houses and school at the village near Taunton. Evidently children were hurt. We saw them in a First Aid Centre. There were crowds of people and cars as if it had been a Bank Holiday. It's just that awful chance in a million.

They were evidently looking for something, because many flares were dropped and several bombs fell in the district. We were in Taunton at 20.40 and at this house by 9 o'clock. I gave Mr. Lamb 12/6 as my share of the petrol. It certainly made a difference.

He had been to school in London and heard about the scholarships. Three of the children here have got them, so we are very pleased. He also told me that a master is needed at the school in London and I feel sure there will be changes after the summer holidays, but cannot tell yet what these might be.

Next week 20 of our children are going to a camp not very far from Wellington so we'll have an easier time. It's run by some Quakers and seems a very good idea.

(1/7/41)

There's the loveliest 'country' smell of hay everywhere. I wish I could find the right adjective for that particular kind of smell. Can you think of it? Honeysuckle too, is lovely now, and has a very special smell – essentially of the country.

(5/7/41)

Miss V was supposed to be going over to see Eric, but he had to go to a funeral - one of his fellows. Three of them have shot themselves since he joined the company. Doesn't that seem absolutely dreadful.

   ... and then took our tea up to the Rec. Helen had been up there to a Sunshine Corner. We watched a cricket match (or rather I did, while Helen played.) It was quite a good match and so lovely up there. One man had his eye split, went and had stitches in it and came back and played. It is the Anniversary tomorrow and Helen says she is already feeling nervous! I've washed and ironed her nurse's uniform for her so she will look smart. The kids went off to their camp at dinner time and would you believe it - two of my girls wouldn't go at the very last minute! I was furious because it has stopped two children who really wanted to go. They really do make me sick.

Bedtime Tuesday July 8th 22.45

My dear one
I think the moon must be almost full, if not quite full, tonight. It is a lovely sight. So peaceful and serene. Last night, it was lovely too, and I stood at the bathroom window, watching it, and longing for you to share the beauty. There wasn't a sound to be heard - everything lay so quietly and peacefully as if the world were at rest - and I felt quiet and peaceful too - a queer remote feeling. It is often very lovely here, isn't it? This afternoon we were up at the Rec and as I looked towards Taunton I saw everywhere hidden under a shimmering haze - the fields near me gleamed like jewels - the sky a cloudless blue. Why is there such evil and such beauty? The beauty can't be just a compensation?
   Half a huge leg of lamb went bad today. What a wicked waste!

(6/7/41)

Mr. Vickery has gone to a great deal of trouble finding out my trains to Aberystwyth. My hat! It does seem an awful journey, but won't be quite as bad if I go to Porthcawl first.

(7/7/41)

There is one other piece of news today. Mr. Warren is going back to London in the holidays and it is suggest that <u>Miss R</u> goes over to teach in that village, which means that she will have to leave here and I will be on my own! I am very relieved, though it may cost me more to live on my own. My own part of the teaching, though, is not going to be so pleasant, because I'm having all the Juniors and they'll be a mixed lot. However, I'm not going to worry about that before I need, and if the children return to London at the rate they are doing now, there won't be very many left. I can see the parents' point of view very plainly, but they do things in such a funny way. Today, for instance, Eva Ward had a letter but <u>she needn't tell her teachers</u> as it would be quite alright. I do think they are an ill-mannered lot. We can't force the children to stay but we like to know what's happening to them.

(10.7.41)

Mr. Morris has a new job in a school in Wales and leaves here in October after 20 years. Quite an upheaval.

BED 22.45 SATURDAY JULY 12TH

Dearest
The soldiers sound very hilarious tonight – shouting and singing outside the white Hart, I suppose. It sounds jolly, but rowdy for this quiet village.

Helen came home punctually at 6.30 from the Rec hot dirty and untidy but she'd had a lovely afternoon and I was glad she had gone – she was taken out of herself. The last Saturday with Eva, too, who returns next week, if her letter to her Mother doesn't make her change her mind. She told her mother that she didn't want to go, that her mother would be sorry later and several other things which would hurt me terribly if I got them in a letter from Helen.

(13/7/41)

It is actually raining and everybody is delighted! It did rain a bit last night but not badly enough for us to come in from the garden. But this morning it really looks settled and we hope it will last all day. I never remember wanting to see rain like this – living in the country makes a difference to the way one looks at things like weather!

I went to communion this morning and gave Mrs V a cup of tea before I went. Mr Palmer is away and the old geezer who took the service gabbled and shouted, but the church looked very beautiful, the flowers were lovely and I find something there which I cannot find in Chapel. As we came out of our church the soldiers were starting out on a trek with all their heavy guns – it seemed such a dreadful contrast.

(16/7/41)

Mrs Vickery is getting about a bit more now, but she seems far from well. She took 2/6 off the bill last week as I had done our room every morning, and I am going to suggest that I do it all the time. A good way of saving 2/6 a week, especially after Miss R goes. We shan't make it very untidy and I have plenty of time in the morning.

(17/7/41)

It is definite that Miss R will be going over to that other village because even if it's Mr Lamb who returns to London then Mr

Darlingest

Warren would have to come over here for the Senior boys. Dr Brettle is coming up to see us at the beginning of next week to get things fixed up.

(19/7/41)

Mrs. V gets on very slowly. I do quite a lot of odd jobs, but have saved 2/6 a week, so it's worth it. Am going on with it while I can.

We had a silly little disappointment this morning. I was lucky enough to get 1/2lb of figs and we had a few of them for breaker yesterday. This morning I was horrified to discover the dish absolutely covered with ants, and hundreds were drowned in the juice – a most revolting sight. Of course we had to throw them away, and poor Helen cried! I tried to get some more, but they were all sold. I broke my pink comb yesterday. Helen gave it to me for my birthday two years ago but it has done very well. Helen was so sad about it. <u>And</u> I laddered one of my two pairs of stockings yesterday! But I think that's the last of my woes.

(24/7/41)

We've had a big day today, one way and another. I was at school by <u>8.30</u> this morning and with Mr. Cann and 20 girls set off for Rivers Farm and had a busy morning picking blackcurrants. Altogether we must have picked well over 200 lbs and the Wimbushes reckon that there are 3½ tons to be gathered! The boys went off this afternoon and as Miss R spent the afternoon at Bradford I had a nasty lot all to myself. Still, it passed alright. And tonight I am going to an alfresco whist drive run by the local conservative Association so it's quite a full day, isn't it? Helen will have to put herself to bed and she doesn't like that.

(25/7/41)

My darling, I didn't write last night, as it was very late when I finally got to bed after the Whist Drive. It was a very pleasant evening – warm and sunny. The garden was so lovely too. I did very badly, but not quite badly enough to get the Booby prize! The 'lady' of the house is an Aunt of Mrs. Vickery – Mrs. Spiller's sister, but younger of course.

(26/7/41)

We had a nice little outing. I went in (to Taunton) *on the 3·45 train which was almost half an hour late, and was lucky enough to march along from the station with a band and a great column of R·A· men. I <u>did</u> wish I could draw, for I've never seen a more comical collection of bandsmen – all shapes, sizes and ages. The men, poor fellows, were worn out. They made me feel so sad. I tried to imagine them all in the thick of it – such young men, hardly more than boys, many of them. Everybody we met had an ice cream so we set off in search of one and found a Walls van on the Bridge and we <u>did</u> enjoy them!*

(28/7/41)

There was quite a lot of excitement because the kids were paid for their blackcurrant picking last week. They gave some of it to the Red Cross so we'll be able to send along 15/- which isn't bad.

(29/7/41)

Eric Muffett had another unpleasant incident of a man who wounded himself because he was refused sick leave! I wish I knew the <u>truth</u> about the company. He blames the Commander.

(2/8/41)

And Mrs. Vickery is in a terrible way. She's got a bad cold and is also very worried indeed about her furnished cottage – the details of which are too complicated to tell you all about. But it really has been the last word here, this week. Miss V has gone away for the weekend – also feeling far from well.

(3/8/41)

Mr. Vickery is home again for the weekend – more himself. He has put that big easy chair out of their room in here and it is lovely and comfy – much better than the others, so I'm lucky.

(9/9/41)

There was a big full-dress funeral today so the whole village has had lots to talk about.
(William Cross of Fairfield Terrace, died 5th September, aged 56 –as a result of a serious operation. He was a wheelwright and had served in the First World War and leader of the bell ringers, He was also a keen member of the British Legion- Report Gazette, 12.9.41)

(12/9/41)

This afternoon I took Helen and a basket and we set off to find blackberries. My word, it was hot and sunny – just like summer. We went past the mill and had a nice afternoon, though Helen groaned rather a lot about the heat and one or two other things like nettles! The blackberries aren't really ripe yet, but we managed to get 1 ¼ lbs so this evening I made some blackberry and apple jam, with Mrs V's help, and it's a great success, so I'm feeling as proud as punch.

(15/9/41)

Didn't have too good a needlework lesson. The oldest girl, a definite pest, wants to go away for 3 weeks and Mr Cann is doing all he can to stop her! I do hope he doesn't succeed. That will make things a little more peaceful.

(17/9/41)

Tonight I paid the milk bill and at the same time told Mrs Grant that she had a bad streak of light showing which I noticed last night. I thought she would have been glad to know, but instead she was really ratty about it! I got quite a surprise because I had no thought of being officious – thought she would like to have it right. You never know how people are going to take things.

(19/9/41)

Helen has been very lively today. Miss R says she's growing by leaps and bounds and she certainly is looking very well. I've decided to drop all thoughts of bringing her to London. Mr Cann is so down on the idea of kids going back for a holiday that I think it would be a bad example.

(20/9/41)

We tried the new National Restaurant for Lunch – a cafeteria arrangement – and very good it was too. One silly thing was to give a child as much as a grown up and so Helen had to leave half hers. But it seems an excellent idea and we had more than we could eat, in clean, pleasant surroundings for 1/7. Not bad.

(27/9/41)

As I write there is a violent storm raging. We haven't had a storm like this since I have been here. It has been dull and heavy most of the day, so perhaps this will clear the air. Helen has slept through it all. I _love_ a storm and always find it most exhilarating, but the Vickeries hate it and think I am slightly potty. The lightning is especially vivid and I had a fine view of it from our bedroom window.

It is Harvest Festival tomorrow at church and chapel. I took an immense bunch of Michaelmas daisies that I got for 1/- to chapel. I am going to communion with Mrs V in the morning so shall see the church. Miss Mills tells me the vicar does all the flowers himself – I've often said how beautiful they are.

Mr Morris leaves next week. A man from somewhere in Somerset has been appointed – youngish, married with two children and quite nice looking. The village has presented him with a cheque for £22. Not bad, was it?

(13/10/41)

School is much the same – no unexpected leavings but there are only about 56 in this village now.

We have had 2 lbs of oranges this weekend so Helen is enjoying herself. There are also some local walnuts about and I like those.

(19/10/41)

Helen and Mary went out to tea to a lady called Gee, so Miss R and I had a peaceful meal and then we went out for a walk and gathered hips and some blackberries. Picking hips is really hard work – I only got 1 1 /4 lbs. We are collecting them in school to sell to the Jam Centre. It was lovely out in the fields. I haven't been out much lately. We saw some <u>very</u> tiny lambs and were able to get quite near them. We also saw what was left after making cider – brown cakes of stuff smelling so strongly. They seem to give it to the sheep to eat. Should have thought it would make them drunk.

(22/10/41)

Mr Cann had a letter from Kenneth May's mother. It seems he's been having an absolutely rotten time in his billet, but you would have thought he would have told Mr C or that his mother would have written to him, but no, she just whisks him off. I don't blame her, but it's a pity isn't it? Poor kid.

(22/10/41) Friday evening

Dear husband, mine,

As I write these words the time is exactly 21·45 – the church clock is now chiming the quarters. I am sitting close to a small red fire, in the big armchair which you have not yet seen.

The chair is decidedly cluttered up with things, like the cane-back chair of mine used to be in the dim far days of life together in the flat. I was too hot and threw my purple cardigan over the back of the chair. My blue bag is here too, open – because I just took my pen out. And I've been knitting – so grey sock and pattern have a corner; while knitting, I was reading, my book balanced on the arm of the chair – and there it is, that strange little story of the Other Wise Man. Inside it is written – To Wilfred with love from Mother, Xmas 1924.

The table doesn't look exactly bare! I spread a cloth half way across it and there is bread, butter, cheese, a packet of Cornflakes, sugar, and actually – an empty milk bottle. At the far end are several knitting patterns that young Helen was studying and the table runner is turned back against a jar holding fresh yellow and white chrysanths put there by Mrs V today.

Just by my knee is the low chair for my supper tray – the remains of my cocoa and a plate of cornflakes. Helen's knitting bag is on the other easy chair – half put away! The iron and the salt cellar are by the fire! I have been eating a few walnuts.

The gas hisses above my head.

(26/10/41)

Helen was ready and waiting for at least 5 minutes – all of a thrill about going to a Parade for the first time in her uniform. The parade went off quite well and I felt happy in the Service. Mr. Palmer was trying his best to make his flock make their confessions to him. Don't know how he'll succeed!

Darlingest

Helen and I had a lovely walk yesterday and we picked 3 ½ lbs. of hips. I've made a nasty mess of my hands and it was real hard work. But I was glad to have an afternoon in the fresh air.

(1/11/41)

I went into Taunton on the 9.30 bus, with the Canns, Mr. Lamb, the new head of the Village School and one of his teachers! There was a very sharp frost and the countryside looked a picture – everything sharply outlined in white. One field was being ploughed – the plough drawn by two fine horses, one dark brown and one almost white, and wreaths of steam came from their rippling sides. Of all the country sights, I think that of horses drawing a plough is the loveliest. I love a ploughed field, the shadows falling across the straight, good lines and the rich earthy smell of the freshly turned furrows, and the dark red is particularly satisfying in this part of the country.

Helen went to her usual Saturday afternoon concert.

Next Saturday will be the last day as the man is going back to Wales. The children do love him. I wonder whether it pays him to take the Hall, letting the kids in at 2d.

After Helen came back from the concert we went for a walk. It was a lovely afternoon and the sun was so warm. We found our way back across fields and I was beginning to wonder if we ever should strike the Wellington road for which I was aiming! You know how good my sense of direction is! However, I was guided by the church and we managed very well. Helen said it was a grand adventure!

(9/11/41)

This afternoon's service went off very well. Most of the Guides turned up. It's a distressing little ceremony, isn't it? But my mind was occupied with the Guides. We were shoved away in the front corner and couldn't see a thing and Mr Palmer preached a sermon which no child could understand. I <u>did</u> think he was mean – not even a child's hymn. I had time to study the memorials to the Spurway family – of the Fort. See if you can find them in any of your books. They seem old enough. What was the naval battle in 1801 – October 21st. Was it Trafalgar? Because a boy of 19 in the RN died then. I spent the time very pleasantly and listened to Mr. Palmer speaking about the power of the saints to help us, with one whole ear. Helen, as usual, was delighted with it all. She went to Sunday School first.

(2/12/41)

I was met at school with the news that the Arnold family is returning at the weekend, to London, and although I know it is very wrong of them to go back to London, I am so very glad to get rid of a few of my beauties and Rita Arnold is one of the worst. I cannot yet believe that the Vickerys have really gone! I'm having a good week. Mr Cann of course doesn't feel as I do about it though I keep my side very quiet (I hope)!

We are very busy with exams, and my class is so varied that it really is rather a farce.

(4/12/41)

It's Rita Arnold's last day tomorrow and aren't I delighted! My heart feels tons lighter already.

Tuesday evening 9th Dec

My dear
News!!! Mr Cann returned from London in almost as vague a state as when he went. But he did tell me that Dr Brettle is writing to <u>me</u>, and I gather that I am to be asked to return to London! What do you think of that? The letter may arrive in the morning and I shall know definitely. But it does seem certain that Miss R is to be left here, after all, and she is very

fed up about it indeed. It's quite definite that nothing is to be done before Xmas, so she'll have to trek over here every day. As far as I go, of course, the problem is Helen, and I wonder what your views are. I fear that you still consider it right for the children to be out of London, and I'm afraid you are right too! So do you think I should get her billeted here? Of course I can't do anything till I hear from Hornsey, but I've been casting my mind about today. I've told Helen about it all and she has promised not to talk about it. She seems perfectly satisfied about staying down here! It will be impossible for her to stay here, but I have thought of asking Mrs Ackland to have her and Helen likes them. They live in that house opposite the gates to Olands. Mrs.A has had an evacuee and threatened not to have any more, but I know she likes Helen. Failing her, I might ask Mrs. Dyte where Eva Ward is.

We have thought and talked about nothing else in school today. Mr Cann is to return early in the New Year, but is to start the school here after Xmas – such as there is of it. He seems fairly sure that it will all be finished up soon. Of course I feel the most sensible thing would have been to push all the kids in the village school and send me there too. Won't it be just my luck to be sent back to North Harringay with Phyllis Vickery and Rita Arnold in the class?

Part Two

MILVERTON IN THE WAR

DEDICATED TO THE MEMORY OF

Shelagh Blackmore
Brenda Horsfield

1. PREPARING FOR THE WORST – THE HOME FRONT 1938-1939

On 6th June, 1939 – The Milverton WI Records state 'An interesting debate took place and was carried – "That husbands should help in the home".' If war came their husbands, of course, were not going to be home.

Over the preceding nine months Milverton's attitude to the threat of war underwent a profound change. Rewind to Parish Council minutes the previous September:

'With reference to the prompt and successful action taken by the prime minister in preventing war, and the signing of the Munich agreement between Germany and Czecho-Slovakia, it was proposed by Mr. Day, seconded by Mr. Glover and unanimously agreed that a letter of appreciation be forwarded to Mr. Neville Chamberlain on behalf of residents of the Royal Borough of Milverton'.[1]

The Parish council members were:
Mr. W. E. Burston – Chairman
Mr. A. G. T. King – (Vice-Chairman)
Lt. Col. C. V. Moberly Bell. Messrs. T. Baker, T. C. M. Day, W. F. Glover, E. C. Kick, E. Redwood & H. Buller (Clerk)

Almost exactly 20 years earlier the Armistice of the 'Great War', the 'War to end all Wars' had been signed. Some of those named above, including

Lt. Col. Moberly Bell had served in that war and would be called to serve again. Indeed the twenty year span meant that in some families, as in the author's, eldest sons served in WW1 and youngest in WW2, whilst the sisters of those who had lost brothers in WW1, had sons who would serve if war broke out again. But now, memories of the horrors of war had taken on a new and more menacing dimension: bombing.

The threat of mass bombing was mooted as early as 1935 when the Government had issued to all local authorities the 'First Circular' on air-raid precautions. This, along with the reporting of devastation caused in 1937 by German bombing raids in the Spanish Civil War, would have increased the sense of threat. When in 1938, 38 million gas-masks were distributed, including 'Micky Mouse' masks for young children, and complete body masks for infants, it rekindled past images of gassed Tommies in Flanders. But this time Milverton itself could be in the front line.

The signing of the Munich treaty promised delivery from this awful fate – the promise evaporated of course. When Hitler broke the terms of the treaty and annexed the rest of Czechoslovakia in March 1939, few of the old soldiers on the Parish Council could have doubted that war was inevitable.

But the Treaty was buying time. Milverton – and Britain as a whole – had six months to get used to the idea of war. And the British government had time to establish a basic infrastructure for home defence. These included Civil Defence, evacuation schemes, registering men and women for war work, agriculture, education and supplies and rationing, all of which will be described in later chapters.

The months between Munich and the outbreak of war saw a surprising amount of activity. The government aimed at drawing together local services including Civil Defence, Police, ambulance and hospital services (pre-NHS) stockpiled building materials and organised the building of defensive positions and trenches. They were to organise casualty centres and mortuaries, canteens, clothing depots, rest centres. The Red Cross and St. John's Ambulance would provide First Aid Centres and training.[2]

The role of the CIVIL DEFENCE SERVICE[3] was to save lives at risk from enemy attack, and to minimise damage, particularly to premises and factories of importance to the community. As early as 1937, the Air Raid Wardens' Service was established as large-scale bombing was felt to be a real risk in any future conflict.

Auxiliary Territorial Service[4] – The ATS was formed in 1938 as a women's voluntary service with the Army having evolved from the Women's Auxiliary Army Corps (WAAC) set up in 1917 and disbanded in 1921. Initially the roles women played in the service were as cooks, clerks, orderlies, drivers or working in the stores.

The Land Army[5] – Learning the lessons from the First World War, the Land Army[3] was reintroduced in July 1939 and in the three months until the outbreak of war 17,000 women had been recruited.

Local Councils would replace lost ration books and issue emergency ration cards. They provided a registration office for identity cards[6] and would collect information about damaged buildings and arrange for air-raid shelters and trenches. Shelters included cellars in many houses. Other houses were supplied with sandbag protection. They also organised sites for road-blocks and searchlights.

In 1938 in addition to the National Fire Service the Auxiliary Fire Service[5] was formed.

From before the outbreak of war, householders had been encouraged to purchase stirrup pumps to enable them to tackle small fires; particularly from incendiary bombs, when the number of fires started during a raid could overwhelm the fire service resources. Many households also had sand bags to enable them to smother incendiary bombs.

In addition villages were encouraged to form fire fighting parties and were issued with two-man manual hand pumps and a few lengths of hose.

Darlingest

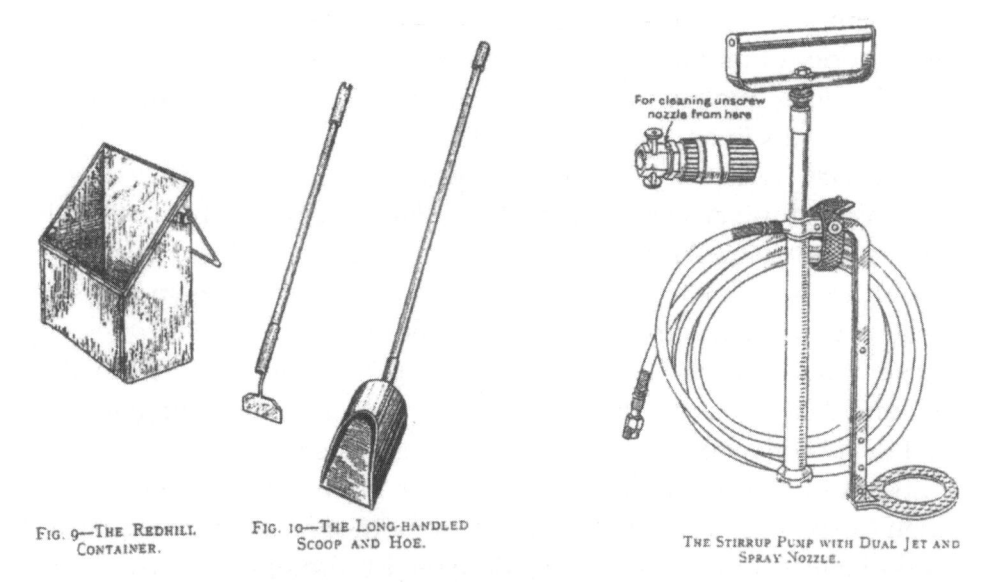

FIG. 9—THE REDHILL CONTAINER.

FIG. 10—THE LONG-HANDLED SCOOP AND HOE.

THE STIRRUP PUMP WITH DUAL JET AND SPRAY NOZZLE.

4. Stirrup pump.
The Fireguard weapons: the Redhill rake, scoop and container, and the Stirrup pump. These put out many of the hundreds and thousands of incendiary bombs that were dropped on Britain. (From the Fire Guards' Handbook, *published 1942, HMSO.)*

Whilst all this information was slowly circulated from the Government at the next meeting of the Parish Council, 19th November, 1938, not only was the reply[7] dated 3rd October from the Prime Minister read out, the Clerk 'reported that on the 12th October last he had been visited by the superintendent of Police (Dunster District) asking what steps the parish council (as the lighting authority for the parish) were prepared to take in case of necessity for the quick extinguishing of all street lamps, should an air raid warning be given? On consultation with the chairman and other members of the council, the following correspondence had been despatched and received from the Taunton and District Gas Company and from the Police Superintendent. Reply 14th October, 1938.'

Dear Sir,

It is quite an easy matter to fit to each street lamp a device so that by lowering the pressure, the lamps are instantaneously extinguished, and on the pressure being again raised, the lamps light, and we have obtained quotations for these appliances in quantities should they be required.

C. Harris (Managing Director)' (Lived at Devonia)

Reply to letter from Parish Council to Police in Dunster on 18th October 1938,

Whilst in time of war street lighting would be extinguished as a permanent measure, it is the desire of the authorities that street lighting authorities should investigate measures to secure their extinction at short notice.

This matter is one for action by your council so far as Milverton is concerned, and unless they move in the matter apparently nothing further will be done.

If such a device as is referred to in the letter from the Taunton Gas Company, were fitted, I am of the opinion that it would be the best method that could be adopted and would result in the lights being extinguished sooner than by any other method. B. J. Brookman (Superintendent).

The Council agreed to move forward and asked who was to pay?
At the meeting on 27th March, 1939, The Parish Council wrote to Taunton Gas Co. saying that 'the best plan for all round safety, would be to ensure that each lamp is extinguished by hand, and that private consumers would not then be affected by the lowering of any pressure.[8] It was thought that two men on cycles could quickly extinguish all lamps in the parish in a very short space of time...'

Apart from this, between 1938-9, local Councils assumed responsibilities for a long list of the government's requirements including billeting and education of evacuees.[9] Mr. William Deacon in Milverton, the Director of Education for Somerset had set up contingencies to cope with an influx of evacuees. And before they arrived, Miss Andrews as Billeting Officer[10] had with her deputy, Mr. Deacon's wife, Gladys, identified those households who could take evacuees.

In 1938 the FANY[11] (First Aid Nursing Yeomanry) along with the Women's Legion and the Women's Emergency Service evolved into the Auxiliary Territorial Service.

THE WVS[12] (WOMENS VOLUNTARY SERVICE) – Also started in 1938 as part of a civil defence unit, was the WVS. They were to attend the nearest Assembly place if bombs were dropped; arrange and appoint persons to attend and assist at feeding and shelter stations; arrange households near such stations for rest, sanitary convenience and ablutions, suitably qualified First Aiders, supply suitable clothing, assist with care of young and infant children. They drew in other organisations to share or take on some of their tasks, one of the most important, with its county wide rural network of members, was the Women's Institute. Undaunted, Milverton's WI took their responsibility to heart as is demonstrated throughout this book. They kicked off, on 28th August, 1939, at a meeting held at the Parsonage at 2.30 p.m. when Mrs. M Bell proposed that if necessary £2 should be spent on wool for knitted blankets for evacuees[13] should they be billeted in Milverton. By this time war was just six days away.

---

1. There is no copy of the letter but there is a copy of the handwritten note in Parish Council Minutes. 24th September, 1938.
2. See 'Doing Your Bit' and Appendix 2.
3. See 'Doing Your Bit'.
4. See 'Doing Your Bit'.
5. See 'On the Fields'.
6. See 'Gone to the Country'.
7. Not in records.

8. See 'Gone to the Country'.
9. See 'Doubling Up – Education'.
10. See 'Gone to the Country'.
11. See 'Doing Your Bit'.
12. See 'Doing Your Bit'.
13. See 'Gone to the Country' and 'Make do and Mend'.

2. 'SUP UP AND CLEAR THE CELLARS' – WAR DECLARED

'It is reported from Oslo that the Norwegian Nobel Committee has decided not to award a peace prize for 1939.'

SPECIAL ARMY ORDER
In all its long and glorious history, the British army has never been called upon to take the field for a cause more just than that which is ours today; it has never entered on a campaign of which the issues were graver or more vital to the future of our race, and indeed, of all civilisation.

I know well that you realise what is at stake, and that, in the struggle which lies ahead, every man in my Armies will play his part with gallantry and devotion. It is my earnest prayer that God will have you in His keeping and grant success to your arms.
GEORGE R.I., 4th September, 1939

At 11 a.m. on 3rd September, 1939, Britain declared war on Nazi Germany.

By then emergency plans were in place, evacuation of children had begun. Ration books and gas masks, had been distributed and identity cards were about to be issued[1] as well as instructions on how to deal with invaders. Food control offices had been set up, and now other emergency plans began to roll out.

1. *Left: Nellie Clemens.*

2. *Below right: Nellie with her daughter Helen, in the garden at April Cottage.*

3. *Below left: Wilfred Clemens wearing his ARP uniform (family archive).*

4. Mr. and Mrs. William Deacon. This photograph was taken to celebrate their 50th wedding anniversary. Somerset Gazette.

5. Cardscroft, second house, next to white house. Home of Mr. and Mrs. Deacon and where Nellie and Helen stayed for a few days before moving to The Lodge (photo 10).

6. Mrs. Vickery.

7. Left: Miss Gertrude Vickery in the garden of April Cottage.

8. Above: Captain Eric Muffett of the 86th Light AA Regiment. Miss Vickery's friend. He went on to join the Royal Indian Army Service Corps, and died of polio in India, in 1945.

9. Sand Street, with April Cottage, three doors from right – with three windows. Milverton Stores in shadow at top left-hand side.

10. The Lodge, the home of Mrs. Bedford, where Nellie and Helen and Miss Rattenbury stayed before moving to April Cottage. Sylvia Perry stayed there with her sister and grandmother.

11. Milverton Home Guard photographed at Milverton School. Permission of Jeffrey Wilson.

Back Row – Henry Hart; unknown; Harold Winter; Unknown; Walter Lang; Bill Locke; Dick Wyatt; John Ackland-Troyt; Lionel Hayes; Bill Gardener; Unknown; Arthur Venton; Jack Rowen; Harold Blue; Harold Rowen; Jack Besley; Frank Sulley; Harold Wyatt; G. Prole; Jack Hope

Middle Row – Bunny Wyatt; Albert Raffel; Unknown; Jack Kingdom; Jack Goss; Don Noble; Bill Mead; Bill Rowe; Cliff?; Tommy Shephard?; Jack Perry; Geoff Gill; Burt Smith; John Tarr; Ike Westcott; Sid Gabham; Cliff Nutt; Tommy Shephard?; Harold Tarr; Ern Tooze

Front Row – L/Cpl. Bill Hawkins; L/Cpl. Alf Cross; L/Cpl. Ern Lee; L/Cpl. John Thomas; L/Cpl. Jack Sharland; L/Cpl. George Bradner; L/Cpl. Maybely Byrde; Sgt. Jack Loosemore; Sgt. Harry Sealey; Lt. Chris Shapland; Lt. Ted Burston; Sgt. Bert Yandle; Sgt. Jack or Walt Jacobs; Cpl. Donald Pulson; Cpl. Cyril Edmunds; Cpl. Jimmy Watts; L/Cpl. Harvey; L/Cpl. Bob Wyatt (Not in photograph Bert and Harry Winter, Jack Stone, Eddie Barter and Ernest Parkman

12. Soldiers of the Pioneer 1942-44 in charge of the QF decoy at Luckham Farm, Milverton. L-R Sgt. C. Boyce; Vic Blacman; Sgt. Harrison; Cpl. Haddington, Cpl. J. Farrell.

13. Thomas and Daisy Ling on their wedding day, married 23rd September, 1939. Thomas Ling had joined the Army after the end of World War One, and served in Egypt, Singapore and Ceylon. He left the Army in 1938 and became a postman. Being on the Reserve, he was called up and had to get a special licence in order to marry Daisy before he went off with the BEF in 'C' Coy, 2nd Bn Middlesex Regiment, with CO. Capt. Edward Bazalgette. After the breakout from Dunkirk he came ashore at Bournemouth where he was reunited with his elder brother, who had also been at Dunkirk. He came to Milverton, as is recorded in 'Military Invasion' and Daisy was evacuated here, when pregnant. She tells her story in 'Gone to the Country'. Thomas, was wounded at Anzio and was being repatriated by ship but died of his wounds and buried at sea. Daisy lived in Milverton for 60 years. She died aged 93 in 2007

14. Ted Perry joined the RAF after a short spell in the ARP.

15. Ted became a truck driver supplying ammunition and petrol to the RAF. His story is told in 'Military Invasion'.

16. Evacuees – the Watkiss family, with back row, Mr. Watkiss, their father, a subconductor with R.O.A.C. (Royal Army Ordnance Corps) next to Bruce. Front row – Robin, Jean, Audrey and Shirley. They are mentioned in 'Gone to the Country'.

Ken Burston, local butcher, remembers his uncle, Ted (Chairman of the Parish Council and in charge of the Post Office) rushing into the White Hart on the day war was declared ordering him and his uncle Ernest Lee (the butcher) to 'Sup up and clear the cellars' in Lottisham House as they had to be used as shelters. 'Hitler won't come today' they protested! As the cellars were used to smoke and salt the pork it was not going to be an easy task to clear them.

One of the Somerset County Council's Home defence preparations was setting up Invasion Committees through Parish or Urban District Councils. These committees would have almost total power. Thus the immediate reaction on 3rd September was that Milverton's Invasion Committee called for cellars[2] to be cleared ready to act as shelters and Wellington Rural District Council paid, an amount of £40 12s., to protect 32 houses in Milverton. Blackout was in place, and the road signs taken down by Tom Greedy, the local water bailiff.

It wasn't until 17th October, 1939 the first bomb was dropped in the Orkneys. It killed a rabbit and one legend has it that that is how the song 'Run Rabbit, Run Rabbit', came about. This song was used in some nursery schools to encourage infants to run to the shelter.

In Milverton, Ken Burston, said people were quite concerned, but were they in danger?

The fall of France in June 1940, signalled the end of the phoney war and Prime Minister Winston Churchill made it clear that Britain should consider itself next on Hitler's list. The threat of Nazi invasion now took centre stage. Invasion by beach, parachute and a major port had to be taken seriously. Of major importance was the defence of the Bristol Channel so a series of defensive lines were built, the Taunton Stop Line[3] being one of the most important. Searchlights were in place, the Home Guard was on look-out and anti-aircraft gun emplacements were ready to protect Yeovil and Bristol. There seems to have been no provision in Milverton for air raid shelters[4] other than cellars. This worried Nellie not long after leaving the air-raid precautions in London who wrote on 26th July, 1940 – 'We've fixed up to use a central passage for our use.'

Darlingest

Milverton, along with other villages and towns was also directly under the flight path of the Luftwaffe from Cherbourg to Bristol and Wales. On 26th July, 1940, a Heinkel He III bomber, mine-laying over the Bristol Channel was attacked over East Portishead Point by a Hurricane from 87 Squadron and brought down on the Blackdown Hills just over the Devon border. Four of the crew were killed but the one survivor was captured and frogmarched several miles by the Home Guard to the nearest Police Station.

According to Nellie, incendiary bombs were only dropped on crops[6] but even so the Parish Council took fire prevention very seriously delivering sand for fire bombs to most houses. Even as late as 2nd January, 1941, it was asking people who had missed their delivery of sand to give their names to Mr. Burston at the Post Office. They discussed whether they should appoint fire watchers but decided against it as no official warning had been given. Nellie mentions having to do some fire-watching at school on 5th February, and that there had been a tear gas exercise in Taunton on 2nd May, 1941.[7]

Concerns about fire threat continued as late as May 1943, when the Milverton Parish Council had invited Mr. Jewell the Senior Commanding Officer attached to Column 1 National Fire Service to explain why the National Fire Service[8] had been discontinued and that fire from enemy action would be dealt with immediately by the local fire brigade until the fire services from Wellington, Taunton and Wiveliscombe could attend. This prompted a discussion about whether Milverton's fire guard had been sufficiently trained. The spat continued with Milverton arguing that they had enrolled a fire guard as requested. However, by August 1943, it was agreed that only the two-man manual pump now stationed in Milverton would be necessary and that each individual (street) section of the fire guard – be provided with stirrup pumps and buckets.

The WI meanwhile was also on the case. Three days after war was declared a letter from a Miss Vernon offered preserving sugar at 27s. 6d. per cwt. It was agreed to order some for jam and marmalade making and for teas. Security was important and just in case photographs of local facilities should fall into enemy hands it was deemed important to collect cameras – a role that Mrs. Jenks, Mrs Deacon's mother took upon herself.[9] Was it necessary given that it was very difficult to get film? It is perhaps the reason why there are few photos of places and inhabitants during the war, Milverton included. This lack of photos particularly affected the photographing of babies and young children unless professionally taken. Mrs. Jenks was a force to be reckoned with as will be seen.

The safety issue arising from blacked out streets was a major problem especially in towns and cities as Nellie mentions on 21st and 27th July, 1940.[10] At a meeting of Milverton WI on 4th February, 1940, a proposal was carried to add 'preferably anklets' to the resolution 'That it should be compulsory for all pedestrians to wear something white when on the roads after blackout'. That a 'Put that light out' warning was heard by Nellie on 19th February, 1941, confirms how active the ARP was. And the pressure of gas continued to be of concern as many houses were still lit by gas light as Nellie mentions, with candles in bedrooms.[11] Electricity was available in some places, including the farm where Land Girl, Amy McGrath worked but she also took a candle to bed. No doubt, moving about with a lighted candle was a fire hazard in itself.

Blackout precautions were adhered to, as Nellie mentions on 19th February, 1941. Twenty yards of material for blackout curtains had been purchased from a company in Taunton for the Victoria Rooms with Mrs. Burston,[12] the wife of the chairman, employed to make them. In September blackout for the large room was deemed sufficient and it was proposed to fix tin shades to the lights and 'that Mr. Marshall fix' new batons to carry the brass rods and rings for the curtains. In November, problems continued and it was agreed that members of the committee should inspect on a dark night. But these problems were ongoing and discussed repeatedly between November 1940 and May 1943 and even as late as 1943 the wiring in the main room had to be renewed and lengthened to facilitate the blackout. The wire netting frames[13] placed over the school windows, as mentioned by Nellie on 18th July, 1940, would have been to prevent broken glass from falling inside She also mentions then that they used a nasty glue to stick cellophane paper on the inside of the glass.

But was Milverton in danger? As we will see it had to cope with an invasion of a different kind.

---

1. See 'Gone to the Country'.
2. See 'Defending Milverton – Home Guard'.
3. See 'Military Invasion'.
4. There may have been Anderson shelters dug in some gardens.
5. See 'Military Invasion' and Nellie – 17.7.40.
6. Nellie 21.6.40. Mrs. McGill believed that farmers were warned of the raid on Bristol so they could watch their crops which were particularly vulnerable at harvest time. She remembers 3 incendiary bombs dropped on Lynch Field and going out with her father to see the damage.
7. On 25.7.40 Nellie mentions a boy losing his gas mask.
8. See 'Preparing for the Worst', 'Doing Your Bit' and Appendix 2.
9. It was the reason why there are no pictures of her grand-daughter, Lavinia, as a baby. See 'Feeding the Nation'.
10. The government produced excellent posters alerting drivers and pedestrians to the dangers. The lack of street lights together with dimmed car lights accounted for many pedestrian deaths. By December 1940, some 1,155 had been killed – 825 during dark hours. There was increased pressure on the Government to do something about it. 'Pedestriancide' was one headline in the Belfast Newsletter for January 1940. The author's Gt. Uncle Tom was one of those that week who died as a result of being knocked down by a car at night in Belfast.
11. Nellie – 19.7.40; 16.9.40; 24.10.40; 22.10.41. Nellie's daughter Helen, remembered the difficulty her mother and Mrs Vickery had in trying to cook two separate Sunday lunches with low gas pressure.
12. Dorothy 'Dolly' sister of Mrs. Vickery.
13. This would have been at the Victoria Rooms where Nellie was teaching see 'Doubling Up – Education'.

3. DEFENDING MILVERTON – THE HOME GUARD

'Those (5 rounds) were to defend Milverton'
William Deacon, quoted by his wife, Gladys

Not, since the Napoleonic Wars at the turn of the 19th century had Britain been seriously threatened by an invading army. The then Prime Minister William Pitt and his Home Secretary, Henry Dundas drew up plans for redoubts around London; they prepared but did not print, instructions to the general populace regarding public safety: and prepared forms to gather intelligence on how many hooved animals, carts and bags of wheat that could be moved away from an approaching enemy; and how many men they could rely on to join the local yeomanry militias that would fight Napoleon's invading armies. These local Yeomanry militias eventually became, The Territorial Army now known as the Army Reserve.

A century and half later – on 14th May, 1940 – the Secretary of State for War, Anthony Eden, appealed for large numbers of men between 17 to 65 to come forward to join the Local Defence Volunteers (LDV) 'When on duty', he said, 'You will form part of the Armed Forces and your period of service will be for the duration of the War.' He thought 150,000 would respond but even before the broadcast ended, men were arriving at police stations to volunteer. The following day 250,000 had joined, this number being doubled within two weeks and by the following month another million had joined up. Of course many of them joined up temporarily whilst awaiting call-up to go into the regular forces, but as the entry requirements were low and there was no check on birth certificates, or specified upper age limit, the old and even the lame soon found themselves 'On His Majesty's Service' – ready to face a very real threat of invasion.

As Nazi armies conquered and held the north coast of France, including the Channel Islands, invasion from Normandy was a possibility and the Bristol Channel – a gateway to the industrial Midlands and North – had to be protected.

Over 6000 volunteered in Somerset that first week. The LDV identifying armbands, officially known as 'brassards' were often the only 'uniform' they had. They were meant to confer protection under the Geneva Convention should they be captured by the enemy.[1] As for weapons – the official directive was that there should be six men to a rifle and those without would wield axes or a heavy stick. The County sent out a request for sporting guns, revolvers or any kind of weapon.[2] Some men in the Home Guard were issued with shotguns. Shotgun cartridge manufacturers, Eley, produced 12 bore and 16 bore shotgun cartridges with one solid lead ball (known as lethal ball). With a broad arrow printed on the side and a small hole in the top end to see the ball they were easily identified as opposed to normal shot gun cartridges with multiple balls known as 'shot'. Shotguns were inspected and marked if they were suitable for firing lethal ball.

Milverton's young butcher, Ken Burston, who joined the LDV with a group of other young lads for three months[3] before he joined the Royal Tank Regiment, said that they were issued with rifles and did not need training as they were already good shots. They practised at a pre-war range north of Milverton Station, near Crowford/Colford.[4] This range was 400 yards long and ideal for Home Guard training although they tended to shoot up to 200 yards. Small-bore shooting took place in the skittle alley at The White Hart, which is where the LDV and later the Home Guard met throughout the War. Grenade practice was conducted at Castle Wood, Wiveliscombe. Ken said that they would stand guard on high points of land and once he and another young man investigated a tunnel from a cave which went from a big dip in the middle of a road right off Butts Way and came up under the Quaker cemetery.

After the fall of France on 22nd June, 1940, the threat of invasion increased. In July 1940, at Churchill's instigation the LDV officially became known as the Home Guard. Volunteers were initially ordered to watch for enemy landings at dawn and dusk, to manning road blocks and watch suspected fifth columnists. In time, some units, but not Wiveliscombe or Milverton expanded their objective to 'augment the local defences of Great Britain by providing static defence of localities and protection of vulnerable and key points and by giving timely notice of enemy movement to superior military organisations'. They mounted guard duties at road junctions, railway stations, bridges and tunnels.

In his book, *The Home Guard*, S. P. Mackenzie describes the tendency of volunteers to be jumpy and nervous – mistaking sounds of the countryside for fifth column or German paratroopers. Tiredness, unfamiliarity and over zealousness caused accidents and even the death of some, including regular soldiers, who were shot when not reacting to a challenge.

Whilst today in the light of the classic TV series *Dad's Army* many may regard the Home Guard with amusement, at the time they were to be treated as a serious military force by civilians and regular soldiers alike.

Administered under the Somerset Territorial Association the original list of kit planned for issue in August 1940, consisted of 'denims' (jacket and trousers), military gas mask, two eye shields, one set anti-gas ointment, steel helmet, field dressings, field service cap, great coat, boots, gaiters, belt, haversack, two armbands, blankets (one per two men), ground sheet (one per four men).

Much of this took a long time to arrive but during the autumn and winter of 1940 serge battledress uniforms and gas capes replaced the denims. Personnel used their own personal vehicles, bicycles and horses (on Exmoor) unless, being transported by locally provided trucks from industry. Military trucks may have been provided when on exercise with the regular soldiers. [6]

Other than rifle practice their training included first aid and taking counter-measures against various kinds of poison gas. Some personnel, but not all, would have been trained in signalling. Communications relied on runners or the few GPO telephones available. Volunteers were also trained in semaphore as wireless communication only became available to some units in 1942-43.

By October 1940 the organisation of the Somerset Home Guard was almost complete. This comprised two groups North and South divided by a line running from Burnham-on-Sea S-E to Street and down to the Wiltshire border. Milverton, part of the Wiveliscombe Company of the 1st Minehead Battalion, (initially named the 1st Dunster Battalion, was in the South Group. Originally commanded by Col. C. L. Norman DSO, MVO, DL South Group was made up of four battalions: 1st Minehead. (2nd) Taunton, (3rd) Yeovil (3rd) and (10th) Bridgwater. Later, in 1943 parts of the 2nd Taunton and 3rd Yeovil Battalions were detached to form the 11th Ilminster and 13th Somerton Battalions.

The Home Guard was initially issued with army Lee Enfield rifles. In early July 1940 they were exchanged for American US P17 and Canadian Ross rifles shipped over from America, in early July 1940, together with 5-10 rounds per weapon. These rifles had been stored in grease and it was left to the Home Guard to degrease them. The problem was that they used .303 bore ammunition whereas the British Enfields used .300.[7] To prevent accidents, a red band was painted round weapons firing .300 ammunition. The Enfields were soon returned to re-equip regular army units on return from Dunkirk, effectively separating both weapons and ammunition from that of the Home Guard. In late 1940 and early 1941 one or two units were issued with Vickers and Browning machine guns and US Savage Lewis .30 machine guns. Milverton would have the normal issue but information is sparse. One local person told me that they did have .303 rifles. Added to their weaponry in 1943 was a Boys anti-tank rifle.

Air reconnaissance in August identified enemy barges massing in the Channel ports and the fact that the tides and weather were favourable suggested an impending invasion. At 22.37 hrs on Saturday 7th September, General HQ Home Forces issued the code word 'Cromwell' to bring forces in the SE and Eastern Commands to the highest state of readiness. Although the Home Guard was not included in the order, Home Guard commanders were informed of the alert. However, not all of them understood what was happening and some called out their men. Church bells were rung as a warning in some places, including Wiveliscombe. Whilst the Home Guard was ordered to stand-down on the Sunday the army remained on alert for several days.

In February 1941 Home Guard commissions and 'ranks' were introduced and from November 1941 – May 1942 some Home Guard were attached to anti-aircraft duties and rocket batteries. By December of 1941 drafting into the Home Guard was made compulsory meaning that those in full-time work were also committed to doing 48 hours Home Guard duty a month. Apart from training, this would be guard duty in shifts of two hours on and hours off duty from 10 p.m. – 6 a.m. A letter[8] from Mr. Shapland of the Wiveliscombe Home Guard stated four men every two hours, which might have been summertime. The 48 hours a month also included drills, musters and training, not just guard duty hours off duty from 10 p.m. – 6.a.m.

Mrs. Yvonne Scott, former pupil at Shaftesbury House School, evacuated to St. Michael's House, tells of a joint Home Guard, ARP exercise to rescue people. 'They chose me to be the dummy. I was taken up to the roof, covered in red liquid (a substitute for blood on my legs). Then they strapped me to a stretcher and lowered me to the ground by ropes. Other pupils took part, plus nurses, ambulances with loud clanging bells and, of course, the occasional spectator. It was all very exciting!' She also remembered a 'smoke canister was mysteriously placed on the front wall to the right of the main gate, emitting clouds of black smoke, to our delight and the horror of the staff!' There are no dates for these events and the smoke canister, too, could have been a Home Guard exercise activity.

The County of Somerset's Director of Education, William Deacon, was second in command. His wife tells this story:

'My husband was in charge of a post at the top of Burn's Hill[9] there, and he was given five rounds of shot and told, that if the enemy came, to shoot back! So, my husband was, not having anything to do with shooting, being in the school corps – so, he had four other people to man the Burn's Hill Post, it was called. And my husband said to Squeaker Wyatt,[10] "Can you shoot?" "Ah," he said, "I know all about ah." Bill said, "You are going to be given by me, five rounds of shot and that's all we have here when the enemy comes."

'He was as brave as anything. I mean he would have shot anybody if my husband had said, "Shoot!"

'Then later on my husband asked, "Now Wyatt that shot I gave you the other day?" "Ah," he said, "Sir."

'"What did you use it for? It wasn't the enemy because they didn't come. I have no more shot and you do realise that Milverton depends upon you." I mean, my husband had to keep a straight face and it wasn't right. It was indeed unfortunate given that Home Guard motto was "to the last round – to the last man". He'd used them for poaching and my husband of course, said, "Well I know what you did with that shot. But it wasn't for shooting whatever you shot with it. It was to defend Milverton and Milverton people." And this was said without a smile I imagine, on either of their faces, so my husband said, "So I'll take that five rounds back please. So bring it to me tomorrow." So I think there was a secret meeting in which Squeaker had to confess he'd used the shot but he'd used it usefully shooting pheasant.'

In the run up to D-Day – Operation 'Overlord' – Somerset figured significantly as a conduit to major ports to be used in the invasion of Normandy. A crucial conference held in the Shire Hall in Taunton discussed the protection of essential lines of communication and identified that certain bridges and tunnels would be guarded. The Home Guard was therefore deployed to cover key points along the railway line to the invasion ports including Somerset Bridge at Bridgwater; the railway tunnels at White Ball and Somerton; the viaduct at Venn Cross and parts of the Southern main line railway near Yeovil.

Milverton's Cyril Loram, according to his daughter, Margaret, would go off at night with his rifle to guard the Venn Cross railway viaduct near Wiveliscombe. Farmers, like Cyril Loram and farm workers were particularly hard pressed as there was a shortage of agricultural manpower and no regular troops to help out as had happened in previous wartime summers.[11]

By the end of July 1944 Somerset was empty of soldiers leaving the Home Guard responsible for defence against sabotage or German raids.

The Allied successes after D-Day reduced the German threat to Somerset. June 1944 saw the transfer of barrage balloons and anti-aircraft guns from the Army AA gun batteries and RAF Balloon Squadrons defending aircraft factories at Westlands, Yeovil and at Weston-super-Mare, to the south coast to help counter the effect of the V1 bomb attacks on London.

On 6th September, 1944 it was announced that duties would no longer be compulsory. On Sunday, 3rd December, 1944 all Home Guard Stand Down parades took place and they disbanded on 31st December, 1945. The photographs show that it was a wet day all over Somerset. But it was not the end of the Home Guard story.[12]

---

1. Apparently Hitler stated that they would be shot on sight.
2. The issuing of weapons for the LDV was hampered because of the loss of 500,000 tons of stores left behind at Dunkirk.
3. Before it became Home Guard.
4. Evacuee, Bruce Watkiss remembered walking across the top of the quarry (probably Whitefields Quarry) when the Home Guard were having firing practice.
5. The author's father served in the Home Guard and said that everything that happened in the TV series was true to life, but having said that he took part in a serious weekend battle exercise, along with regular soldiers, defending an important West Country city.
6. There was one Home Guard Transport Company in Somerset.

7. The Canadian Ross rifle was an extremely accurate weapon firing the standard Mk7.303 round but it did not like the mud of the trenches!
8. See 'Doing Your Bit' – There is some discrepancy about this and it might be due to summer time.
9. Clive Perry said his father, Ted, saw the Home Guard burying bottles (Phosphorous or Molotov cocktails) at the top of Burn Hill.
10. Author has not been able to identify 'Squeaker'.
11. See 'On the Fields'.
12. See 'Silver Linings and Dark Clouds'.

4. DOING YOUR BIT – WHAT DID YOU DO IN THE WAR GRANNY?

by Jane Woodland

'That in the opinion of this house, trousers are much more useful than skirts'.

WI debate 5.11.40

The civilian population contributed to the Second World War effort on a scale never known before. This highly effective mobilisation resulted in one third of all civilians playing their part by 1944, including over seven million women. Men who were not conscripted, and women, worked in a variety of roles, paid and unpaid.

On 22nd May, 1940 the Emergency Powers (Defence) Act passed into law giving the government complete control over people and property. In the wake of this Minister of Labour and National Service, Ernest Bevin introduced the Essential Work Order (EWO). This became law in March 1941 and meant workers doing jobs deemed essential to the war effort had to continue in their employment. Employers were similarly constrained, having to seek permission from the Ministry of Labour if they wanted to sack one of their priority work force. Reserved occupations included engineers, railway and dockworkers, miners, farmers, agricultural workers, schoolteachers and doctors. The age at which a job was designated as reserved varied. Many pacifists and conscientious objectors opted to work in reserved positions.

Darlingest

BOROUGH OF TAUNTON
EMERGENCY POWERS (DEFENCE)
REGISTRATION FOR CIVIL DEFENCE DUTIES

Notice to men born between 7th September, 1881, and 6th September, 1923.
Requirement to Register on Sunday, 14th September ; Saturday, 20th September ; and Sunday, 21st September, 1941.

NOTICE IS HEREBY GIVEN by the Council of the BOROUGH OF TAUNTON that all male British subjects who, on the 6th day of September, 1941, are resident in the BOROUGH OF TAUNTON and are not less than eighteen but under sixty years of age, are, unless they are exempted persons as specified in the Schedule hereto, required to apply in the manner hereinafter mentioned to be registered under the Civil Defence Duties (Compulsory Enrolment) Order, 1941.

The application for registration is required to be made in writing on a form which will be provided, and the applicant is required to state his names in full, his home address, his age, the date of his birth, his National Registration Number, and his occupation or profession.

The application is required to be made in person on the appropriate day as specified below according to the applicant's age, at the following places, namely :

Applicants residing in the Castle and Wilton Wards—The Employment Exchange, 45, Bridge Street, Taunton.
Applicants residing in the Priory and Trinity Wards—The Employment Exchange premises, Revenue Buildings, Billet Street, Taunton.
Applicants residing in the Staplegrove and Rowbarton Wards—St. Andrew's School, Rowbarton, Taunton.

The form on which the application is to be made will be supplied to the applicant when he attends for the purpose of making his application for registration. **APPLICANTS WILL BE ASKED TO PRODUCE THEIR NATIONAL REGISTRATION IDENTITY CARDS WHEN REGISTERING.**

To avoid waiting, applicants should, as far as possible, attend at the appropriate place mentioned above and on the day and at the time indicated below, namely :—
TIMES

5. *Emergency Powers*, Somerset Gazette, *1941.*

Many men and women, some too old to be on active service, had 'reserved' occupations, where their skills were required for the job they were already doing or required elsewhere and moved to specialist factory or other work. The result was that some of the most talented people were co-opted to work for government departments such as the Ministry of Information and Ministry of Food. Here their considerable talents produced some of the most dramatic and iconic posters, cartoons, catch phrases and propaganda films of all time. But wherever people were working whether it be in banks, in shops or factories they still had to do their bit for civil defence as fire wardens, often in their own workplace or be attached to the ARP set up before hostilities[1] or Home Guard, in 1940.[2]

The ROYAL OBSERVER CORPS (ROC) – set up in 1925, was a civilian volunteer corps working 24-48 hours a week. The observers were issued with RAF uniforms and high quality Royal Navy binoculars, and were well trained, having prepared for war since 1938. They worked in pairs – requiring a lot of people to cover each 24-hour period. To alleviate the pressure on volunteers, women were recruited from 1941. The original observation posts were nothing more than sheds situated next to telegraph poles so as to enable communication to a control centre either directly or via a local telephone exchange. The sheds were positioned 10-16 km apart – in fields or on top of buildings. Each centre controlled 35-40 posts. In Avon, Somerset and Devon there were three centres: 23 Group (Bristol), 22 Group (Yeovil) and 21 Group (Exeter). Whilst the Corps' main task was to spot, locate and report the approach of enemy aircraft, observers also kept watch for parachutists; troop carrying aircraft, and all types of marine craft – including submarines, and ships laying mines in coastal waters. They also aided in search for lost aircraft and reported crashes. ROC alerts triggered air raid warnings both in residential areas and areas with 'permitted lighting' such as ports or factories.[3] Given a 'purple' warning, if under threat of imminent attack they could extinguish lights. After the war, the Royal Observer Corps came under the administrative and the operational control of the Home Office. It eventually disbanded in December 1995.

By the outbreak of war 1.5 million volunteers had signed up for the ARP. Controlled centrally by the Home Office, the AIR RAID PREVENTION WARDENS (ARP) was to 'minimise the effects of air raids once the enemy had penetrated the active defences'. They watched for fires, advised and checked on black-out precautions and shelters and issued information about protecting people from gas attack. After a bombing attack they were to help restore services, deal with heavy casualties and dispose of the dead. Originally most ARP wardens were part-time volunteers, the few full-time[4] wardens being paid £3 a week for men and £2 for women. During the phoney war – when it came – the ARP were often greeted with abuse, accused of being paid to interfere.

But was rural Milverton going to require all these services? Whilst waiting to be called up, the late Ted Perry did his bit as an Air Raid Warden, with a helmet as his only uniform. Their HQ was in the former Committee Room at St. Michael's Rooms (Felton Hall) where they had a phone, bed and blankets to sleep at night. 'We'd take it in turns for this duty. It was our job, as soon as we had a red alert, we used to have to go out, up in the churchyard and parade around there and look around to make sure no one was dropping out of the skies. "Red Alert" came from Headquarters, which, as far as I know was Taunton. Often the planes were going over to Exeter and Plymouth over here. We used to hear them. It was a terrible sound… it's difficult to describe… But, then, often you could see all the Ack Ack.[5] We had searchlights all the way around here, and as the plane came over they would pick it up and then they'd pass it on to the next.'[6]

In the cities, however, once the bombing began it was soon realised that there were not enough personnel to respond to the frequency of air raids. In 1941 the Ministry of Home Security issued its first Civil Defence Enrolment order stating that all males of 16 – 60 not already engaged in Home Guard or Civil Defence duties must perform up to 48 hours fire-watching a month.

The question of which occupations should be designated as reserved jobs was reviewed throughout the war and men previously thought too old to fight, were recruited into the forces to replace younger men in non-combatant roles. Retired military personnel were called up for home-based military duties. In Milverton, the Parish Council asked that Col. Moberly Bell, who had resigned on 16th December, 1939, be excused attendance at Council meetings while on military service in Preston but that as no election was due he should retain his seat.

Some, but not all teaching posts were reserved. Men up to the age of

35 could be called up, unless a head teacher and women teachers were not assured of returning to their jobs if they enlisted in the WRAC, WRNS or WAAF.

But a raft of legislation determined the contribution women were expected to make to the war effort and in May 1940 trade unions agreed to let women work in trades previously barred to them. So, as they had in the First World War, women began to take a more active and important, sometimes strenuous role in urgent war work such as munitions, transport and heavy industry, including ship building to free men needed to join the forces.

In the early summer of 1940, Mrs. Nellie Clemens, a teacher in North London had applied for war work and unbeknown to her was accepted by the Board of Censors, but before its letter arrived, she had agreed to accompany children from a North Harringay School who were to be evacuated to the safety of rural Somerset.

On the day the National Registration Act of April 1941 came into effect Miss Florence Hancock of the Transport and General Workers Union gave a rousing speech at Leeds, 'This day is a red-letter day for women, for it is the first time in history of the country that they have been called on to register for work of national importance. If we believe in equality there can be no reason to oppose similar provisions being applied to women as are already operating for men. There are a number of women who are well able to work in the factory or go into one of the Services, but who are evading their national responsibilities and are not rendering any useful service to the community. The country must say to such women you can no longer live on the work of others.'

Nellie had signed up months before this Act came into effect whereby all women aged 18 to 50 had to register as 'mobile' or 'immobile'. Immobile women were those who had a husband at home or were married to servicemen. They were directed to local war work. Theoretically though, Nellie was classified 'immobile' as her husband remained at their home in London.

December 1941 saw The National Service Act which enforced

conscription for all unmarried women between 20 and 30. Women had the choice to be a) auxiliaries i.e. WRN, ATS, WAAF, National Fire Service, civil defence forces and police war reserve or b) workers in industry or agriculture. Married women were not compelled to join the services but were expected to play their part in the war effort and could be directed to work in industry.

Exemptions could be granted in cases of special hardship, including cases where single women had adopted or illegitimate children under 14 living with them.

The Employment of Women Order 1943 controlled the movement of 'mobile' women workers aged 18 to 40. The country was divided into zones of different colours; scarlet areas were deemed in urgent need of unskilled women, red areas were able to recruit locally, so women did not have to leave these areas and green zones were said to have spare labour and women workers living here were moved to scarlet areas.

The age limit for conscription for women was later extended to 43. Women who had served in the First World War, including Wrens, could be conscripted up to the age of 50. By mid-1943 almost 90% of single women and 80% of married women were working in factories, on the land or in the armed forces.

Throughout history as today, child care is a problem for working women. Addressing this issue, Ernest Bevin, Minister for Labour, stated in 1941 that 'the provision for the care of children is a matter of the first importance for the war effort'. For women working full-time with no one to look after a small child, nursery facilities, both day and boarding, were made available. State funding was provided to establish about 1345 wartime nurseries, a huge increase from the 14 such nurseries which existed in 1940 and by the end of the war 62,000 children were in day care. For some women, working in towns and cities, this meant they only saw their child at the weekend if he/she had been moved to a safer area.

Married women with only one child could be called up[7] and their children put in a nursery. It was difficult for mothers and for some children it affected their relationship with their mothers for the rest of their lives. There was no such nursery in Milverton but in addition to her day to day teaching duties Nellie mentions, on 21st October, 1940, to being asked by Mr Cann (head teacher for Evacuee North Harringay) to 'do a bit of supervision' and that he 'is going to tell the office that I shall get paid for it. It's really very decent of him and I don't mind because it's only a case of looking into the Victoria Rooms a bit, as the children are going to be allowed there, they are not wanted in their billets.'[8] The intensity of this work varied, on some days she 'wandered' down to the rooms and there were no children to supervise but in poor weather she earned her money. On 30th October, 1940 she wrote, 'It was wet and I thought I'd better get me to the Victoria Rooms in good time. It was as well that I did because I had quite a mob there. They were there all morning as well. What a din there was! I'm hoping it's not going to be as cold and wet tomorrow. It's too much like work meetings!' Women were offered the choice of forces, factory work or working on the land:

AUXILIARY TERRITORIAL SERVICE (ATS) – As the war years drew on, the need emerged for women to play a more extensive role in jobs which were previously all male domains. All women serving in the auxiliary forces had equal status as men. ATS women were considered part of the

MIDDLE AGED CALL UP

Men of 50 and women of 45

By TREVOR EVANS

MR. BEVIN, reviewing his man-power programme for the summer, has decided to exercise his power to call on women up to 45 and men up to 50 to register for employment.

The last women to be registered were the 41's, the last men the 47's.

Events in Libya and our commitment to a Second Front are reflected in this move to extend registration to middle-aged men and women, and in a simultaneous overhaul of the cases of all younger men and women who have not yet been called to national service.

The registrations will take place fortnightly for the next three months, as follows :—

July 11 .. Women born in 1900
July 25 .. Men   „   1894
August 8 . Women   „   1899
August 22. Men   „   1893
Sept. 5 .. Women   „   1898
Sept. 19 .. Men   „   1892
Oct 3 .... Women   „   1897

Tomorrow women born in 1923 will register, unless exempted because of their present jobs.

6. Daily Express, *26th June, 1942.*

army, they wore uniform, lived in Nissen Huts, paraded and learned a great variety of skills, which eventually included signalling, decoding, observing, even manning anti-aircraft guns and maintaining and driving cars and trucks. During the war more than a quarter of a million women served in the ATS, including Queen Elizabeth II, making it the largest of the women's services. On 3rd June, 1940, at the height of the Dunkirk crisis, paragraphs of the County letter were read, appealing for recruits to the ATS. On 3rd February, 1942 the WI sent good wishes to a Miss Chapman who had joined the services, though it doesn't say which. On 3rd July, 1945, Mrs. Jagger gave 'an entertaining account of her experiences in the ATS to Milverton WI.

The WOMEN'S ROYAL NAVAL SERVICE (WRNS) – Originally founded during the First World War, this service was reformed in April 1939 and by 1943 there were 74,000 WRNS members or Wrens as they came to be known, working both in the UK and overseas. They helped plan and organise naval operations and some worked at the Government Code and Cypher School at Bletchley Park where German and Japanese codes were broken. Few served at sea, but some Wrens did pilot small ships across the channel on D-Day.

The WOMEN'S AUXILIARY AIR FORCE (WAAF) – was founded in 1939, to enable RAF personnel to take front line positions, by 1943 there were 182,000 members. Women in the WAAF, with few exceptions, did not fly. But they did get to know aircraft as they helped to build them, becoming acetylene welders, fabric makers, flight mechanics and fitters as well as doing the very specialised work of parachute packing (rigging). They also compiled weather reports, served on airfields and worked in intelligence. Many worked as radar control operators and guided night-fighter aeroplanes against German bombers. Huge barrage balloons (66 feet long and 30 feet high when inflated) were used to deter enemy bombers and members of the WAAF took responsibility for raising and lowering the balloons, operating more than 1000 balloon sites across the country.

The AIR TRANSPORT AUXILIARY AIR FORCE (ATA) – was formed in 1939 to free pilots for active service. Women took over the role of ferrying aircraft from one air station to another. Whilst having transported new, twin-engine aircraft from the factories to where they were needed, they were never allowed near Spitfires and Hurricanes!

Whilst, of course, nurses were recruited into the forces in Queen Alexandra Nursing Corps – Army, Princess Alexandra's Royal Naval Nursing Service, Princess Mary's Royal Nursing Service – RAF. The Army nursing service could draw on VADs. The VOLUNTARY AID DETACHMENT began in 1916 comprising volunteers from the Order of St. John and the Red Cross working with the newly formed Territorial Army. Before the Second World War the VAD had been recognised as being able to supplement the general medical services. They drove St. John and Red Cross ambulances and not only worked on the Home Front, they also travelled to the Far East. VADs had to defer to Army sisters.

Milverton people will remember the diminutive figure of Beatie Hayes (Beatrice Perry). Her nephew, Clive writes that she held her own amongst her brothers – climbing trees helped by Perce (Percy) and Cyril who then ran away leaving her up there. She left school at 14 and went into service and worked in the kitchens of the Red Cross convalescent home (for the Army and RAF) at Abbotsfield, Wiveliscombe. She used to sneak out at night to go down to the pub hiding her nightclothes under a bush to change into on her return in case the cook found her outside. 'Just popped out for fresh air' was the planned reply to enquiries as to what she thought she was doing out at that time of night. She had met Albert 'Tib' Hayes at a dance in Milverton before the war and they married on his return from service in the army in Italy. They lived at Hayefield at the top of Wood Street.

To become a FANY was a ticket to a myriad of jobs disguised as FIRST AID NURSING YEOMANRY had developed in 1909 from the Royal Army Medical Corps. The FANY recruited middle and upper-class young ladies who underwent training in first-aid, home nursing, horsemanship and veterinary work. During the First World War, they drove ambulances as well as giving first aid in the field. Whilst volunteers, the government called upon them as drivers during the General Strike of 1926 and the following year recognised them officially as the FANY (Car Ambulance Service). Reconvened in 1938 the FANY interlinked with the ATS, but, they had an additional group – a volunteer corps, the 'free' FANY who wore a different khaki uniform. They led a very different life acting as driving escorts, hostesses and cover for the Special Operations Executive (S.O.E.) including parachute jumping.

Men and women joined SOE parachuting into occupied Europe to help the Resistance and carry out guerrilla activities. Women agents in SOE wore FANY uniforms to give them military status. At home, some men became involved in the very secret Auxiliary Units of the Home Guard,[9] hid away in bunkers, underground tunnels trained in guerrilla tactics and to work behind the lines of an invading army.

AUXILIARY FIRE SERVICE – The Auxiliary Fire Service was formed in 1938 and by the outbreak of war over 5,000 AFS women were serving in London. Even with the additional man and woman power, great strains were put on the fire service when German bombing began in earnest. On the night of 29th December, 1940 1,600 fires were at one point burning simultaneously in London. May 1941 saw the nationalisation of the fire service in a bid to improve its efficiency; the National Fire Service was created. In 1942 compulsory fire watching duties were imposed on women under 45.

Locally, a fire guard was set up in Milverton. It is unclear how many of the local force were women though Nellie does write on 5th February, 1941, that a school fire-watching scheme had been discussed but didn't think it necessary. The parish council minutes record a lengthy discussion about the responsibilities and training of the Milverton Guard.[9] The response to fires caused by enemy action was to come primarily from Taunton, Wellington and Wiveliscombe fire services but if there was a delay, action was to be taken by the Milverton Fire Guard. Apparently 'a good number of volunteers have been enrolled to form a fire guard in Milverton'. There was a two man manual pump in the village and stirrup pumps and buckets were placed at intervals on the streets. A training ground was set up in a Mrs Bere's garage at Old Halls and the yard beyond it.

Women played their part in CIVIL DEFENCE, both as volunteers and some as paid ARP wardens. The normal working week was 72 hours for men i.e. 6 12 hour shifts and 48 hours for women. Men were paid £3 a week and women's salaries were £2 a week with a 5s. rise in July 1940. By June 1940 there were more than 50,000 women in full time civil defence work and at the height of the Blitz one in six wardens were women.

In April 1943 the War Office withdrew its ban on women serving in the Home Guard and they took on non-fighting, domestic and medical duties.

Heavy industry in Somerset was dominated by the aviation industry, and particularly centred on Westlands in Yeovil and the Royal Ordnance Factory at Puriton – a long way from Milverton.

Elsewhere in the country, many women worked in ship building as welders. A *News Chronicle* article of 5th June, 1944, states that by the end of the financial year 1943/44, the proportion of women in the aircraft industry had risen from negligible to 40%.

In terms of lighter industry in Somerset, an unexpected increase in demand was experienced in the withy trade, which had been in decline for a number of years before 1939; willow baskets were required for air drops.

Working on the land and the story of providing growing and producing food during the war is described in chapters, 'On the Fields, Dig for Victory' and 'Feeding the Nation' and includes the Women's Land Army. A pamphlet produced during the war titled *Eve in Overalls* by Arthur Wauters, evaluated the success of the nation's efforts to increase food production. 'The area under cultivation has increased since the war by six million acres. The quantity of corn grown alone has risen by a third, potatoes by 60 per cent and sugar even more. At the present time 4 million tons of vegetables are produced whereas in 1938 this figure was only two and a half million tons. And there are three million small private gardens, which supply between ten and fifteen million pounds' worth of vegetables every year.'

The LAND ARMY – women marched and trained as an army, though not with guns. Locally, training took place at Cannington College. The *Somerset Countryman* publication (January 1940) stated during the four weeks training here 'the girls have specialised in milking and livestock, in general farm work with tractor driving or in horticulture. Very delightful has been the month spent at the Farm Institute and afterwards these recruits have been allowed extension training to learn how to set about things on a Somerset farm.' The women were either billeted at the farms where they worked, or lived in hostels or taken to farms when they were needed. Their 'dress' uniform of breeches, socks and a green sweater with flat brimmed hat has remained a dominant image of women in the war, though they did their work in overalls and many of them did not get rubber boots for months. By the end of 1939 there were 4,500 Land Girls and by 1943, 87,000. In Somerset there were 163 Land Girls by December 1939, a figure which climbed steadily over the next couple of years but saw an exponential increase to 1,298 by the end of December 1942, finally peaking in December 1943 at 1,794.

Statistics from a university study show that, across a range of tasks, the Land Girls produced on average 79% of male output They were least efficient in heavy tasks such as loading potatoes (44%) and manure (46%), but came close to matching performance in tasks such as milking (91%) and turning hay (92%) and in some areas exceeded their male counterparts e.g. poultry tending (101%) and picking peas (103%) and runner beans (101%). They were paid by the farmers, and the pay rate was fixed by the Board of Agriculture – 28s (£1.40) for a 48-hour week, though girls under 18 received 22s. 6d. (£1.12). The wage went up slightly in 1944.

Some Milvertonians volunteered to help local farmers. The Milverton WI records for 7th May, 1940, state that Mrs. Morris volunteered to give part time help in response to an appeal for volunteers for the Women's Land Army.

Others were moved into the area and employed as full time Land Girls, living and working on local farms. One such was Amy McGrath[10] (nee Mason) who, over the age of 17 and no longer needed at the Tootal

Factory as an embroiderer and finisher of garments was offered the ATS, munitions factory or Land Army. She chose the latter. From Bolton she was sent to Manchester for six weeks' training and then Taunton ending up working at Cormiston a small-holding at Preston Bowyer for four and a half years. Jacquie Keates' mother, Olive Yesford arrived in Stogumber on 21st December, 1942. She had also been working in the textile industry in Bury.

Interesting social comment at the time comes in Arthur Wauters' booklet, *Eve in Overalls*. He writes 'Farmers were at first a little afraid – many on account of their crops and no doubt a few on account of their morals – of these women pertly dressed up as men. A member of the House of Commons tried, however, to convince them by recalling that after all, from the beginning Eve had shown a great interest in the cultivation of fruit.'

Arthur himself is won over by the Land Girls. 'I have never been so struck by joy of living, suppleness of gait, vivacity and moral balance. They look gracefully gay in their riding breeches and they are happy. The majority of them have only one desire: to continue their work on the farms after the war. Their health is excellent; their food is more varied and more abundant than in the towns. They have a variety of jobs to do, of far less monotonous character than in the factories – and out in the open air!'

Amy Mason wrote that she was met at Milverton Station by the Hon. T. H. Watson's secretary a Miss Hincks accompanied with her two dogs – Roy and Colin. She recorded memories of working at Cormiston, and they paint a vivid and often humorous picture. She worked alongside another Land Girl, Barbara Williams who came to Somerset from Liverpool. After a month's probation, spent at Olands Lodge, staying with Mr and Mrs. Ackland (where the Dakowskis now live) she was given a bicycle to get to Preston Bowyer where she 'made good progress – very different, very tiring – but I did love it'. She eventually moved to the Mill with Mr and Mrs. Jacobs, Capt. Watson's bailiff and their school girl daughter, Joan. 'Yes, I was homesick – but we just had to get on with the job, along the way there was a few tears. I wrote home – eagerly awaited the post for letters – and so month after month went by. Leave was one week in six months and a long weekend. Barbara and I and Joan, all became like sisters. I couldn't honestly say it was easy – it wasn't. Living at the farm had its good parts – we did have electric light but only candles at bedtime… Mrs Jacobs was an excellent cook so we did enjoy good food. When I think of the girls who were in hostels who were given sandwiches daily – Barbara and I were very lucky indeed. Mr Jacobs was a good boss – quite strict with us – but I feel, got us into shape. He knew we were tackling far different lives than our nine to five jobs. Up we would be 6.30 in the morning. The Ministry of Food decided that Somerset should continue to produce milk. Registers had to be kept of all the milk, butter and cheese produced.'

Amy and Barbara had a variety of daily tasks. Collecting the eggs from the hens was occasionally enlivened by drama. 'We used to go and let the hens out and then once we went, and you know nothing came out – they all were, on their perches, with their heads off… dogs, perhaps a fox or a badger got under and got (them) and we had the job of burying them. Miss Hincks said she would not dream of eating them.'

Work required skill and was often physically demanding. Amy recalls scything grass for the bull, a task she seems to have managed, but loading and controlling the barrow was less easy. I 'filled the barrow and was taking it down and there was a bit of an incline there and I'd opened the gate and blinking barrow slipped down, just as a convoy of Americans were coming round the corner. Down it went on, "Oh, hi there Land Girl, Oh what's the matter?" And three of them got out and such a to do. Oh was my face red! Oh I thought I'd never get out of this. It was pouring down. I'd got my sou'wester on. I must have looked absolutely dire. And they just said, "Need we bother about this? Are you just alright with the barrow?" "Yes I've been as quick as I could." "Yes, that's it." And so, we got it back in the barrow and ultimately, excuses to Mr. Jacobs. And he said, "That bull's going to be so thin!" Oh I got into trouble for that.'

Ploughing was another skill that it took time to master: Mr Jacobs' comment on the furrows Amy made when she first handled the plough was, 'Well, I hope no one passes there when the wheat's growing in that field.' Milking came more easily to Amy and one of the cows, Lettie, 'would only give me her milk'. The Land Girls did have time off but it was limited and dictated by the farmer. Amy usually had a half day on a Thursday and would take the bus to Taunton where she'd shop, have tea at Maynards on Bridge Street and go to the cinema, but she never met other Land Girls. They had to do their tasks though and milk before they went off duty half past two or three but had to be back home by 8.30p.m. Despite these restrictions, a necessary corollary of war, Amy had a good relationship with her boss, she appreciated his kindness and mentions his gift of a box of Cox's apples, sent on the train to her mother. She remembers having fun she enjoyed as a Land Girl and reflecting in 2005, when visiting Milverton, she likened her Land Army years as being her 'Gap Years'.[11]

TIMBER CORPS – Other women worked in the Timber Corps which again was a tough physical job. Locally, trees in the fir plantations planted at the top of Huish Cleave and spreading down to Waterrow were cut down by women and farmers' sons in 1939. The timber was used for pit props in the mines, and later on for telegraph poles. The trees were cut down with axes and dragged out by shire horses and then cut in 6½, 4½ and 3½ foot lengths with handsaws. A women working in the Taunton Timber Corps recalls, 'We were always washing our hair, as in spite of wearing scarves, turban fashion, we got so much sawdust, lichen and dust raining down on us as we sawed away at the trees.'

But if not conscripted to do war work there was still essential voluntary work to do. Once war was declared and over time the WVS took on more duties including escorting evacuees,[12] staffing fixed and mobile canteens,[13] knitting for troops,[14] organising libraries and Housewives Service to even making camouflage netting. It was organised county-wide and in Somerset a local MP's wife, Mrs. Wickham led the Centre in Taunton. They were also to assist Police by providing cars and loudspeakers for which a local mobile service of three cars was provided by Mrs. Gregory of Bradford on Tone, to assist with a messaging service. (No mobile phones.) The organisation lives on today as the Women's Royal Voluntary Service.

The WOMEN'S INSTITUTE – The Milverton WI was vigorous in its efforts throughout the course of the war. The Milverton WI Committee Record Book 1939 – 45 illustrates well the tasks that members were asked or volunteered to take on. As successive meetings were held, in different venues every few months as the war rolled on, the minutes record the diversity of war effort areas to which the women of the village contributed, as will be revealed in other chapters. It is significant that at on 5th October, 1942, Milverton's Women's Institute having realised the great role played by women during the past very difficult and somewhat frightening years, agreed to add a rider to their Council's Autumn meeting – Resolution 4 'that all manual workers without canteen facilities should be allowed an extra cheese ration' proposing that the words 'man or woman' be inserted after the words 'manual workers'.

As you can see, women took on a variety of jobs. Whatever it was, they were doing their bit! Everyone was involved in keeping everyone fed and safe! As at end of the First World War, and again at the end of the second, women had been tested and shown their worth. On 9th March, 1945 Milverton's WI held a debate 'That there should be equal pay for equal work'. The words echoed the speech of Miss Hancock of the TGWU exactly four years earlier. The motion was carried, but the debate continues 70 years on.

---

1. See Preparing for the Worst' and 'Sup up and clear the Cellars' chapter 2.
2. See 'Milverton's Militia'.
3. See 'Military Invasion'.
4. Wilfred Clemens, Nellie's husband was a full-time ARP warden. See, Biography at front of book.
5. Nellie mentions – (17.7.40). There was a searchlight on high ground behind Houndsmoor Farm.
6. See, 'Military Invasion' for searchlights.

7. Nellie had applied for war work – the letter from the Board of Censors, dated 18th June, 1940 – arrived after she had gone to Milverton. It offered her a job working in several cities – all of which were severely bombed!
8. Milverton WI on 6.9.39, agreed to close the meeting at 4p.m. 'as many members had evacuee children billeted with them'. See 'Gone to the Country'.
9. See 'Sup Up and Clear the Cellars'.
10. See' On the Fields'.
11. Her experiences of attending the dances at the Victoria Rooms are recounted in 'Raising a Laugh'.
12. Sylvia Perry recalls being given tea by the WVS in Salisbury when she was travelling down to Milverton from London, as an evacuee – 'Gone to the Country'.
13. Military Invasion.
14. 'Make Do and Mend'.

5. MILITARY INVASION – DEFENDING THE WEST COUNTRY

'Belgian officer informs me King of Belgians has signed separate Armistice with Germany. Shall I blow bridge on my front?'
                                                                    Maj. E Bazalgette

On 20th November, 1939, Mrs. Enid Moberly Bell wrote informing the parish council that her husband, Col. Moberly Bell could no longer attend council meetings 'as he is now commanding a training centre in Lancashire'. The Military Training Act of April 1939, decreed that all men between the ages of 20 and 21 had to register for six months' military training. But this was rapidly superseded by conscription. By October, all men aged between 18-41 were liable for military service for the duration unless in reserved occupations.[1] The first called up were the 20- 23 year olds who had their pick the Army, Navy or RAF. One by one Milverton's young men began going off to war. Ken Burston (who had briefly joined the LDV[2] in May 1940) left to join the Royal Tank Regiment ending up in North Africa. John Fouracre joined the Royal Engineers ending up in Burma, Edward (Ted) Perry left his ARP duties to join the RAF. His son, Clive, writes that Ted's initial training was at RAF Locking, a Trades Training Centre. He was originally scheduled to land on Gold Beach[3] on D-Day+2 but the engines of his ship or landing craft failed. They had to wait overnight mid channel for a tug as lights of German e-boats passed by. He was rated as an emergency driver of different types of vehicles including those supplying fuel and ammunition.[4] The airfields were so near to the front line that during the battle of the Falaise Gap he saw that no sooner had Hawker Typhoon fighter bombers taken off and dived to fire their rockets they immediately turned to land again. He remembered bullets whistling by his head that were fired by pockets of German troops nearby. There was always the danger of being shot by your own side as RAF blue could be mistaken for German Feldgrau at a distance. He remembered a front line rule: 'When the RAF flies over, we stand and watch. When the Luftwaffe flies over we stand by our trenches, but when the Americans fly over we get into the trenches!'

His brother, Cyril, had tried to follow his eldest brother Percy into the Navy, but was rejected as unfit because of heart problems. He was however, accepted in the Army. After initial training, he was posted to the Pioneer Corps. Their cap badge of crossed pick and shovel gives an idea of the type of work they did! Nothing is known of his war service but he finished the war in Germany. There was always friendly rivalry between the brothers and one night after drink had been taken there was a heated discussion about which was really the senior service: the navy or army.

Sadly, Percy did not survive. His nephew, Clive, said that Percy joined the Royal Navy in the mid-1930s as a Stoker. 'After serving on minesweepers and destroyers, he transferred to motor torpedo boats in 1940. Sent to the Far East he landed at Singapore in early 1941, as the Japanese were closing in. He was last seen the night before the surrender but was not at muster the next day. The Japanese bombed and shelled the shrinking perimeter into the early hours so he could well have been killed then. His memorial on the Hoe at Plymouth with an "unknown grave on land" is shared with at least four other stoker mates from HMS Sultan who died at the same time. Perhaps, like many others they took their chances with a small boat that night but did not make it. Whatever his true end, he was definitely never a prisoner of the Japanese. This is confirmed from the list of Far East POWs held at the National Arboretum near Tamworth.'

Clive revealed that in his last letter to his parents in October or November 1941, Percy had said that he was going to settle down when he got home as 'he had his eye on someone'. The identity of the 'someone' has remained a mystery.

Basil Jennings joined the RAF serving in Coastal Command being stationed in Scotland some of the time. He remembered getting on a train in Plymouth packed with sailors sleeping on seats, in corridors and even on luggage racks. He saved up for barley sugars when going on 'ops'. Looking back, Basil came to regard his war years as the best time of his life thanks to the sense of comradeship which he could never recapture in peacetime.

The Maunders brothers, Ralph and Thomas from Houndsmoor also chose the RAF. Ralph used to tip his wings when flying over Milverton, but sadly Thomas, was killed when just 20 years old. His funeral was held on 14th July, 1942 at St. Michael's Church by the Vicar, the Rev. Palmer, who unusually added a comment in the burial book 'Thomas Victor Maunders RAF. A brilliant Pilot officer who crashed in Sussex'.[5]

Not everyone went to war. Whilst Herbert Tucker joined the submarine service, his younger brother, Jack, remained to work at Baghay Farm, in a reserved occupation, much to his chagrin.

Throughout the country a great many camps were either quickly built or adapted to fast track training the massive influx of raw recruits. Three training camps were in the Taunton area during the summer of 1939: Norton 'militia camp', now home to 40 Commando; Sherford[6] and Middleway. So urgent was the need that the 950 men involved in the construction worked an 88¾ hour week with the average overtime being 42½ hours.

Before the outbreak of war, militia camp accommodation was good, significantly better than later wartime camps. Like Norton, many had sets of six sleeping huts linked, like spokes in a wheel to a central hut (nicknamed 'spiders') that contained baths, ablutions and latrine facilities. In the SE corner were two 30-yard rifle ranges. Norton Manor house was used as the Officers' Mess.

In the late 1980s, when the Dr. Barbara Bond and her husband moved to Milverton, she could not understand why her father, Jack Garside, knew all the pubs in Taunton! Being a telegrapher he had been classified as having a 'reserved occupation' but was determined to serve in the forces. From Manchester, where he enlisted in the Royal Corps of Signals as a Telegraphist, he travelled south to Norton in 1940 for training.[7] He explained that Taunton was near enough to be able to discover the pubs on foot. He went on to serve in Italy from Messina to Venice. Being 'non-combatants' they had just two rifles between 38 of them!

The young conscripted men who went away from Milverton were replaced by a 100-250 men of 'C' Company, 2nd Battalion, Middlesex Regiment (the 'Diehards') who had experienced a traumatic withdrawal from Dunkirk.[8]

According to Clive Perry, his Uncle Percy was a changed man after his return from helping in the Dunkirk evacuation. Percy was there as the organised withdrawal gave way to a final free for all. He didn't talk much about it but did say how awful it was hitting desperate men with a boat hook to stop them climbing onto an overloaded vessel that was nearly capsizing under the weight of the troops already on board.

After regrouping, the 2nd Bn. Middlesex Regiment, went first to the Isle of Wight; then to Langport; and finally to Taunton. 'C' Coy. arrived in Milverton on 7th August a month before Nellie's first reference to the C.O. Major Edward Bazalgette. He attended a dance on 11th and on 28th September, a whist drive, where he gave out the prizes and said 'goodnight to her most cordially'. Milverton's community spirit shone through at this time as the population welcomed and entertained these soldiers who had been through so much.

'C' Coy's arrival was part of a massive movement of people throughout the summer of 1940. As civilian evacuation began gearing up in May,[9] General Headquarters Home Forces decided to establish nine corps headquarters across Great Britain each with a responsibility for the field force troops in its area and for the active preparations to repulse any German invasion. Large numbers of troops soon took to the road.

Darlingest

Nellie noted on her first night in Milverton, 17th June, 1940, that she was kept awake by heavy military traffic along North Street – the main route from Taunton to Wiveliscombe and Exmoor.

The 8th Corps was formed after Dunkirk and assigned to Southern Command with responsibility for Somerset, Devon, Cornwall and Bristol. Southern Command's HQ was at Salisbury. The 8th Corps included two divisions – 3rd Division (in which were the 2nd Bn. Middlesex Regiment) and 48th Division. On 25th July, 1940, the staff and soldiers assigned to form the HQ of 8th Corps assembled at Bhurtpore Barracks Tidworth. The advanced party left for Taunton on 29th July followed by the main body on 7th August.

A Corps HQ in the field normally splits into two parts; Main Corps HQ and Rear Corps HQ. The Main HQ of 8th Corps was sited in Pyrland Hall (now King's Hall School). This contained the Corps Commander (Lieutenant General Sir Harold Franklyn, KCB, DSO, MC[10]) together with his Operational, Intelligence, Artillery, Engineer and Signals Staffs, whilst the Corps' Rear HQ, commanded by Brigadier Berry, was at nearby Hestercombe House with the Personnel and Logistic Staffs, together with their supporting services.

8th Corps had a big job on its hands. On 25th June, 1940, Winston Churchill had agreed and implemented immediately a plan put forward by General Sir Edmund Ironside, Commander-in-Chief of the Home Forces to construct defensive lines across the country to prevent an invading army approaching London and the Midlands. The task of designing the pillboxes for these defensive lines was the responsibility of the Fortification and Works Branch of the Royal Engineers.

With the fall of France in June 1940, the West of England became the third most vulnerable area for invasion. Had the naval ports fallen into enemy hands – access to the Bristol Channel and up to the Midlands across the narrow county of Somerset could have been rapid. It fell to 8th Corps to construct defences running from Burnham on the north coast of Somerset to Seaton on the south coast of Devon following rivers, canals, and railway lines. Virtually slicing through the west of

England from the main bulk of the country, the Taunton Stop Line, as it was called consisted of pillboxes, anti-tank obstacles following roads and rivers or beach defences. Some of these defences can still be seen in the countryside today. If a German West Country push was going to be halted, it would have to be here.

Milverton and Taunton were on the 'wrong' side of the Stop Line – locations likely to be subject to direct enemy assault. Eyes began turning to the sky anticipating a softening up aerial bombardment, or even a parachute attack.

Set up in September 1938, the nearest Observer Corps[11] observation post was W of Little Jurston Farm, Chelston Heathfield. The role of the post was to track and report enemy aircraft.

Before October 1940, there were no searchlights west of a line roughly between Burnham on Sea, Yeovil and Bridport. From October 1940 there was one placed at Bathealton (Leigh Farm) and one at the top of a hill just behind Houndsmoor Farm. Alan Winter recalled that the soldiers manning it were billeted in the Old Chapel (now a private house) from where the cable for the light ran through the trees to the top of the field. There was a generator on the farm. Soldiers also manned a gate on Oak Road that led to the light. Alan Winter also said that the 'searchlight soldiers' had access to tinned bully beef they would give to the locals.

But Nellie mentions, on 17th and 25th July, 1940, seeing a searchlight before this. Its location is a mystery, since at that time the nearest would have been Yeovil 28 miles away and Weston 22 miles. Given there were no Luftwaffe raids reported in the area on those dates, it was likely to have been at Norton Camp for a training exercise. In September 1939 Norton Camp was occupied by 22 Searchlight (SL) Militia Depot Royal Artillery (RA). But by 26th September the unit was renamed 222 SL Training Unit RA. By February 1940 this unit had 1500 men. In June, 1940, 222 SL became the 'redistribution location' from where all RA searchlight personnel having returned from Dunkirk were dispersed back to their original unit or to new SL units being formed.

By late 1940 after the success of the Battle of Britain the threat of invasion receded – though anti-invasion defence continued until 1943. Somerset became a training and assembly area for troops to deploy from south coastal ports on subsequent operations in North Africa and north-west Europe.

Whilst not targeted for deliberate bombing,[12] both Milverton and Taunton were on the flightpath for bombing raids from Cherbourg to Bristol and South Wales, the Admiralty Hydrographic office at Taunton and Army Supply Reserve Depot at Norton Fitzwarren would be particularly vulnerable.

Controlled by the Commanding Officer of 3 Supply Reserve Depot at Norton Fitzwarren, an A-series (Army) bombing decoy was operational in February 1941 at Nynehead just south of Luckhams farm and known as the 'Donald site'. This had QL and QF decoys. QL decoys simulated the low level of lighting permitted to keep factories working at night. A 'purple' warning would be given and the lights switched off, whilst lights at the decoy site would be lit, to simulate the real target, and lure the bombers towards it. QF decoys were activated when a target had been set on fire. The fire would be extinguished and a fire at the decoy lit to fool the enemy bombers into bombing where they could see fires.

After heavy 'Baedeker' air raids on Exeter and Bath between 23rd April and 4th May, 1942, Taunton was thought the next likely target and the site was moved to Castlemans Hill, south west of Taunton as a temporary starfish decoy to protect the town and the depot for which 120 basket fires, including those transferred from Nynehead, were in place on 12th May, 1942. Starfish decoys simulated burning towns, setting off fires in elevated baskets replicating houses and were considered effective. The decoys were eventually controlled by the American forces when they took over the supply depot at Norton Fitzwarren.

During this period, 'C' Coy. Middlesex Regiment embedded itself into village life. Major Edward Bazalgette, lived in Fore Street with his wife and baby son. Evacuated teenager, Sylvia Perry[13] worked for them as a nanny. Unconfirmed sources place other officers at The Court, Lockyers and at Rocklyn. The enlisted men were billeted in tents at Lottisham house, at Milverton Court, and in the fields at Doltons – wherever they could find a perch – including the skittle alleys. Alan Winter, as a boy, remembered that Nissen huts were erected in Doltons whilst lorries and other army vehicles were parked along Houndsmoor Lane and up the hill blocking access, so that the only route was via Huntash Lane.

Mrs. Daisy Ling,[14] an evacuee from North London in 1940 came to Milverton to join her husband who was in 'C' Coy. Middlesex Regiment. Whilst she was billeted at the home of George Cridlands opposite the Globe, her husband was billeted in the skittle alley at the then George Hotel opposite the shop (County Stores).

From the records of the Mother's Union we are led to believe that the men had access to a Reading Room at Winkley House, where they could write letters. On 1st October, 1940, Nellie mentions soldiers coming for baths at Mrs. Vickery's, and it was likely that they availed themselves of bathrooms in several houses for their ablutions!

Bathed or not, the soldiers had to be fed. Evacuee Bruce Watkiss recalled that the Middlesex Regiment had a cookhouse in a field behind the Victoria Rooms (Creedwell Orchard). 'Village boys', he said used to 'badger the cook for a helping of plum duff until they became a nuisance and were banned.' These were perhaps temporary arrangements as on 27th January, 1941 Milverton WI agreed to take responsibility for running a canteen for the week 29th January to 6th February. By 5th March, the WI had agreed to a formal request from the Women's Voluntary Service to organise a canteen. We do know that eventually the military canteen was in the reading room at the Victoria Rooms because Parish Council records on 12th September, 1941, note a meeting between the finance committee and the military to discuss the charge.

Both the Middlesex and later the Cheshire Regiments were machine gun regiments, though they eventually became mechanised and lorry-borne infantry. Alan Winter says that 'a big pit was dug near the telephone exchange in Rosebank Road for ammunition. But (Alan's father) said "it would flood and it did".' After that, ammunition was stored, along with ordnance and vehicles, under guard at the Court.

Until recently removed, a pile of bricks had lain by the field gate at the junction half way up the High street, suggesting that this might have been the remains of a sentry box.

The Middlesex Regiment moved out on 16th January, 1941.

Local Colonel Tony McMahon has traced the progress of Major Bazalgette. He went to North Africa, then to Sicily and to Italy but after 1943 there is no further mention of him in the Army List (or on a war grave list). Sadly, Daisy Ling's husband was killed in Italy.

There was to be no let up for the residents of Milverton. As they bad farewell to one group of soldiers, another was on its way. On 1st February, 1941, 'C' Coy. of the 2nd Battalion of the Cheshire Regiment (the 22nd of Foot) left Skegness travelling by train to Wincanton. From there, 'C' Coy, with CO, Capt. Anderson, travelled by coach, arriving in Milverton on or about 3rd February. Nellie mentions the arrival of what must have been an advance party of the Cheshires as early as 23rd January, 1941 – 'We have a Cheshire Regiment here now – a quiet lot they seem.' The quiet stoicism of the sentiment is typical of the village's attitude to their visitors in khaki.

It appears that the 2nd Bn. Cheshire and Middlesex Regiments followed one another about. They had also been part of 3rd Division in the BEF. We can therefore assume they took over the same billets. They also continued their training. Whilst the public were being warned that 'Careless talk costs lives' and to 'Keep Mum', Nellie was surprisingly open in her letter writing. There are one or two instances where she clearly withheld details of places and events, such as her journey to Milverton on 16th June, 1940. However, what is surprising is that she knew so much about troop movements. For instance, on 12th February, 1941, she mentions '80 soldiers have come for tonight sleeping in the Victoria Rooms', and then the following day 'Thousands of troops have passed through here today. The lorries have only just stopped now and there has been one long continuous stream since 9 o'clock this morning. Everybody has a different tale, but there's some big stunt on Exmoor, I believe.' Her indiscretions were worryingly accurate. On 12th February, there was an 8th Corps Field Firing exercise[15] on Exmoor involving all Rifle Companies. The route was from Highbridge, Milverton, Wiveliscombe, Bampton to Dulverton. The logs note that Coys., 'A' and 'B' had excellent weather, whilst 'C' & 'D' had practically no visibility but performed well on the Compass march across Exmoor.

On 16th January, as noted, 'C' Coy. 2nd Bn. Middlesex Regiment, were packing up to move to Wimborne to be replaced by 'C' Coy. 2nd Bn. Cheshires. They would not have taken part in these exercises.

At this stage in the war, Churchill badly needed to contain the Germans in North Africa. Exmoor Exercise, No. 2, 21-22nd January, 1941, was based on the planned North-Western Desert Advance.[16] It's purpose was to repel the enemy – 'Italian advance troops (were) in touch with British frontier troops on line Hurstone Point to Exton and air recce shows enemy has line of defended localities Porlock Common to Exford common. Strength unknown. Estimated two Italian Divisions in Ilfracombe – Barnstaple area. Morale of enemy weak – in desperation will probably use gas'. As Nellie's letter shows, Milverton folk were aware of the build-up of troops in the area. For this exercise The Green Howard's Battalion HQ was established at Bishop's Lydeard and the buses transporting them left from nearby Ash Priors at 0845 on 21st. It was deemed a great success and the 5th Bn Green Howard's reported that it 'proved valuable training – the whole of Exmoor being bleak and practically roadless making administrative details a big problem. The exercise terminated at 1200 hrs on 22nd but snow had begun to fall heavily earlier in the morning and the Bn. was stranded, snowed up, in the Lynmouth area but helped by "local" unit 67 C.H. Coy. R.E and billeted within three-quarters of hour. The Bn. returned to billets the following day.' Gas was used and 'unfortunately 2 men of 'A' Coy. became contaminated with mustard gas, apparently from sitting on a contaminated net in a vehicle'. By 24th February the two men were evacuated to hospital with large blisters – 'all men on the vehicle had to be decontaminated, as was their clothing.' The 7th Bn. The Green

Howards reported enemy bombing of Swansea, 19-20th and Bristol 26th-28th February. 'C' Coy .of the Cheshires did not take part, and no doubt were grateful, given the bad weather.

The Cheshires, continued their training and other defence duties. They seem to have been giving the villagers cause for complaint – about what Nellie does not say – but it's clearly an ongoing issue, as she had noted on 18th February, that 'the Cheshires still can do no right.'[17] Nellie is upset that nothing is being done to entertain them, and then says that they will leave in two to three weeks. Before that they took part in another 'stunt' on 2nd March, 1941. But by 27th March, Nellie comments: 'I think the whole of the army went through our village last night'. Evidently, the troops stationed at Milverton left at 4 p.m. but there followed a continuous stream of noisy motorbikes and even tanks being cheered by the children. She reports that they were going off to Egypt on 25th April and the advance party of the Royal Artillery is creating a good impression. On Sunday, 27th Mollie says that whilst three soldiers were at chapel, camouflaged buses full of soldiers went through the village. This ties in with the 'Movement Instructions' for the 2nd Bn. Cheshires, dated 25th April, 1941. 'C'Coy. having to stack their blankets, paillases and bolsters by 0900. But, on 2nd May, Nellie writes that the Cheshires were to return, as there was no room for them in Greece! There is no evidence of this but 10th July, 1941 Nellie mentions soldiers singing outside the White Hart who could have been from the Royal Artillery who were here for a while. A few days later, on 13th July, Nellie mentions that coming out of church she saw 'the soldiers were starting on a trek with all their heavy guns'.

The Cheshire Regiment[18] went out to North Africa, as part of Montgomery's 8th Army and were tasked with holding the Alamein line to the East of Sidi Barrani and thus prevent the enemy from reaching the Suez Canal. The exercise on Exmoor, mentioned above, mirrored an area south of Sidi Barrani, East of Tobruk, which consisted of a narrow strip of about 30 miles wide from the coast to unnavigable salt flats in the South. This strip was the only navigable route to Alexandria and the Suez Canal. Milverton is probably the southern most part of the so-called 'navigable' area on the Exmoor map.

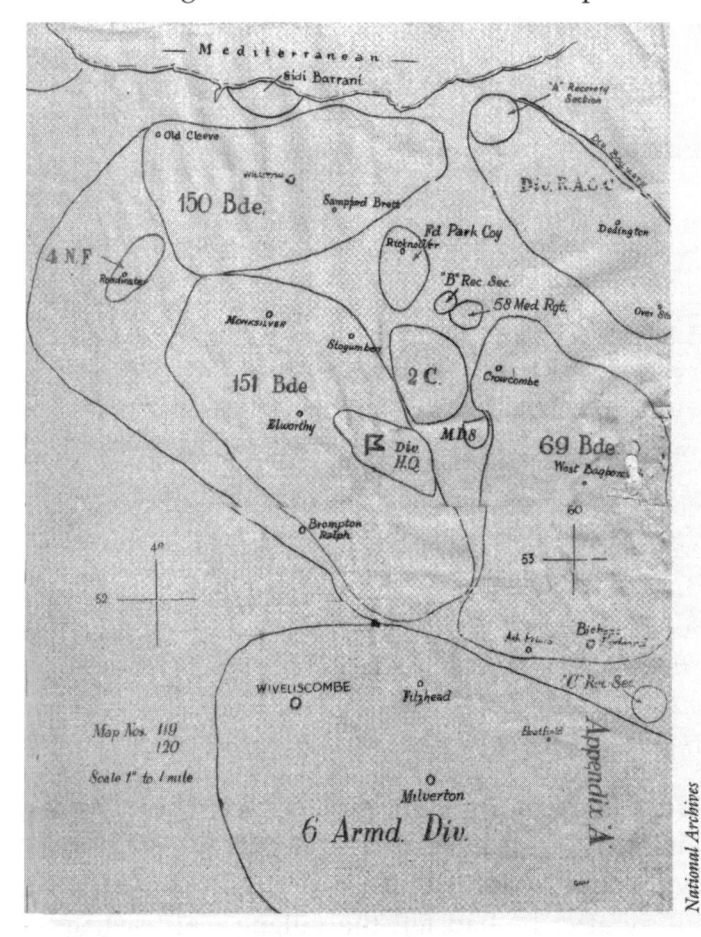

7. 8th Corps Exercise, showing Milverton in relation to Sidi Barani (Watchet) on the Egyptian coast. National Archives.

This narrow pathway had been held, taken and retaken at various times by the Italians and British. In 1942 the German Army under Rommel succeeded in recapturing it. But, a few months later Churchill got his first victory at the second Battle of El Alamein on 11th November 1942, for which the bells were rung (not in Milverton) and gave rise to Churchill's speech at the Lord Mayor of London's banquet on 10th November, in which he said 'This is not the end. It is not even the beginning of the end. But it is, perhaps, the end of the beginning'. Two days earlier, on 8th November, Operation 'Torch'[19] the combined British-American invasion of French North Africa had also begun.

```
              8 CORPS EXERCISE NO.2.              EXERCISE.
                                                  SECRET.
                                                  Copy No.. 22 ..
              4 G. H. Operation Instruction No.1.
INFORMATION.
    1. Enemy: ITALIAN adv. tps. are in touch with BRITISH frontier
       tps. on line HURSTONE POINT 3371 - LUCCOMBE 3566 - CUTCOMBE
       3660 - ELTON 3655.
              Air recce shows enemy has line of defended localities
       on line PORLOCK COMMON 2067 - EXFORD COMMON 2962. Strength
       unknown but not more than an Inf. Bde. or Inf. Bde. Gp.
              LUCOTT MOOR 2865 does not appear to be held.
              Approaches to LYNTON 1571 and SIMONSBATH 2161 probably
       covered.
              Estimated two ITALIAN Divs. in area ILFRACOMBE 9569 -
       BARNSTAPLE 9955.
              Morale of enemy weak - In desperation will probably use
       gas.

    2. Own Tps: 101 Div. has formed series of defended localities
       about MINEHEAD - DUNSTER 4265 - WATCHET.
              BRITISH frontier tps. are in touch along line PORLOCK
       COMMON - EXFORD COMMON.
              R.N. have command of sea.
              R.A.F. have air superiority and have destroyed most of
       enemy aerodromes.
```

8. *'Operation Instructions 1, for 4th Bn Green Howards, 8th Corps exercise, No. 2 – showing that the 'Italian advance troops are in touch with British frontier troops.' National Archives.*

Of course, there were romances when the soldiers were here. Nellie mentions an officer visiting Gertrude Vickery and that she continued to correspond with Lieutenant Muffettt of the 86th Light Anti-Aircraft Regiment, Royal Artillery after he had left the village – at least until September 1941.[20] In fact, as recorded by Nellie, Eric Muffett was often at April Cottage. It has been difficult to find evidence of his whereabouts in the area, as the 86th is recorded as being stationed mainly in the Wraysbury, Weybridge area. However, some 86th went for Anti-Aircraft firing practice at Watchet. This could be where he was at one stage. Muffett had a difficult time. Nellie writes on 25th May, 1941, that 'Miss V was supposed to be going over to see Eric Muffett. But another soldier had shot himself, making 3 since he joined the company'. According to Nellie, he eventually went up to Nailsea. Ethel Jennings' friend Vicky Bundy became friendly with Ernie Green of the Cheshires. Here there was a happy ending as, after the war, he returned and they married.

After the British Troops had departed, vast numbers of Americans were moved in to train and prepare for the D-Day landings. They came in such numbers that it might have been easier to evacuate some areas altogether. It is a tribute to the security measures and strict censorship that few people realised the area's importance to the war effort. That story comes later.

---

1. Reserved Occupations, Dock Workers, Miners, Farmers, Scientists, Merchant Seamen, Railway Workers, Utility Workers – Water, Gas, Electricity – see 'Doing Your Bit'.
2. Local Defence Volunteers, later Home Guard – see 'Defending Milverton – Home Guard.
3. Gold Beach was the middle of the five beaches assaulted on D-Day. It covered the area between Port-en-Bessin and La Riviere. To the west were the American beaches Utah and Omaha; to the east were the British and Canadian beaches Juno and Sword. As such Gold was a vital link in an invasion front 80 km long. XXX Corps' commander Lt. General Gerard Bucknall was in overall charge of the assault. Under his command was the 50th (Northumbrian) Infantry Division (which included 2nd Battalion, The Cheshires, 8th Armoured Brigade and 47 Royal Marine Commando. These were combat-tested troops who had fought in North Africa and Sicily. In comparison to Omaha, the operation went relatively smoothly. Naval bombardment neutralised 3 out of 4 of the German heavy gun emplacements prior to landing. Earlier reconnaissance – including clandestine diving operations under the Germans' noses – had established that the beach near La Riviere could not support the weight of tanks, and other areas had newly-built underwater anti-tank obstacles. The first wave therefore included special 'AVRE' vehicles to lay matting for the tanks. Demolition teams meanwhile removed the obstacles. While the first wave took heavy fire from fortified houses and pill boxes, the second wave focused on linking up with Omaha and Juno capturing the town of Arromanches. Commandos meanwhile targeted Port-en-Bessin. By the end of the day Arromanches was taken and contact had been made with the Canadians. But Omaha remained

out of reach. Casualties were between 1000-1,100 with 350 dead. The number of German casualties is unknown. On D-Day +1 the first sections of the Mulberry Harbour were brought over. At Port-en-Bessin the joint Anglo-American oil depot – 'Tombola' – began operations fed by buoyed pipes from tankers moored offshore. This was eventually superseded, in late August, by the underwater pipeline 'Pluto'. John Kiacz and Ted Perry would both have refuelled here. See below and 'Over Here'.
4. As above.
5. This is a mistake – he crashed at Diss in Norfolk.

It is not possible to give an account of the wartime achievements of all local Milverton people, but as there is a memorial pew end in Milverton church for Air Commodore Michael Wight-Boycott, C.B.,ED.,DSO and Bar, MA, RAF (rtd), (1910-1998) it is worth relating his wartime career. Though he was born in Wiveliscombe – he retired to Milverton. On the night of 17th/18th January, 1943, he commanded 29 Squadron – a Beaufighter Night Fighter Squadron – stationed on the Kent coast. Expecting a raid of some 80 enemy bombers, his radio observer, using MK airborne interception radar was guided in the dark to a Dornier Do217 which he shot down. He returned to base, to have an early breakfast, took off again, before dawn and shot down another Dornier. Whilst taking avoiding action, he accidentally switched off his oxygen supply. Nevertheless he was still able to attack a third Do217. His oxygen restored, he further downed a Junkers Ju88. He was awarded an instant DSO for this night's achievements. In 1942 he was flying Mosquitos, in 'Mahmoud' sorties – the Mosquitos posing as bombers, to lure enemy fighters. In 1944 he shot down two V1 flying bombs after which he joined no. 12 night operations staff at 12 Group Fighter Command.

Devon-born Rear Admiral Anthony Follett Pugsley, CB, DSO & Two Bars (1901-1990) retired to Javelin House, Wood Street, and is commemorated by a plaque in St. Michael's church yard. He also played his part on D-Day. The destroyer on which he was Captain landed the 3rd Canadian Division on Juno Beach. Later in 1944, he was responsible for both planning and carrying out amphibious landings, on Walcheren in the Battle of Scheldt.
6. Sherford Camp – served as training militia camp for expanding army prior WW2. (It continued in use after Second World War and was occupied by HQ SW District and HQ (Wessex) Division in the 1950-60s.) Middleway Camp, now built over, also believed to have been training camp.
7. Why he was at Norton Camp is a mystery as it was used for 222 Search-Light training Regiment. Barbara does not know when and for how

long he was at Norton Manor camp but does know that her parents got engaged on the occasion her mother visited Taunton for a weekend to see her father during his training. When they married in Manchester in May 1941, Jack was in uniform. He may well have been involved in training for the North African Campaign as he served on the front line in Italy and survived a critical injury. He died in 2003 at the age of 90.

8. Operation Dynamo' (27th May-4th June, 1940) managed to evacuate 338,226 troops of which, 98,780 were lifted from the beaches and 239,446 from the mole at Dunkirk harbour. Nine hundred and thirty-three ships from various countries took part including an unknown number of small vessels who had crossed the channel to ferry soldiers to the bigger ships. Such was the bombardment by the enemy that 236 ships were lost and 61 put out of action. On 31st May, at 2030 hours the final withdrawal orders were received. Read their experiences in Appendix 3.
9. See Minister of Health, 'Gone to the Country'.
10. Replaced by 1941 by Lt. General Kenneth Anderson (later Sir Kenneth Anderson KCB, MC) who became GOC-Eastern command in 1942. See 'Hestercombe in the War' published 2007.
11. It was through information from the Observer Corps (see 'Doing Your Bit') – together with the eventual ability to monitor radio communications of enemy bombers and using radar – that fighter command was able to give specific area air-raid warnings. There was also a system of sending up 'red' rockets to denote enemy on land and 'green' – the approach of enemy vessels. But 'Granite' starburst flares could be lit to warn friendly aircraft approaching high ground when visibility was poor. There was one of these 'Granite Stations'; at Wellington, presumably to warn aircraft of the proximity of the Blackdown hills.
12. Nellie, 26.7.40. 'It takes 12 mins from Lyme Regis to Bristol.'
13. See 'Gone to the Country'.
14. See 'Gone to the Country'.
15. The Field Firing exercise does not mention which Regiments took part. Other exercises and movements of troops for 8thCorps, mainly Green Howards: On 2nd January, 1941, Lt. Col. W.E.Bush, DSO, MC, commanding Officer of 5th Bn. Green Howards, had, as the log reports – 'Inspected all Coys. in tropical Kit – oddly enough there was a fall of snow on the ground and the weather turned definitely colder'. This was followed on 18/19th January, by a 4th Bn. Green Howards Exercise No. 1 in the Weston-Super-Mare and Clevedon region, the opening narrative being 'Somerset is one of the German States'. On 31st January, the 7th Bn. Green Howards (based at Castle Cary) were given Operational Instructions, as to their roles item (g) of which was 'to occupy a sector of the Taunton Stop Line to stop enemy advancing from SW England'.

16. This preceded Operation 'Torch', which was a joint British and US Operation. The US did not come into the war until December 1941, after the bombing of Pearl Harbour – see 'Over Here'.
17. See Nellie 15.1.41 and 23.1.41 Boy and a Middx. Soldier.
18. Milverton's 'C' Coy. of the 2nd Btn. Middlesex and Cheshire Regiments took part. The 2nd Bn. Cheshire Regiment eventually went from Benghazi to Sicily but returned from there to take part in the D-Day landings on Gold Beach. See 3 & 4 above.
19. See 'Over Here'.
20. Capt. Eric Douglas Muffett went on to join an Indian R.A regiment where he died of polio in 1945. He sent Helen, via his sister in London, an ivory necklace and a red plush stuffed elephant for her sister, Linda. Helen wrote to Miss Vickery's daughter, Nicola Forgan, in 2002, to say she remembered her mother receiving notification of Eric Muffett's death from his sister who asked her to pass the news 'to the girl in Milverton that he was fond of'. Helen continued – 'I remember how upset my mother was and how difficult she found it to tell your mother'.

6. GONE TO THE COUNTRY

'It is a gesture of solidarity which all the fighting men will understand, that children from the cities should continue to enjoy the friendship and the comfort of the firesides in the villages and the country towns.' Walter Elliot, Minister for Health,[1] 15th February, 1940

The word 'Evacuee' in WW2 evokes images of black and white photos and newsreels of children boarding trains, carrying a small suitcase their name on a label attached to their coats, but evacuees of all ages and from different groups went to the countryside. Long before war came to Britain, refugees particularly Jewish, had fled here from the Nazis.[2] Once war was declared many of the men, were put in holding areas, either for the duration, or eventually screened and their education and abilities drawn in to aid the war effort.[3]

All over Britain people would be constantly moved about in trains and trucks to military camps, factories and to safety. For security reasons the government had to find ways of keeping track of this disrupted and displaced population. On 5th September, just two days after the declaration of war the National Registration Act, 1939 passed into law. Every individual living in Britain had to register their details. And they were given three weeks to do it. In pre-computer days, collating all this data was a massive undertaking. 62,000 people were involved, checking and issuing everyone with buff coloured cards that recorded, name, sex, age, occupation,[4] address, marital status and whether or not a member of a military service. Each person had an identifying number the same as their National Insurance number and these are still valid today.[5] By1943 blue cards were issued to adults; green to government officials who also had a photograph and by then military personnel had their own separate cards. Identity Cards had to be carried and shown upon request with addresses officially changed as people moved around. In use until long after the end of the war, the Act was eventually repealed in February 1952.

Whilst some children had been sent to the USA and Canada, by the time war was declared plans were in place to evacuate children, expectant mothers and adult or blind people from vulnerable parts of London, major cities and ports throughout the country. Milverton classed as a 'compulsory' area meant that if inhabitants had room they had to take evacuees. On 28th April, 1939 the Board of Trade had sent a letter to all local authorities outlining the plans in place for the additional supply of emergency food rations. [6]

Immediately, of course, women reacted. Realising the potential problems that could come from the Government's Evacuation Policy they founded The Women's Group drawing in some 20 voluntary organisations from industrial, social, religious, educational groups but mostly the other women's organisations. Way back on 4th May, 1939 the Clerk of Somerset County Council, wrote to all District Councils advising them that Miss Vernon the Hon. Secretary of the Somerset County Federation of Women's Institutes was organising helpers in all reception areas who would be willing, if needed, to help in mending, cooking and laundering. The WVS, via the Civil Defence produced a leaflet to be handed to all those taking unaccompanied children. Also that May, the County Council convened their first conference of billeting authorities.

So serious was the threat of danger that in the first week of war 1½ million people were evacuated to reception areas in four days. Somerset received 44,956 people from 1st September, 1939. The County Council stated,[7] that there were far more mothers and children amongst this group than the 'official' unaccompanied children but they managed to deal with them. Milverton School Log, dated 18th September, 1939 reported that on 1st and 2nd of September a party of children from Denmark St. in Bristol had arrived in the care of a Miss Smith, and by 29th September several unofficial evacuees had arrived and 11 children from Canning Town, London on 28th February, 1940.

This period became known as the 'phoney war' and by the spring of 1940 1 million had returned to their homes – for the time being. On 15th February, 1940, Walter Elliot the Minister of Health in a broadcast, praised those who had taken in children and those continuing to care for the remaining 400,000 still billeted in reception areas. 'Winter', he said, 'has gripped all Europe and halted the war in the west; but when winter passes, the danger comes again. We must look ahead.' He went on to say that they would not try to move adults at all but plans to remove children were being set up when and 'until air warfare is developing in such a way as actually to threaten our civilian population'. His rallying cry paid tribute to those who had helped earlier with the migration – 'It is their kindliness, patience and thoughtfulness that has achieved so much. We are authorising the most extensive use of empty houses for sick bays, for housing of difficult children. Camps will be filled as soon as the better weather comes' and 'We are increasing the billeting allowance from 8s.6d to 10s.6d for all children over 14.' They were even going to extend allowances on similar terms to the Government schemes for private 'unofficial' evacuation to relatives.[8] He urged people to enrol as hosts:[9] 'It is a gesture of solidarity which all the fighting men will understand, that children from the cities should continue to enjoy the friendship and the comfort of the firesides in the villages and the country towns. All the world is watching…all those who sympathise with our cause will rejoice when we succeed as we mean to succeed.'

Somerset County Council's Report of 21st June, 1941, stated that 'After the evacuation of Dunkirk, the county had six hours notice to make plans to receive virtually the whole of the population of Hastings[10] the reception of which went on for two days and nights without stopping.'

Darlingest

They also had to liaise with the military about billeting soldiers and requisition of buildings.

Then, as forecast, once London was bombed, the report says 'The government plans completely broke down as refugees poured into the county at the rate of 700-1000 a day.'

Figures showing the breakdown of population and evacuees;
Population of administrative county (Somerset)   504,000
Official evacuees   60,000
Unofficial evacuees   59,000

Evacuation of unaccompanied children to Somerset
Wellington Urban   200
Wellington rural   250

The Government Evacuation Scheme memorandum made arrangements also to move disabled not only from danger zones but those in safe areas when their homes had been requisitioned. One such was Sandhill Park which had become the British 41st General Military Hospital, later leased to the American government as a neurological hospital. Evacuated from there to The Parsonage (the Old House), in September 1939 came 30 slightly mentally handicapped[11] men and boys in the care of Mr. Frank Butler. Whilst to The Fort, nearby went 30 women, aged over 16 under the care of Miss Ann Cornaby[12] the Sister-in-Charge. These inmates were well looked after and some were employed[13] in the village.

William Deacon, (Cardscroft, North Street) as Director of Education for Somerset had, in June 1939, received instructions from Somerset County Council and together with his wife, Gladys, deputy billeting officer, returned early from holiday to action his plans. The School(s) in Sand Street (now private homes) was to be Milverton's reception area. Young Beatrice (Beattie) Perry (later Hayes) who had been helping with the children was disappointed to cut short her stay in Cornwall whereas her fiancée, Lionel, was delighted to have her back!

Whilst her husband busied himself organising the education for the expected extra children, Gladys and the billeting officer, Miss Mary Andrews who lived at Bank House, immediately put into practice their plans, made just a few weeks before, to house the 'official' evacuee children. Each area had to have as many children as would match the children already in the village. At that time the large houses in North Street were mostly occupied by elderly ladies who Mrs. Deacon told, 'Oh yes, you can put up, you've lost two indoor servants, and you've got seven bedrooms, you can have yes, seven evacuees. They had no choice but there they were.'

As the threat of evasion increased, the West Country, far removed from London became the pressure point for safety and thus evacuation.

'A danger line has been drawn from the Tweed, along the east coast, round the corner and along the south coast, and a number of miles inland, into this area no children will in future be evacuated,' was the opening paragraph in the *Daily Mail* of 14th June, 1940. Then, on Saturday, 15th June, the local press[14] announced that 16,000 evacuee children would be arriving in Somerset the next day of which 600 would be arriving in the Taunton area. Government photographs show hordes of children with names on baggage labels attached to their clothes. They carry their gas masks, bags or

JUNE 15, 1940.

EVACUATION THIS WEEK-END

HUNDREDS OF CHILDREN FOR WEST SOMERSET

SUNDAY ARRIVALS

Sixteen thousand evacuee children are expected in Somerset this week-end.

It is expected that 600 London children will arrive in the Taunton rural district to-morrow (Sunday).

Detailed plans, based on the arrangements and experience of the last evacuation scheme have been made by the chief billeting officer, Mr. P. O. Cowlishaw, and his staff, which now includes a billeting officer for every parish in the district.

9. Somerset Gazette, *15th June, 1940.*

small attaché case holding no more than a change of clothes and a few toys and food such as 1 tin of Ideal milk, 1 tin of bully beef, 1 packet of biscuits and 1 bar of chocolate. It was with a group such as this that Nellie and her daughter, boarded a train at Paddington[15] on 16th June, 1940 and it is the day her letters begin.

Also to Milverton came Shaftesbury House School[16] from London. One of the children, a Mrs. Yvonne Scott, described her time in Milverton, as very happy.

Nellie Clemens had taken up a post as a teacher accompanying children from the North Harringay School (still in existence) that feature so vividly in her letters. But, why had the telegram sent to her husband confirming her safe arrival been dated 17th and not 16th June? There is no indication of anything wrong in the beginning of the letter, written whilst on the train on 16th – later finished on 17th with the explanation. She had been expecting to go further west to Cornwall from where her husband's family originated and Milverton had expected children from the East End not the North of London.

For some reason either the points failed, or it was sheer incompetence but a great number of trains transporting evacuees from London bound for the safety of the West Country on 16th June, 1940 ended up in the wrong place and for Nellie, it was Wellington.

But on the evening of 16th June, 1940 Gladys Deacon reports 'We were all there in time with the allocated uncles and aunts who had agreed to put up, some protesting madly that they couldn't have so many children, and we said, "Come on, they'll be alright. It'll be quite fun, you know…" They were all sitting round, these prospective uncles and aunts on this particular evening and the train was due to arrive about 6 o'clock. But Mr. Hoare (The Headmaster) came panting up, in the dark, whispered to myself and Miss Andrews – "It's not children, they're pregnant women!" We were aghast! All those pregnant women, we couldn't possibly…'

'It was the wrong train load but Mrs. Lloyd Fox of Gerbeston Manor, Wellington … 'rang me up and said, "It's only going to be for tonight," because of course, Wellington is the place arranged for these pregnant women[17] because of the maternity home there. "I will arrange for them to come immediately if you will perhaps arrange to keep them overnight?" So Miss Andrews and myself said, "We must, we must." So we just said to prospective uncles and aunts, "I'm afraid there's been some mistake in Paddington or wherever. You're going to have to, and please agree, to put up a pregnant woman just for the night. They can rearrange things and Mrs. Lloyd Fox has assured us that she's got spaces for them." She'd arranged to have them. So moans and groans and an awful five minutes to pacify them and finally these poor, tired pregnant women came into Milverton School and we just had to allocate – "Mrs. Jones you have this one" – because it was only going to be for one night and it was only one night and breathed a sigh of relief when we did our swap and everybody laughed over it.'

Whilst the pregnant ladies slept well in Milverton, 113 children and teachers, as Nellie explained, went to Fox's Mill. One of her charges, Bruce Watkiss, also remembers sleeping on the sheepskins.

Nellie seemed oblivious about the swop with the pregnant ladies and does not say where she and Helen stayed on Saturday, 16th. She accepted that she'd be in Wellington and seems surprised that they were, children and infants moved to Milverton on the Sunday, arriving at '9 o'clock' – presumably morning – and were dispersed.

Bruce Watkiss, with his siblings went first to Love Lynch for a couple of days and then to Bill Andrews in Sand Street just a few doors away from April Cottage where Nellie and Helen were eventually lodged. Twin boys went to stay with Mr and Mrs. Greedy at Courtfields one of them asking about the shelter! Also from the same school was Barbara Wood (née Buckland) who with her sister, Jean, stayed with Mr and Mrs. Mead at a farm worker's cottage at Houndsmoor. Mrs. Deacon said, 'that Milverton people were wonderfully kind and good and most of the, well I should say, more than 90% of the children, were as happy as they would have been anywhere. But it was a wilderness of happiness in some ways. They were sad at leaving father and mother and sister and brother or whatever but – children are very resilient aren't they? And uh, there were very few who were truly unhappy. I don't think you could say any of them were, because they had their schoolteacher with them.'

Parents did occasionally visit their children and were allocated train tickets but as Gladys Deacon said: 'Dad was probably in the army anyhow and Mum had younger children at home. Miss Andrews and myself, thought it could unsettle the child to see their mother and want to go back to London.' It was probably easier for the 'unofficial' evacuee children who either had a parent with them, or were staying with relatives.

Children were billeted, if possible, where there were other children but not in North Street, as the large houses earmarked to accommodate many children, were the homes of mainly elderly single women. 'And yes, we squeezed them in quite tightly, but we found spaces for all the evacuees we were allocated.'

After a couple of nights staying with the Deacons at the bottom of North Street Nellie and Helen with another teacher, Miss Rattenbury moved to The Lodge at the top of the street, on 18th June. Her letters indicated that they weren't very happy as the landlady, Mrs. Bedford was a snob and whilst it took some cajoling of the authorities she eventually moved to what is now called April Cottage in Sand Street on 28th July. Mrs. Bedford was threatened with soldiers and other evacuees which she avoided until September when another large influx of evacuees were expected.[18]

It was on 11th September, 1940, at the height of the Battle of Britain that Sylvia Perry (having witnessed RAF dog fights overhead) got on the train at Bexhill-on-Sea[18] where she lived. 'There were notices round, telling people they ought to be evacuated, as everybody thought the Germans were going to invade. We went to the station in Bexhill-on-Sea – my grandmother, my sister, who is younger than I. They asked our ages when we went through.

'I was 15. We got on the train. We weren't told where we were going and the train set off. We didn't go up to London of course. We kept going along the coast as far as I remember. And we got to a station and the train pulled in. So a porter said "Where are you going?" and we said, "Well, somebody said Wiltshire." "Well," he said, "you are here." So I think it was Salisbury, and... we had tea, and I suppose something to eat from the WVS, and the train set off again. We finished up at Wellington Station and the train stopped and we were told to get out. When we got out, there were a number of school children there and they sang "Sussex-by-the-Sea", which was wonderful. We got in the coaches with our luggage and we went a little way up the road in Wellington, Station Road, and back again down to Fox Bros' factory. And I can't remember who welcomed us but up in the canteen, they'd laid the sheep's wool all the way round with blankets but anybody with small children had to sleep somewhere else downstairs. Anyway we spent the night there, and in the morning we were given breakfast, which I can't remember, but an elderly gentleman stood up and he thanked Fox Bros for having us and he said we were "Wanderers on the face of the earth". I can't remember, what else he said, but that stayed with me.'

So another tranche of evacuees had to be dispersed by Mrs. Deacon. 'I think most of the people in Milverton were extremely co-operative, were all very nice except I think to Sylvia Perry.[19] We unwittingly put her with an unwilling person who met her, I think, at the door.' This time Mrs. Bedford was not exempt.

Sylvia records that 'When we arrived at the house, the lady living there – she was a solicitor's widow – always dressed for dinner. She was deaf, which was a little worrying because she always banged the doors and it made one think of perhaps, bombs dropping, or German planes flying over. She took one look at me and she said, "I don't want you," which was a bit of a shock. My grandmother did the cooking for the three of us. We were on our own in what was the servants' quarters... three beds in a room. There was a door that shut the front of the house off. The servants had a sitting-room and a very, very large kitchen. We were told to use the side gate, not the front door. I can't remember how long we stayed there. I worked as a nanny[20] to start with.'

In a few weeks Milverton had absorbed an influx of mentally

handicapped people from their homes, two large tranches of evacuated school children plus Company 'C' of the Middlesex Regiment but as the danger in London and the south-east increased there was a continuous 'dribble' of 'unofficial' children either accompanied by their mothers or sent to relations already living here. Those, like pregnant Mrs. Daisy Ling, had to find their own accommodation. Her husband was here in the Middlesex Regiment and asked her to come away from the bombing. She arrived at Taunton station in November 1940. 'He borrowed an army lorry against the rules – that's how he met me, and he drove me to the Globe Inn and it was half-past-ten at night and they were just closing. He'd already been in and I suppose he knew the people and he said, "Would they, had they got room in the inn that I could stay in, because he was full up?" Londoners they were and "Very, very sorry he hadn't got a bit of room." And while we were in the bar talking there was a gentleman standing behind us, and he said to me, "You looking for a room for the night?" And we said, "Yes." So he said, "Don't go any further." He says, "Come across the road." And we went across to Mr. Cridland's – George Cridland was there and he lived in a little cottage right opposite The Globe, in the main street.

'They had a bed already. But they had lost their evacuees a couple of days before and his wife had had a new baby at the same time, so she was a busy woman, but she said, "You can stay for a fortnight," which I did. So during that fortnight we went out and looked for a better place. I was very happy there. She was very, very nice but we had to go and look for something more, less temporary. We went to about three places on the Sunday morning and they were all full up but Milverton was under compulsory order – that if they'd got a spare bedroom in their houses, they were compelled to take evacuees – cos it was pretty full-up. And one voice went for another and said, "Go somewhere else," so we ended up in Wood Street, in Mrs.Pepperill's. Mrs. Pepperill had lost her two people. They had gone back that morning and her house was empty so they knew her evacuees had gone. "So go and call on Mrs. Pepperill." So on the Sunday morning we called on Mrs. Pepperill's and we were met there with open arms. They didn't have any bathroom and (had) outside loos. I thought I'd better be straight and tell them I was pregnant. And the husband turned round and said, "Oh, Ada, you are going to have a baby in the house!" I thought he didn't know how long the war would last. He was tickled pink and that encouraged us. So he brought our bags in and we moved in and I was there – John was born in the nursing home, from there. Milverton itself found out I was pregnant and they made all the arrangements for doctors and nursing homes and they done very well. Mr, Pepperill[21] had a car and he and his wife went to Bristol and bought a cot from war damaged property for the new baby.'

In 1940 also, as a year-old baby Diane Taylor (née Rooksby) moved to Milverton with her mother after their home in the East End of London had been bombed. They stayed at the College with Mrs. Vickery's aunt, Mrs. Georgana Totterdell, and her husband. Diane said her father would come down about twice a month to see them. A monthly bill would be given to him that included a penny halfpenny for kindling. Diane's mother told her that, Mr. Totterdell grew his own vegetables and, of course, had chickens, and charged his wife for them. He said that what "I grow, I grow. It's saving you buying it from the shop so you can pay me." But tight though he might have been he would fill a sheep's horn with rough cider which he'd hand to Diane's father and then fill it again for himself, after which the ladies would join them in the parlour. Diane and her mother returned to London in about 1942.

Other adults avoided the bombing, including Mr. and Mrs. Summerfield who took over at The Globe.[22]

The WVS leaflet issued to hosts[23] gave sensible advice on how to care and feed the children, dealing with clothing, shoes, entertainment and visiting a Doctor, for which pre NHS days, the fee would be reimbursed. The children were to be given breakfast and an evening supper, the main meal being provided at school.[24] 'Uncles and aunts' who had their own children were told to treat them as their own and would have known how to feed them, but what about the ladies in North Street?

Darlingest

The redistribution and social mix of population during WW2 must have been difficult for some to handle but of overall great benefit. In one swipe domestic servants had been removed[25] and those who had never done housework or cooked found themselves having to be 'below stairs'. Gladys had to deal with this.

'They used to ring me up because Miss Andrews wasn't so used to cooking as I, or was then, and well, Miss Mills was classic. She lived at the top of the village (The Mount) she had her hair in a toupee, and skirts down to her feet and she was one of the school managers – Milverton School Managers. She had four indoor servants and I think two outdoor men and she was confronted and I said "Now Miss Mills, you've lost two indoor servants and you've got two or three spare rooms, I'm going to give you x number of children." So, being very co-operative she didn't actually refuse and I said, "And I'll help you with anything." I think she said they ate quite a big packet of shredded wheat when they came – because they loved it and she had five evacuees. So she said, "I can't do it on the ration money." So I said, "No, alright, you'll make them porridge." "Oh, I love porridge," she said. After a few minutes she rang back and said, "Yes, but I can't make the porridge you know. How does it become porridge?" She said, "I've got the oats." So I had to go and show her. So after about a week she rang me up and said, "Would you like to come and have breakfast with us?" She sat one end of the table, I sat at the other and five evacuees sat around and she ladled out, as I'd instructed her to do, two ladles each.'

But according to Mrs. Deacon the children thought cows' milk 'horrible! 'Yes, they thought that milk from cows was horrible. They were amazed that apples grew on trees and the potatoes came from the ground. You know, they had never seen vegetables growing or fruit being picked, and some of them disliked the thought of – something that was a rare treat in those days – chicken for food, and they couldn't get used to it not being cruel and they'd never seen a chicken in its feathered form, you see. So to see them all stripped of feathers and that was a nasty shock and they had never seen wellington boots!'

But it wasn't only those with evacuees who suddenly found themselves having to cook, as Gladys described a conversation with the doctor's wife, the sister of the Bishop of Winchester. 'She rang up and said, "Byram (Dr.Blackman) wants sausages and mash." I said, "Yes, well you are not restricted very much on the sausage part and you've got plenty of potatoes." "Yes," she said, "but how does a potato become mashed?"' Mrs. Ling however, had done well. 'Our food was very lovely – all home-made. She (Mrs. Pepperill) was always cooking. She just loved cooking. So I did the housework and she did the cooking.'

Evacuee children got used to the changes and were absorbed into school and village life as described in other chapters. Bruce Watkiss remembers gardening on the allotment and singing in the choir where he also 'pumped the organ frantically for Purcell's Trumpet Voluntary'. He remembered walking across the top of the old quarry when the Home Guard were having a firing practice! And also helped with collecting.[26]

All children, of course, whether local or evacuees were drawn into collecting items for saving, raising funds and picking fruit. They took part in entertainments and integrated into village life. They must have been happy as the records we quote here have come when, as adults, they returned to visit the village and made themselves known to Milverton people who recorded their stories.

But even as late as June 1941, the parish council was asked to make a report of the business transacted at Wellington in connection with the necessary accommodation and feeding of persons who may be sent to Milverton when evacuated from other places following enemy action. 'Mr. King gave a very clear outline as to the necessary procedure should such occasion arise ...' This ties in with the Somerset County Report of 21st June, 1941 (quoted earlier) para 7 – 'the dispersal of industry for war work has presented another major problem in the billeting of war workers. The available accommodation is kept constantly under review and action taken at short notice – even at night.'

There were, at that time, 127,000 evacuees or war workers in Somerset but more pressure was to come. Later that year, the *Gazette* on 1st,

November, 1941, reported a visit by the then Minister of Health, Mr. Ernest Brown, to the Shire Hall in Taunton. There, he addressed a large group of officials of local authorities, thanking them for their response in dealing with the evacuees but warning of more billeting ahead particularly where war factories were in production.

Gladys Deacon does not mention them or any role she had in billeting war workers, though she did comment on the great upheaval of people doing war work. She did, of course, take Nellie and her daughter for a few days and later on a mother with three infants and by then, Margaret, one of the inmates from The Fort, is mentioned as helping in the house.

Early in the new year of 1942 Nellie returned to London leaving Helen with Mrs. Vickery. Helen stayed on at school. Nellie would visit Helen and by late 1942 take her new daughter, Linda. When the doodlebug bombs were dropping on London, Nellie would have liked to return to Milverton but by then Mrs. Vickery was looking after her son who had been injured in the RAF and her mother had needed more attention. Nellie took her children to a family in Liverpool out of range of the V1s and V2s but she and her family continued to visit Milverton for several years.

But Milverton continued to

HEALTH MINISTER'S VISIT.

'MR. ERNEST BROWN AT TAUNTON.

" HEAVIER BILLETING " WARNING.

LOCAL AUTHORITIES' WORK PRAISED.

The Minister of Health, Mr. Ernest Brown, who is spending the week-end in the West of England, yesterday met Somerset Mayors and chairmen and officials of local authorities in Taunton.

The gathering took place at the Shire Hall, where the Minister briefly addressed a large assembly of public representatives. He was welcomed by the chairman of the Somerset County Council, Mr. A. L. Hobhouse, who, in his introductory remarks, spoke of the large part which Somerset had played in the reception of evacuees. No less than 35 of the 36 local authorities in the county were reception areas. " We have taken our share of evacuees, whether that share was fair or excessive, with readiness and goodwill," Mr. Hobhouse declared. He described the services which had been set up for the care and welfare of the evacuees, and, mentioning that the county's school population had practically doubled, said that on the county's educational department had fallen a great deal of administrative work of a detailed nature, apart from the organisation of a schools' feeding scheme. The co-operation which had been received from local authorities and voluntary organisations, particularly the W.V.S., had been of the greatest help.

10. Somerset Gazette, *1st November, 1941.*

care for its guests and more evacuees as they arrived. In December 1943, when Doodlebugs were terrorising London, Pat Bishopp came to stay with her grandparents, Mr and Mrs. Piper at 11 Sand Street. She had spent most of her 'war' with an uncle and aunt in Cornwall. Her grandparents were friends of the Acklands who lived nearby. They in turn were acquainted with two ladies of the name "Boots and Toffee"one of which was the actress Eleanor Summerfield.[28] Pat went to Milverton School. She wrote to her father describing her life – bathing in a tin bath and having a ride on the milkman's horse 'Tommy'. But sadly her grandfather died in June 1944. In a matter of fact way, rather than deliberately being humorous, she tells how his coffin had to come out of a window, rather than through the door. She does not say when she went home. But even in late 1944 Mrs. Marjorie Simpson, née Sumpter, arrived in Milverton with her mother to stay with Mr and Mrs. Bond, relations of Fred and Ruth Casley who ran the Post Office in Wiveliscombe. Her mother returned to London to care for the older step-children. Marjorie herself returned to London in time for victory celebrations.

Sylvia Perry remained here and married her Ted[29] and Mrs. Ling returned here when she was widowed.

The Somerset Council Report of 21st June, 1941 was written before the bombing of Pearl Harbour in December 1941 and before, therefore, any indication of the even greater invasion of US troops that was to arrive in Somerset and the west country. It is therefore poignant that at the end of the report, Para.12 pays tribute to two men who were crucial in facilitating the government evacuation scheme. 'There are many other aspects of evacuation which have not been covered but it is pointed out that all this additional work has been undertaken at some time during the twenty-four hours of the day by Mr. Cooper and Mr. Strickland without any additional assistance apart from the Welfare organisations.

Darlingest

1. See, On the Fields'.
2. Some 'Aliens' were allowed to join the Pioneer Corps.
3. Author's father as Labour officer for WARAG committee, Gloucestershire,
4. Housewives were classified as 'Unpaid domestic work' no mention was made if they were also mothers, especially of young children. No doubt the word 'unpaid' was to differentiate them from domestic servants. Whilst today the term 'Housewife' might be derogatory, the term 'Unpaid domestic work' suggests slavery!
5. Those of us still with cards need to keep them safe against identity fraud.
6. See 'Feeding the Nation'.
7. County Council Record of events 21.6.41.
8. HM Queen was going to send to each household hosting children a personal message as a token of her recognition of their service to others.
9. Mrs. Pat. Bishopp.
10. Sylvia Perry.
11. 'It is important to understand that at that time a lot of the people being kept in such places were not intellectually disabled as we know it – they were defined as socially deficient – so in theory could have gone to university. Most of those in the institutions then were of low average intelligence and not severely mentally disabled and thus wrongly stigmatised.' He went on to say that 'In the war, in Brentry Hospital, the medical superintendent gave a talk complaining that many of the staff were less intelligent than the inmates.' (Quote from Local Psychiatrist and Historian, Glenside Museum.) This is still the era of a pregnant mother on poor relief being classified as mentally deficient, or a place where unmarried mothers could be hidden away. Nellie 21.7.40 – sale at The Fort – suggests that the women from Sandhill Park arrived at this time rather than at the same time as the men in 1939.
12. See 'Raising a Laugh – Entertainment'.
13. See Godber Ford 'Feeding the Nation'.
14. Gazette date 15.6.40.
15. The 'official' train was due to leave Ealing Broadway (Paddington Line) at 12.12 to arrive in Milverton at 15.55.
16. See 'Doubling Up – Education'.
17. Report, dated 21.6.41 para 10 'The billeting of expectant mothers has always been a very difficult problem … and the County Council suggested a scheme of earmarking billets was extended to other counties'. The *Gazette* of 15.6.40 states 'It is probable that some expectant mothers will be evacuated to Wellington but the date of their arrival is not certain'.
18. Nellie 11.9.40.

19. Nellie 24.7.40 and 26.9.40 and 30.3.41.
20. See 'Military Invasion'.
21. A baker in Norton Fitzwarren.
22. See 'Raising a laugh – Entertainment'.
23. Information on Evacuation for Households taking Unaccompanied Children.
24. See 'Doubling Up –Education'.
25. See 'Doing Your Bit'.
26. See 'Waste Not Want Not'.
27. See 'Raising a Laugh – Entertainment'.
28. Ted Perry – See 'Sup Up and clear the Cellars – Military Invasion', 'Doing Your Bit', 'Feeding the Nation', and 'Make do and Mend'.

7. DOUBLING UP – EDUCATION

BY JANE WOODLAND

We are the children of North Harringay,
We came down to Milverton on a bright summer's day,
We had all the brawn but no brains some they say,
We work in hall with Gables so Tall
But at History and Geography we're no good at all.

Down at Kingsham we went and had fun
They say that rheumatics in water does run
We found that the waters was not a bit cold
But we will have screws when we are ever so old.

The school song written by North Harringay School evacuees about their time in Milverton provided by former evacuee Bruce Watkiss.

In June 1939 Somerset County Council sent out a letter urging local councils to work out the detail of how evacuated children were to be educated. School units were to be kept together as a 'cardinal principle' of the evacuation scheme: as most London schools were much bigger than Somerset schools it would usually not be possible to accommodate a London school in a single Somerset school but efforts were to be made to place London pupils in schools in the same vicinity so that the London head teacher could supervise his schools and preserve the identity of the school in the reception area as far as possible. The number of school

17. Brendons in North Street, where the WI made their jam and preserved fruit.

DIG FOR VICTORY

18. Left: Poster.
19. Above: Milverton's War Funds Board, found in cellar of Carlton House now in Milverton Archives.

20. Poster designed by Bruce Watkiss when an evacuee schoolboy, redrawn from memory as an adult.

21. Mural above fireplace in St. Michael's Rooms. The original picture had been damaged, and this picture, copied from a box of chocolates, was painted by an American soldier.

JOHN KIACZ JR
35523857 T43 43 0

C

22. Dog Tag found by Julian Dakowski.

23. Selene and Shona Withers holding the photographs of Vincent Tuminello they had taken to Milverton School, without realising the significance or what his story would reveal. They are sitting on the gate to Doltons Field, where many of the American soldiers lived in tents.

THANKSGIVING DAY
ENGLAND
CO "M"
513th QM. TRK REGT

MENU
****

CIDER
FRUIT COCKTAIL

ENTREE
******

* ROAST TURKEY WITH GIBLET GRAVY AND CRANBERRY SAUCE *

* ROAST PORK WITH DRESSING *

MASHED POTATOES   SWEET & SOUR PICKLES
SWEET POTATOES   BUTTERED PEAS

VEGETABLE SALAD

BREAD   BUTTER   ROLLS

           PLUM PUDDING WITH WHITE SAUCE
FRUIT CAKE   CANDY   APPLES   PEARS

COFFEE

24. *Above: Menu for a Thanksgiving meal given to people in Milverton. Date and time unknown, but the venue was a tent by the Recreation Ground.*

25. *Right: Victory certificate given to Erica Tucker when she was a schoolgirl.*

Erica M. G. Flaggett.
Form Vx

8th June, 1946

TO-DAY, AS WE CELEBRATE VICTORY, I send this personal message to you and all other boys and girls at school. For you have shared in the hardships and dangers of a total war and you have shared no less in the triumph of the Allied Nations.

I know you will always feel proud to belong to a country which was capable of such supreme effort; proud, too, of parents and elder brothers and sisters who by their courage, endurance and enterprise brought victory. May these qualities be yours as you grow up and join in the common effort to establish among the nations of the world unity and peace.

George R.I.

26. *Photograph taken at the Victoria Rooms, after the 'Telling the Story of Milverton in the War' event as part of the 60th Anniversary of VE Day, in 2005. L-R Amy McGrath, former Land Girl, Helen Amy (Nellie Clemens' daughter), and Bruce Watkiss who was evacuated to Milverton from North Haringgay School in Nellie Clemens' group.*

children to be evacuated to the various parishes was to match the school accommodation available as far as possible.

In each billeting area a head teacher was appointed Education Liaison officer. Miss Hardcraft was the headmistress in charge of the local district which included Milverton and Wiveliscombe. Miss Smith was in charge of the Denmark St. School but eventually, Mr. Cann – who arrived on 17th June, 1940 – as Head of the North Harringay School became responsible for all evacuated children in Milverton.

One and half million people were evacuated of which 750,000 were school children with their teachers. In Milverton, a senior teacher from North Harringay – Miss Ursula Rattenbury, together with Miss Mills and Mrs. Clemens remained. But not all teachers could stay – needed at home, they had to return. Teachers were in short supply as is clear from the School logs.

The value of teachers accompanying their school children from the South East was expressed by Mrs Deacon, the assistant billeting officer for Milverton, 'They knew the teacher and the teacher knew their background and the teacher knew who was a difficult Tommy and who was a sweet little girl. She knew they were not being difficult just because – but they are difficult children to cope with...that was a wonderful help to us and a wonderful consoling, yes, consoling fact for the children'.

The majority of school aged children evacuated to Somerset attended elementary schools. By February 1940, 34,000 elementary and 2,800 secondary evacuees had arrived. Elementary schools, such as Milverton, took pupils up to the age of 14. Secondary schools catered for children over the age of 11: pupils were mostly fee paying, though a proportion received scholarships meaning fees were waived, partially or completely.

Secondary school children were received in the larger Somerset towns including Bridgwater, Yeovil, Minehead and Street. Coburn School for Girls, Poplar (199 pupils) was accommodated in the premises of what was termed the old Bishops Fox's School in Staplegrove Road in Taunton and Bishops Fox's Girls' School moved to Kingston Road in October 1939.

Less successful was the evacuation of Barking Abbey School, Essex to Weston Super Mare Grammar School. The 344 pupils returned to London when the Weston School was blitzed.

The logs for Milverton School and the neighbouring Bathealton, Kittiford and West Milverton Schools plot the arrival of evacuees during the war years. All Somerset schools were closed on 1st September, 1939, by order of the Chief Education Officer, William Deacon. Schools then reopened after the arrival of evacuees when initial arrangements had been made for educating them and the local children.

Bathealton and West Milverton School reopened on 13th September, 1939, having received a group of evacuees in the first phase of the country's evacuation scheme. The log recorded that 'the Bathealton School children are working in the Main Room, the class room being given up for the present to the London evacuee'. By 20th November, 1939, it was noted that owing to the Assistant Master of the Evacuees and the five senior evacuee boys having been moved to Wiveliscombe, the junior and infant evacuees with their teacher in charge, and Miss Clements[1] with the Bathealton infants, are working in two groups in the Main Room, to allow for more freedom in movement while the Bathealton Seniors and Juniors are working in the classroom'.

Milverton School reopened on the 18th September. The log records the following arrivals over the course of the war years:

> September 1939 a school party from Denmark School, London
> February 1940 11 evacuees from Canning Town
> September 1940 Bexhill and District evacuees
> October 1940 more than a score of evacuees admitted
> March 1941 Shaftesbury School evacuees [2]
> May 1941 20 Bristol children
> September 1942 7 evacuees billeted at Fitzhead
> June 1943 2 more children from Dagenham
> July 1943 a group of children from Kent

Not recorded, is that on Sunday, 17th June, 1940 Mrs. Clemens and children from North Harringay arrived in Milverton.[3]

Also not included in this list was the constant dribble of 'unofficial' evacuee children, who came with a parent or to stay with relatives and had also to be absorbed into the school.[4]

Private schools were evacuated as a whole to large houses in safer areas. Milverton accommodated one such London primary school – Shaftesbury House School – at St. Michael's House. It also used St. Michael's Rooms (Fenton Hall) until they were requisitioned by the Army.[5]

Village schools were not, as a general rule, requisitioned for civil defence but where villages took in evacuees additional premises often had to be found to accommodate the expanded school population. An extra 451 premises were used for education purposes in Somerset during the war.[4]

In Milverton, the village children continued to be taught at the Old School House, [6] Sand Street (now private houses). Occasionally the school was required for billeting purposes and the school day was disrupted. Over time all the evacuee children, from whatever school, were merged with the North Harringay School under the Head, Mr. Cann.

The evacuees were taught in the Victoria Rooms where the classes, including Nellie's were divided by a curtain. Other premises were occasionally used. Helen Clemens was taught at one point in the pavilion at the recreation ground in Butts Way until it was too cold and they moved to the school room at the Methodist Chapel. Games lessons were sometimes held at the Recreation Ground.

Local school children also had some lessons in the Victoria Rooms. Mrs. Scott, who lived in Houndsmoor during the war years and was then Miss Redwood, recalled having cookery lessons there. This may have been a temporary arrangement as the Milverton School Log dated 16th March, 1943, records Miss Butler, Assist. Organiser of Domestic Science paid a visit to the school in connection with a possible re-organisation of domestic science and the possible use of the school instead of the Victoria Rooms.

Occasionally Nellie's class was displaced by the traditional function of the Victoria Rooms. She mentions having to teach the children in the small room because villagers were preparing for a jumble sale in the big room. 'One of the boys left his mac and cap there, and he found them on the table marked 9d and 3d.'

The Victoria Rooms as well as the school house were used for billeting troops.[7] On 12th February, 1941, about 40 soldiers came just for the night. Nellie says this necessitated a 'grand clearance and the Sergeants had the doubtful privilege of sleeping in the cloakroom'. The minutes of the Victoria Room committee meetings refer to payment of rent (£3 a week) being received for accommodating the new school. This charge was met by the government and visiting schools were not charged for any of the routine costs of education.

Safety was important and whilst Milverton was not really under threat from bombing.[8] The County Architect surveyed all Somerset schools and advised on optimum protection against air raids. The evacuee children, of course, would have been aware of Air Raid precautions in London, and one evacuee who arrived to stay with Mr and Mrs. Greedy, immediately asked where the air raid shelter was.[9]

Protection mostly took the form of 'fitments of close mesh wire screens to guard against dangers from flying glass and fragment'. The Education Committee paid for fitments in Voluntary as well as Council schools. Nellie writes on 18th July, 1940, 'our school windows are being protected with wire netting in frames and are having cellophane strips on as well. What a messy business it seems, sticking it on with some peculiar mixture!' Less than a year later, Nellie comments that all the cellophane is being pulled off 'what a waste of money'.

The teachers were advised that where possible all children should be kept in the school during an air raid but no more than 50 children were to be in any one room. Where accommodation was insufficient older children were to 'scatter in open ground near the school under discipline or with neighbouring householders'. Children needed to 'gain cover within five minutes of leaving their desk'.

In July 1940 they had an air raid practice which Nellie described as 'lively' as there were 20 girls in one small room and just enough space to lie on the floor, though it was not possible to get any distance from the windows.

School was occasionally interrupted by the threat of bombing. On 27th September, 1940 children were sent home very rapidly at dinner time because of an air raid warning in Taunton.

Teachers were responsible for checking gas masks and ensuring school children could put them on properly. The Bathealton, West Milverton, log records on 7th January, 1941, 'The ARP wardens have been advised this morning that the enemy is likely to use gas at any time. I have consulted the teachers on the need of a few gas masks drills in order to find out any defective masks, and the teachers have consented to carry out the drills.'

Asked how the children got to school, Mrs. Deacon said: 'In those days children had to walk two miles to school wherever they lived in Somerset. They weren't collected.' She explained that most evacuees lived with a family where there were children, or there might be a child next door, who would escort them to school. It is not clear how this worked, given that, in line with practice throughout most of the country, the school day was split with Milverton evacuees being taught from 8 a.m. to noon and local children's lessons from 12.15 – 4.15 p.m.[10]

The head teacher for Milverton School was Mr. Emlyn Morris, a keen singer and mentioned by several evacuees. But whilst the aim of the two-school system was to co-ordinate and to teach the same curriculum, lack of resources and equipment made that very difficult as Nellie records on 25th June, 1940. Within a week of the children in her class arriving in Milverton, trestle tables and pencils were in place enabling school to start. But she pines for a decent blackboard.

Maintaining the Curriculum was important. Nellie's letters give a flavour of some of the lessons. Singing appears to have featured regularly as mentioned above. Patriotic songs were on the curriculum such as 'There'll Always be an England' which prompted Nellie to comment, 'You've no idea how stirring the words really are.'

In June 1940, before Nellie arrived, William Deacon, Chief Education Officer, had sent a letter to schools, stating that Nature Study lessons should teach children the injurious effects of certain weeds on the food supply of the country. Children were to learn to recognise weeds such as ragwort, thistle and dock. Were they amongst the 30 different kinds of wildflowers collected on 20.6.40 during one of the numerous walks? On one occasion Helen picked primroses with Miss Rattenbury's class on the Wimbus (now called Rivers Farm), the 'big place on the Wiveliscombe Road'.

The novelty of the countryside for inner city children and their teachers is depicted well by the Percy the caterpillar incident: 'We had the most exciting find today. The children all rushed at me on the way to school with a creature in a box and I could not believe it was real – an immense fat caterpillar – about four inches long and pale yellowy green with bright blue spots on! Nobody had ever seen such a thing. After several enquiries I've got as far as discovering that it is probably the caterpillar of a death's head moth and quite rare! So when we go into Taunton on Saturday morning I'm going to take it to the museum and see if I can find out all about it. The death's head moth takes about two years to form! We have christened him "Percy"! It has made quite a lot of excitement and I'm almost tired of watching the uncanny creature.' The watching did not, however, last long: four days later Nellie's letter carried the news 'Percy is dead! I don't know what I'm going to tell the children. It's really very disappointing.'

Girls did needlework. On 19th January, 1943, the County Organiser for needlework visited the school to inspect the needlework arrangements. Three days later the log records that 'Certain re-arrangements in the timetable were started today to allow for two periods of needlework for the senior girls. All girls of seven and over will now be having needlework.'

The school logs show all boys from seven had to do gardening and there were regular gardening lessons as well as extra afternoon gardening periods from time to time for planting.[11] Nellie occasionally helped the boys with their vegetable cultivation.

On 24th July, 1941, described as a 'big da', Nellie and Mr Cann took 20 girls to Rivers Farm and had a busy morning picking blackcurrants. They picked 'well over 200 lbs'. The boys did the same in the afternoon. The children were paid for this fruit picking and gave some of their pay to the Red Cross. They also involved themselves with other national activities along with the village efforts in saving and salvage.[12]

Milverton School was a Council School[13] but the Vicar, would visit the school to test the children. On 4th November, 1940, J. D. George wrote 'The school is reported generally Good and Very Good where conditions permit.' By January 1943 the Religious Instruction for 1942 reported 'Generally speaking and in the two top groups in particular, the written work is up to a sometimes very high standard of performance and definition, the children explaining themselves better with pen than with tongue.' Some extra-curricular activities were laid on for evacuees. Helen attended a Sunshine Corner for about a week. Nellie described it as 'a sort of happy go lucky meeting for children. The missioner told them stories but most of the time they were yelling hymns of a revivalist nature, "I'll meet you on the other side of Jordan", etc.' Helen appears to have loved it. She was so excited that she could not eat her tea one night. About 70 children took part and sang regularly in the evenings. Nellie was less than enthusiastic by the end, referring to the 'hell of a din' (as) they gloried in the chance to be able to shout at the tops of their voices. On 2nd July, 1940, Nellie mentioned that Helen was thrilled with a feeling of adventure at going alone to a Lantern lecture after tea today, given by Church Army sisters.

Some pupils went to local camps. These camps were self-supporting, and children were paid at an agreed rate which went to the cost of running the camp. Nellie mentions that 20 of the children were going to a camp not very far from Wellington, to be run by Quakers in June 1941. She welcomed the camp as it would make teachers' lives easier with smaller class sizes.

The Government took the Welfare of the evacuee children seriously making sure that a medical check was carried out on all children at the point their parents registered them for evacuation. An Evacuation Medical Card was completed for each child. A medical examination was then undertaken on the day before departure. This was to ensure that all children 'handed over to the care of a householder in the reception area… shall be clean and free from disease'.

Over the years several cases of scarlet fever were recorded at Milverton School, as well as cases of measles, chicken pox, scabies and suspected ringworm. Occasionally more serious illnesses affected the pupils. Nellie writes on 1st April, 1941, that 'one of the little infants, Gerald, is very seriously ill with pneumonia' and she clearly fears for his care 'this village doctor is a damned fool'. Children needing to be in isolation were cared for at what is now called 'Pemberley' at the end of Sand Street.

There were regular visits from the health visitors to check for nits or Head Trouble as the school log rather coyly terms it. Doctors visited to inoculate pupils and regular dental checks for school children were held in the Victoria Rooms.

Accidents happened then as now. One boy broke his wrist very badly in July and needed hospital treatment. Dog bites and cuts are recorded. Sometimes the doctor was available in Milverton at other times – particularly for Bathealton School – the staff had to take the child to Wiveliscombe or Wellington to see a doctor, fees for which, pre NHS, for evacuated children, would be covered by the government.

Examinations went ahead as normal and despite the disruption of evacuation, the need to use temporary school accommodation, overcrowding and lack of equipment, efforts were made to offer students the same chances to learn and take exams. Nellie refers to exam preparations in early December in the two years she was in Milverton and the need for teachers to mark the exams. On 9th March, 1942, nine children took exams – six of them of them the Somerset County exam and three the London Metropolitan exam.

The logs record a good pass rate for both local children and evacuees, which enabled them to go on to secondary schools. In 1943 local children scored notable academic successes. Muriel Gould passed the County

Special Place Exam and won a place at Bishops Fox's (Girls), whilst Michael Edmonds, Laurence Jones and Royston Nutt secured places at Huish's Grammar School (Boys). Evacuees meanwhile took the exams relevant to their home town. For example in 1944, evacuee Diana Goodwin was awarded a Foundation scholarship to Hornsey County School. Brenda Stock passed the Middlesex Special Place Exam.

Class sizes constantly varied. We get a feel for the regularity with which the evacuee pupils came and went from the school logs and Nellie's letters. Just after she arrived Nellie mentions that she had 28 children in her class, 14 girls and 14 boys, all two years older than she had taught previously but they came and went which must have been unsettling for teachers as well as students.

As early as 28th July, 1940, only just over a month after the Haringay contingent's arrival, Nellie writes of a boy from her class and his younger sister returning to London: their parents had come to Milverton to collect them – 'a great pity'.

In a January letter in 1941, Nellie mentions that two of her pupils have left in one week as a girl called Winne ('who was very good at composition and was keen on her tummy') is going up North with her sister as her father had a new job there and wanted his family to be together again. Nellie remonstrates that her class is fast disappearing and she hopes she will not lose her job too soon.

Most of those who left went home but some were destined to travel further afield. Nellie refers to several of the Haringay children having their medical examination for Canada in July 1940 but her letters do not say if or when they left.

Teachers sometimes got little notice of changes. Eva Ward had a letter from her parents telling her she was to return home but needn't tell her teachers as it would be quite alright. Nellie is irritated by this: 'I can see the parents' point of view very plainly but they do things in such a funny way. ... I do think they are an ill-mannered lot. We can't force the children to stay but we like to know what's happening to them.'

Some of the evacuee children too were less than enamoured by their new situation. A Kenneth May was unhappy in his billet and his mother according to Nellie 'just whisks him off'. Others took matters into their own hands. Nellie's letter informs that one of the Bristol children had run away. The boy's younger brother was in Nellie's class and he announced that he intended to run away 'next weekend'. Three days later a letter states that the runaway has been found but might not return to the evacuee's school as he was already on probation for stealing £20.

Nellie clearly had pupils she enjoyed teaching and others who were more demanding. She stated at one point that 'Mr Cann thinks they have sent us all the criminals. The reports of the children that he has received are appalling'. The letters show her pleasure at the departure of the Bristol children 'most of the Bristol children have gone back – we are not sorry' and also of certain Haringey children: 'I was met at school with the news that the Arnold[14] family is returning at the weekend to London and although I know it is very wrong of them to go back to London, I am so very glad to get rid of a few of my beauties and Rita Arnold is one of the worst. I cannot yet believe that the Vickerys[15] have really gone. I'm having a good week. Mr Cann of course doesn't feel as I do about it though I keep my side very quiet (I hope).'

A notice from the Ministry of Health dated April 1941 contained in full in Nellie's letter of 31st March 1941 shows the pressure put on parents not to request that their children return to them for the holidays.

Evacuee children were to spend Christmas Day with their hosts but otherwise volunteers would organise games and other activities. As war continued, children became involved in summer activities particularly in the countryside.[16]

As well as the organisational demands put on the system by children going back and forth from billeting areas to homes in holidays, it may have been that the upset caused to the children was also a reason why such ventures were frowned upon. One boy, according to Nellie, did not want to go home at Christmas.[17]

In September Nellie wrote that she had decided Helen should not return to London for a holiday. 'Mr Cann is so down on the idea of kids going back for a holiday that I think it would be a bad example.' The author's father was billeted to Nottinghamshire from Worthing in 1941.

Government advice contained in the Plan IV Evacuation Scheme on holidays and closures dictated that the Leaders of Evacuee Groups should inform the Divisional Dispersals Officers in London of holiday addresses of teachers, with dates and also note the holiday addresses of the voluntary helpers on their lists. If a crisis arose during the holidays all teachers would be recalled. All teachers and helpers were to keep within reach of the radio throughout all holiday and closure periods and return promptly if recalled.

In 1941, The Ministry of Health sent this plea to parents: For the sake of your children's safety, do not bring them home for the Easter holidays. They would be running great risks in the Danger areas; and while they were away, their billets might be filled, and then they would be unable to go back. The Education Authorities and School Governors have been asked to keep the school premises and playgrounds open in the holidays so that the children may be kept happily occupied. Leave them where they are until the government says it is safe for them to return – 'Keep them away from the danger areas.'

The number of former evacuees who have returned to Milverton over the past years suggests that on the whole the evacuees seem to have been fairly easily assimilated into village life. The references to potential differences are few. Nellie writes that a villager commented that she could not understand what the London children said at the Harvest festival. Mrs Scott's family had an evacuee from Bristol billeted with them. She recalls they got on quite well: 'I don't think we did an awful lot of fightin'.'

While education was generally segregated between locals and evacuees during the first part of the war, there were some joint events. In October 1941, the log reports that the senior boys (nine in number) went to the Recreation Ground at 3.30 p.m. for games joining with the senior boys of the evacuated school – at the Victoria Rooms under the control of Mr. Lamb.

Inevitably there were tensions and Nellie relates one incident, involving Mr Cann, Head teacher of the Haringey School in January 1941. 'Mr. Cann has had a strange, not too pleasant experience. Plastered all over the village this morning were little notices, with nasty things about him on them! One said he was a spy. All very mysterious. He has decided it must be one of the soldiers. You see, one morning this week, he was caning a boy and a soldier who happened to come in, interfered in a very rude way and of course Mr. Cann was furious and reported him to the Major. It happened that this particular soldier has defended the boy before. One night Mr. Cann turned the boy out of the canteen and this soldier turned on him. All very peculiar. Dirty deeds in a village!'

The government took on responsibility of feeding a main meal[18] to all school children, evacuees of course, were only to be given breakfast and supper at their billet. The Log of 7th August, 1940 refers to the distribution of milk having been arranged for those who wish to have it.

A hot schools meal service was introduced, alleviating some of the hosts from giving a hot meal to their evacuees. It was to provide one third of the child's daily dietary needs. No meal was to be pre-heated or re-heated. The Milverton School log records the commencement of the service on 29th November, 1943. The School Dinner service began today when 72 children were served with hot meals. Owing to some delay at the central kitchen, the food did not arrive till 1 o'clock but otherwise the service was satisfactory. At the end of 1943, 14,000 meals were being made daily across Somerset. An average of 23,000 children took milk. In Somerset 71% of the cost of providing food came from the Treasury. Coupons were not required for school meals. If a hot meal could not be provided the 'Oslo sandwich' was provided, this was cold with cheese and salad and a glass of milk.

Newspaper adverts sought recruitment to the service 'for the sake of

Britain's children, the nationwide School Meals Service must grow bigger still, now and after the war. This can be done only with the help of an increased number of Domestic Workers, to whom its present success is so largely due.'[19]

The period between children leaving school aged 14 and being able to do 'proper war work' was not to be wasted, so boys and girls had to join other organisations. The Girls' Brigade was one and there is good mention in transcripts of Milverton's brigade.

Mrs Scott recalls being part of the Brigade: 'We thought we were the cat's whiskers because we all had a uniform and we did from time to time, parade through the village. What actual good we did, I don't know. But we learnt lots of things, you know, we did First Aid, and Red Cross and things like that. We went once a week.' They also went to camp at Blue Anchor on the train for a week but for Mrs Scott the experience was not a pleasant one: 'I hated every minute of it.'

Mrs Scott remembered the uniform was a peak cap, a navy blue skirt, a white blouse and ankle socks, and the image produced was, she felt, 'rather fetching'.

At the end of 1941, the government stipulated that the local Education Boards set up a register of all young people between 16 – 18 who were not attached to any youth organisation, or pre-service training. A County Youth Committee interviewed these young people, to make them aware of the way they could serve their country. Interviews were conducted by School Managers with representatives from the Home Guard, Armed Service Cadets and Civil defence. 6,800 boys registered of whom 1,000 were in full time education and 3,000 were already undertaking an approved activity. Students at universities or other places of higher education who were pursuing specified scientific or technical courses were to be granted a deferment of national service on the recommendation of the University Joint Recruiting Boards. Those still at school but who were intending to take such courses were able to do so in 'suitable cases'.

Continuity of teaching staff was hard to achieve during the war years.

Evacuee teachers were called back to the South East from time to time or moved on to different evacuee schools and there were changes in village school staffing too. The village head teacher, Mr Morris left the school at the end of the summer term 1941 after 20 years at the school to go to a post in Wales. He was replaced, temporarily by Mr. Lamb from North Harringay who was himself recalled to London[20] and then Mr. Ronald Hoare[21] arrived to be permanent Head in October 1941.

Nellie herself was told in early December 1941 that she was to be recalled to London and her last letter dated 9th December, 1941, is full of thoughts about the future of the evacuee school. She advocates a merger of the evacuee school and Milverton School and this did take place the following year. The school log states on 14th March, 1942 – 'The North Harringay School has been joined with the local school and today the children assembled here. There were 26 from the Hornsey Schools and 2 from Bristol.'

Even with the smaller numbers of evacuee children the pressures on the school and its staff were considerable and the school log makes several references to lack of staff: the Head teacher had to take classes 1 and 2 together[22] as no supply teacher turned up, a total of 69 children. Teachers from Kent were called to the school on two occasions in 1944 for a stint of six weeks each. Miss Mills,[23] Helen's teacher, was finally recalled by the Hornsey authorities on 13th July, 1945 and her colleague, Miss Jacoby returned a week later.

Educating the next generation of young Britons during the war was an extraordinary feat. Nellie's letters give a clear picture of the difficulties stacked against teachers and educators in the war years. Maintaining or extending educational standards was a near impossible task against a backdrop of damage to one in five schools nationally, requisitioning of almost two thirds of town schools for civil defence, one million children evacuated, overcrowded classrooms often in non-school accommodation, split school days, constant changes of staff and pupils in evacuee schools, air raids and the need for children as well as adults to support the war effort as well as lack of equipment and evacuee children coping with absences from their family. There were also a large number of children in the early war years who were not evacuated but remained in inner city areas where the schools were closed. They were often left without the supervision afforded by schools or families as their fathers were called up and their mothers worked for the war effort. (The Government reopened some schools in these areas when the impact of school closures became clear.) Despite the efforts of teachers, a significant number of children failed to reach the require levels of literacy and numeracy. In education, as in so many other aspects of life, the post war years saw politicians grasp the initiative for change and the 1944 Education Act[24] raised the school leaving age to 15 and created the first nationwide system of state-funded secondary education in England and Wales.

> 'We are the children of North Harringay,
> We came down to Milverton on a bright Summer's day
> For all you dear people who gave us a bed
> (Punch line forgotten in the mists of time!)
> *Evacuee – Barbara Woods (née Buckland)*

---

1. Not Mrs.Nellie Clemens.
2. (& 5) See 'Gone to the Country' – Shaftesbury House School was evacuated to St. Michael's House, but as there are no records it remains a mystery even more so, as an old pupil said they were taught privately and did not mix with the village, which conflicts with the record showing their arrival in the school logs. Emily Meare's school project discovering the history of her home – St. Michael's House, records memories of a former pupil, Mrs. Yvonne Scott. She described an incident that eventually led to the school being closed in 1944. See also' Over Here', 'Defending Milverton – Home Guard'.
3. See 'Gone to the Country'.
4. Wiveliscombe school took in 120 evacuee children from the dockland district of London's East End. The school logs states '4 rooms were being used by us (ie for Wiveliscombe children) and 3 by West Ham authorities. There is considerable

congestion in two cases more than 60 children are crowded into 1 classroom.' This was resolved by children being taught in the Constitutional Rooms (now the Community Centre), the Liberal Club (number 32 and 34 Silver Street) and the Old Church School Rooms.

5. (see 2 above.)
6. The school logs show that first intake of children from Denmark Street were taught in the upper part of the school with tables borrowed from the Victoria Rooms.
7. See 'Military Invasion'.
8. See 'Militaty Invasion'.
9. See 'Gone to the Country'.
10. See 'Gone to the Country'. The author's father was evacuated to Nottinghamshire and attended Newark Secondary School in the afternoons. Mornings were supposed to be used for doing homework, but he recalls many enjoyable cycling trips in the sun, which on one occasion resulted in being given a black ticket, the punishment for lack of completed homework!
11. See 'Dig for Victory'.
12. See Waste Not, Want Not'.
13. Although it had its foundation closely linked to the church, in the 1870s Rev. Fowle caused a major rift and set up in opposition in St. Michael's Rooms. There is a convoluted tale but the outcome led to Milverton becoming a Board School and hence a County Primary School today. The Vicar would have gone in to examine the children's RE knowledge but there would not have been the same curriculum as in a Church School.
14. Not only Nellie, as Margaret McGill (née Loram) wrote that the Arnold children stayed with her parents at Lovelynch Farm and that her mother found Rita and her father very difficult.
15. Joan Vickery, not related to the family where Nellie was billeted.
16. See 'On the Fields'.
17. The author's father was billeted to Nottinghamshire from Worthing in 1941 and describes how he was very well cared for by his new family and enjoyed the whole experience initially, without any worries, but a visit from his mother, grandmother and sister, arranged out of kindness by his billet family, upset him greatly and thereafter he was very homesick and unsettled and longed to return home.
18. 2nd September, 1946, the log stated that 1/3 of a pint of milk was available free to all school children. (For Secondary schools free milk continued until 1968 and for children, over 7, until 1971.)
19. The author's father recalls the school meals being good. They had plates of what was termed national wholemeal bread to start with, which was a peculiar grey

colour but tasted fine. He ate his as did most children, though he remembers some of the less appreciative pupils made bread pellets which they fired around the dining hall.
20. Nellie, 17.7.41 and on 10.7.41 Nellie mentions that Miss Rattenbury might be moved to another school to replace Mr. Warren who was being recalled.
21. Both Mr. Morris and Mr. Hoare were remembered by evacuees visiting in later years and by Milverton residents today.
22. Nellie 4.1.43.
23. Miss Mills eventually returned and settled here.
24. See 'Clearing Up to move forward'.

8. RAISING A LAUGH – ENTERTAINMENT

'Tuppence worth of chips and a shilling for the pictures'. Mrs. Ling, evacuee

Life had to go on regardless. An increase in population often living in difficult circumstances had to be entertained and in a self contained village as Milverton, this was going to be home grown fun!

During the War the Victoria Rooms was the main hub of a variety of activities, as it still is today. At one time or another they were used as an overflow school room for evacuees; played host to various parish council committees convened to organise money-raising events such as 'Wings For Victory'[1] and 'War Weapons Week'; was the venue for cookery classes; and even saw service as a troop kitchen.

A revised charge list[2] of 12th September, 1941 reveals the wide variety of social and cultural events held there:

> *'Hire of Large Hall'*
> Local concert and plays   £1.0.0
> "Outside hirers   £1.5.0
> Local Dances   £1.10.0
> "Outside hirers   £1.15.0
> Local Whist Drives   12.6
> "Outside hirers   17.6
> Jumble sales   10.0

Extras
Piano Dances 5.0
Piano Socials 2.6
Piano Concerts 2.6
Lighting 2.6
Heating (per hour) 1.0
Preparation of Room 2.6

Reading Room
Whist Drives 7.6
Committee Meetings or
any similar use 2.6

Nellie regularly went to whist drives but doesn't say whether she attended the weekly Houndsmoor Club or the Home Guard Snow Ball whist drives at the Victoria Rooms, both of which were held during weekdays, though she specifically mentions one on 25th July, 1941, in a private home organised by the Conservative Party. Land Girl, Amy McGrath, also mentioned going into Milverton to play whist.

The WI was again quick off the mark in that a few weeks after the troops arrived it was proposed on 28th October, 1940, that the C.O.[3] should be approached as to whether the troops would appreciate Folk Dancing Classes. A month later they were planning a party, eventually held on 16th January, 1941 to which troops would be invited at half price and asked to provide some entertainment. But it was the dances that became the highlight of the week. The WI organised occasional dances – a very successful one reported in the *Gazette* was held on 29th November, 1941, with an attendance of 250.[4] Meanwhile the British Legion and Home Guard organised the regular weekly Saturday dances. According to newspaper reports, and the recollections of Land Girl, Amy McGrath, [5] the only refreshments were sandwiches and cups of tea. Nellie mentions a Friday night dance for the Cricket Club on 4th October, 1940, when the Secretary Mrs, Vickery provided the refreshments. According to Nellie the soldiers were tipsy so maybe they had first visited the several public houses in Milverton that included the White Hart and the George almost next door. Many soldiers were billeted in these pubs and both stood just a few doors down from April Cottage where Nellie lived.

The music would have been a live band – Edgar's Smith's Orchestra, or Sydney Frank's Orchestra and Sylvia Perry remembers two ladies who played accordions accompanied by a man at the piano. Could they have been The Adainians? According to Sylvia, 'One band leader played the musical saw, which was most unusual, but it was absolutely packed. Someone used to make paper flowers for the front of the stage. When the Americans came it was fuller than ever as everyone wanted to see the Americans that weren't in the village and it used to get so hot the damp used to drip from the ceiling… it was condensation. It was so hot you could feel it dripping.' Nellie's descriptions of dances do not include such details and it maybe that Sylvia's memories relate to dances that took place after Nellie returned to London at the end of 1941 and refers to dances once the American soldiers arrived.

Amy McGrath the Land Girl[6] echoes Sylvia's memories, in her description of dances in 1942: 'they, (US troops) came from Norton Fitzwarren. They came in their jeeps and their trucks… must have been about 40 came in, all from there because they used to know where all the village hops were… so they would arrive in. And the little band we had, ordinary, they took over. They said, "OK, mind if we get on." And it was all hell let loose when they got on. Everybody was dancing away there and they'd got cigarettes and nylons, and then about half past ten, I think it was, ten to half past, up Mr Jacobs would come, spoiling all the fun and would shout our names "Joan", that was his daughter – "Joan, Barbara,[7] Amy, come on." No chance of getting escorted home and any … business going on because we had to get home. We walked down together… down the long walk from you know, the station.'

Whether the WI's folk dancing classes ever took off is not recorded, but some kind of dancing classes must have taken place as on January 1943, they had decided to postpone proposed dancing classes and social 'owing to the troops leaving'. This must have been a temporary situation as dance continued until after the end of 1945.

In July 1944, the Parish Council Chairman stated that 'the police had been in communication with the management of dance rooms throughout the county, with reference to late night dances asking that their numbers should be reduced. It had therefore been decided that dances at the Victoria Rooms should be held on Saturdays only and should close at 11.30 some dancing classes had taken place as the WI agreed on and troop numbers in the county were greatly reduced. Though towards the end of the war, on 15th February, 1945 the WI booked an RAF band to play at a social they were organising. Whilst these were public occasions, the WI arranged entertainment for their 'social hour'. One such was 7th April, 1942 when there was an 'excellent display of physical training by girls[8] now living at The Fort (now Lancaster House) followed by club swinging by their matron.

Apart from social events the Victoria Rooms hosted more intellectual and educational entertainments. Nellie mentions a concert on 18th September 1940 with visiting artists and this is likely to have been presented by CEMA (Council for the Encouragement of Music and Arts – forerunner of the Arts Council) who ran a travelling exhibition 'Art for the People' which performed *The Merchant of Venice*[9] in the Victoria Rooms on 7th March, 1941, and on 12th March, 1943,[10] a performance of 'The Market Theatre'.

Just as today plays or shows were put on by the WI, the school children and the Amateur Dramatic Society. Mrs. Frances Pryor, of Fitzhead, was friendly with the young actress Eleanor Summerfield[11] who, with her parents, had fled the London Blitz. Whilst her parents had become proprietors of The Globe Inn in Milverton, Eleanor was doing office work for Norton Fitzwarren Depot (now the Langford Mead development and also the site of the Somerset Heritage Centre). Later, she worked for the US Army at Hestercombe House where she is remembered by Betty and Joyce Rockett[12] Frances, a dancer (stage name – Vera Dick) and Eleanor took part in a Troop show, called 'Stand Easy' with members of the Royal Artillery, who were billeted here. The show was performed for three days at the Victoria Rooms, followed by two days at the Wellesley Theatre, Wellington after which it toured around various military convalescent homes in the vicinity.

But whatever else was going on at the Victoria Rooms, Friday night was always film night. The *Gazette* of 18th October, 1941 lures punters to a forthcoming visit of the free mobile film unit with the promise of 'Famous films such as "Britain at War" that have thrilled thousands'. Evacuee Mrs. Ling remembers also a local Milverton man, Don Davies who would screen films in the Victoria Rooms every Friday night. 'You could get tuppence worth of chips and a shilling for the pictures – that was high living on Friday!'[13]

11. *'Milverton, Free film show'*, Somerset Gazette, *18th October, 1941.*

MILVERTON.
FREE FILM SHOW NEXT MONDAY.—The Ministry of Information Mobile Film Unit is visiting Milverton on Monday to give a Free Film Show in the Victoria Rooms at 7 p.m. Famous films of "Britain At War" that have thrilled thousands will be shown. Unaccompanied children will not be admitted.—Advt.

HOME GUARD.—The local Home Guard are running a succession of Saturday evening dances and snowball whist drives on Thursdays in the Victoria Rooms. The snowball whist drives commenced last week and met with good support. The proceeds are in aid of the Hut Fund of the local company.

But all these were local activities. War news and entertainment from outside the close-knit Milverton community would have come via newspapers and most importantly the radio, known as the 'wireless'. By 1939 over nine million radio licences had been issued making it possible for 90% of the population to have access to radio broadcasts. The BBC[14] was the sole provider, its charter decreeing that it should 'Inform, Entertain and Educate'. Whilst it remained independent of Whitehall, the Government was allowed airtime to broadcast important speeches; information[15] that included warnings; information for farmers; the daily food facts; the Radio Doctor; and coded messages to the Resistance in occupied Europe.

Many older residents will remember that as children they listened to 'Uncle Mac' introducing *Children's Hour* with the words 'Hello children everywhere' whilst the Schools programmes kept children up to date

– whether they had schools to go to or not. These early radio nature lessons were given by Frank Gillard then a teacher at Taunton school.[16]

In 1940 – at the height of the 'invasion scare', BBC newsreaders identified themselves for the first time. It was felt that if the public could link voices to names they would not be duped by fake German broadcasts giving misleading information. The news was read at a specific pace to enable it to be written or taken down in shorthand. Unfortunately for sport lovers, outside sports broadcasts were discontinued to economise on use of telephone lines.

The naming of newsreaders[17] quickly spawned the 'radio personality' – one being Wilfred Pickles with his northern brogue so very different from the precise received English of news broadcasters. With personalities suddenly at the helm, radio entertainment quickly came into its own as a major morale booster – but lighter Radio entertainment was the major morale booster – with dance band programmes introduced by Billy Cotton and Henry Hall; variety shows such as *Bandwagon; Crazy Gang*; and the comedy series – ITMA (*It's That Man Again*!) with Tommy Handley in charge of the Ministry of Aggravation and Mysteries. The population particularly identified with the satire in this programme and with its many catch phrases – 'Can I do you now Sir' and 'It's being so cheerful what keeps me going' from Mrs. Mop – interspersed with the threatening and mysterious 'This is Funf speaking'. Other popular daytime programmes were made to cater for those in factories including *Music While you Work* and *Workers Playtime* broadcast from a secret factory on a Saturday morning, increased eventually to three times a week. One of the two

DAILY MIRROR 4th September 1939

Don't Let Your Radio Blare

The B.B.C. appeals to listeners on behalf of night workers.

"Will listeners please remember," they ask, "that, in the house or flat next to them, there may be someone who has been working all night and who has to sleep during the day.

"Will they, therefore, see that the volume of noise from their wireless sets is as little as conveniently possible."

12. *Daily Mirror, 4th September, 1939.*

resident pianists, who travelled the country coping with the late arrival of pianos, or piano legs missing, was Jack Clarke, the uncle of Mrs. Wenda Moon who lived in Milverton until 2004.

1940 also, saw the introduction of the Forces Programme which produced special programmes such as *Forces Favourites* that linked families with their loved ones serving overseas.

Nellie writes to her husband on 23rd March, 1941 (not included in the extracts) that 'This afternoon I will bake a cake and listen to Beethoven's Fifth symphony and then a Shaw play.' This shows the diversity of radio programming. What would now be on Radio 4, and very successful were *The Brains Trust* and *In Your Garden*. And to counter the traitor Lord Haw Haw's broadcasts 'Germany Calling – Germany Calling' J. B. Priestley's fireside chats – *Postscripts* – were introduced in 1940 and broadcast after the news on a Sunday evening.

William Joyce, Lord Haw Haw, was an Irishman, but naturalised US citizen who in 1938 had obtained a British passport that was renewed in 1939 – despite his being Co-founder of the National Socialist League. Named Lord Haw Haw for his upper-class sneering[18] tone, he broadcast propaganda from Hamburg during the phoney war. In the early part of 1940 he regularly had an audience of six million[19] as people thought them funny when there was little news. His talks often based on half-truths spoke of social division and inequalities. When the war turned serious in late 1940 the audience dropped off.[20] *The Vale of Taunton Past* (p.113) mentions Lord Haw Haw reporting a concert in the Victoria Rooms at Milverton[21] that had taken place a few days earlier. Arrested in May 1945, he was prosecuted as a British subject under British law and hanged for treason on 3rd January, 1946.

Together with radio broadcasting, the Government Film Unit's information and propaganda films were shown alongside the Gaumont, Movietone and Pathé Newsreels. These kept people abreast of the progress of the military aspects of the war as well as informing them of new regulations. They soon became an important part of any visit to 'The Pictures' to see UK and US made films. Mrs. Ling said: 'the main cinemas, – the Gaumont, Odeon, and the Gaity[22] were in Taunton' where Mrs. Ling's son, John, would go as well as evacuee Marjorie Sumpter who sneaked off unknown by her hosts. Nellie mentions taking Helen to see *Gulliver's Travels* on 16th July, 1940. Amy McGrath, Land Girl recalled that on a half day, she'd go into Taunton on the bus, look round the shops and go to the cinema having had tea at Maynards on Bridge Street.

All newspapers local and national broadsheet newspapers were reduced to four pages – but were full of stories reflecting normal everyday life as well as reports on the war and military matters. Books were precious since paper was strictly rationed for new publications, but there were new books for children and lending libraries or subscription libraries that Boots the chemists provided.

As well as going to concerts and dances at the Victoria Rooms, and listening to the radio and gramophone, people also made their own music themselves. Sheet music was reduced in size to save paper but it was still possible to buy records.

Sporting activities continued at the Recreation Ground of course for adults as well as children. On 5th June, 1941 Nellie mentions going to watch a cricket match.

All in all, the picture that emerges of life in Milverton during the war was anything but dull. In fact in some respects there may have been more entertainment and greater opportunities for socialising and meeting the newcomers – whether they be evacuees or soldiers – than before the outbreak of hostilities.

1. See 'Waste Not Want Not'.
2. By 3rd September, 1942 charges must have increased as the Management Committee agreed to reduce the charge from £1.17s.6d back to £1.10s for dances, from 8 p.m. to midnight, after Major Harvey RA had made a complaint. The heating would be extra.
3. Major Edward Bazalgette.
4. Today only 120 allowed.
5. Amy McGrath – See 'Doing Your Bit' and 'On the Fields'.
6. See 'Doing Your Bit'.
7. Other Land Girl, Barbara Williams.
8. There is some confusion about where these evacuees came from. It is believed they were from Sandilands. The men and boys were at The Rectory (the Old House) – See 'Gone to the Country' and 'Feeding the Nation'.
9. Nellie 27.2.41.
10. School logs.
11. Eleanor Summerfield(1921-2001). Nellie's son-in-law remembers Nellie referring to her as 'Boots Summerfield' but doesn't know the reason how she got this name but evacuee, also Pat Bishopp also remembered that name. (See 'Gone to the Country'. Eleanor was an 'all round' performer. She had a long career on stage and in films and a witty contributor on radio panel shows. The *Daily Telegraph* Obituary in July 2001, stated 'she first appeared on the professional stage at 18, in a touring revue for ENSA. Her career however was interrupted by the Second World War, during which she worked for the War Office.' The 'War Office' we, know employed her at Hestercombe House and at Norton Fitzwarren Depot. She married Leonard Sachs, 1947 who presented TV's *Old Time Music Hall*.
12. See 'Hestercombe At War' booklet published 2007.
13. See also 'Doubling Up – Education' (Shaftesbury House School).
14. WI Minutes for On 2nd April, 1945 Z Mr. Milliken of the BBC gave an interesting talk on broadcasting.
15. It also appealed to listeners the day after war was declared – 4th September, 1939 – to be careful about volume as 'there may be someone who has to sleep during the day'.
16. Frank Gillard, CBE (1908-1998) originally a pupil of Wellington School, went on to have a distinguished broadcasting career, first as a war correspondent in North Africa, Italy, Normandy and Berlin, and ultimately as Managing Director BBC Radio 1963-70.
17. Amy McGrath. Land girl recalled listening each morning to War news with Alvar Liddell.
18. Nellie 17.9.40.

19. *Daily Telegraph*, 27th March, 1944 – Lord Haw Haw silent.
20. He also read out a list of Prisoners of War, which was sometimes the first indication that missing military personnel were alive.
21. Without listening to the many tapes it is impossible to confirm this story.
22. The Gaumont (now Mecca) by the bus station, the Odeon, on the corner of Staplegrove and Station Road, demolished in 1998, the 'Gaity' nearer the station in Kingston Road.

9. FEEDING THE NATION

'During the course of two hours I received five signals that food ships had been sunk – all bacon. In order to keep the pledge of rationing – stocks of bacon kept in easy reach of Liverpool were to be reallocated to other parts of the country as the one solitary ship with bacon came into the port of Liverpool – the cargo was brought off with speed and went into distribution.' Lord Woolton, Minister for Food[1]

When Nellie, who could only get her rations from the County Stores, remarked on 28th March, 1941, that she had managed to get a jar of marmalade[2] – one per month – she was at the end of a very long rationing chain that began with convoys. That the rationing system could order and distribute food, so that one person at one shop in a small rural village could get her allotted ration was extraordinary achievement in pre-computer days.

Pre-war Britain had been dependent on imports for 92% of requirements for fat, 51% of meat and bacon, 73% sugar, 87% flour and cereals as well as a large proportion of cheese, eggs, vegetables and other foods. Manufactured food such as bakery products, breakfast cereals, canned and bottled food and sauces took up a large amount of the household food budget. With the war reducing imports to absolute necessities, ensuring that people got a nutritional and balanced general diet was a challenging undertaking.

Bread accounted for 20% of food consumption in Britain during the war, and, with potatoes, remained un-rationed. Only after the war was a bread ration finally introduced.

In 1940 bakers were able to increase the flour content of bread from 73% to 85% just by retaining the germ and bran (containing Vitamin B and iron), during milling. The result was a greyish loaf – the National Wheatmeal Loaf – that first went on the market in March 1941. Even with the Government promoting its extra nutritional value it was not popular; so for a while a white loaf 'fortified' with vitamin B1 was also made available. However, increasing shipping losses during 1942 meant that fortified loaves could no longer be provided. It was the 'National-Loaf' or nothing. And even this was restricted and could only be sold a day old, being easier to cut so it would therefore go further. Sliced bread had not been introduced.

13. Mrs. Vickery's bill for supplying food and laundry to Mrs. Clemens and Miss Rattenbury, 6th July, 1941.

After the Munich crisis the Government had had time to build up stocks of various imports including large quantities of whale oil for the manufacture of margarine.[3] In 1940 the Ministry of Food added sufficient vitamin A and D to mimic the level of that in summer butter with the result that when Denmark was invaded and imports of butter ceased, there was sufficient to distribute to everyone. Eventually all margarine production was rationalised and was the same wherever it was made and sold.

Quality control of various foodstuffs by the Ministry of Food protected the consumer especially from low value substitute products imported during 1941 when shortage of eggs, onions and milk was particularly acute. The Food Substitutes order of October 11, 1941, prohibited the sale of any food substitute except under licence. Together with the Food Standards Labelling of Food Order issued in 1944, this gave the Minister of Food power to regulate composition, labelling and advertising of food.

Ration books had been issued after the declaration of war and the public were therefore not surprised when the rationing of bacon, fats and sugar commenced in January 1940. By March meat (not offal) was rationed although the amount was pretty much like normal. In July tea was added to the list. Cheese followed in May 1941 and even soap (one bar a month) by February 1942.

The permitted list of rationed basic foods varied with supply. When an issue of cheese was reduced, this was balanced with an increase in another protein food such as dried eggs or dried milk. Those working in the fields requiring packed lunches were given a larger ration, but they had to fight for this causing some hard debate.

The ration for meat varied between 1s and 2s.2d. but mainly 1s. 2d. (about £2 today). It was the quality and not quantity of meat that determined what was bought as obviously the amount would buy a tiny piece of steak against a larger amount of cheaper slow cooking cuts. Bacon varied between 8 ozs. (200 g) and 3 ozs. (75 g) (generally, 4 ozs. or 100 g); cheese between 8 oz. and 1 oz. (25 g); sugar between 1lb (400 g) and 8 ozs. (200 g); and tea at 2 ozs. (50 g). Vegetarians and those with religious dietary needs were given different amounts. The variation in amount was geared by availability.

The Ministry of Food maintained a large number of supply and distribution depots next to railway sidings, holding food for about six weeks. They no longer exist as modern supermarkets now control the food supply holding about enough for two to three weeks!

A point system allowed a purchaser to choose to buy additional un-rationed foodstuffs including tinned meat, fish, fruit, vegetables and beans. Some spices were permitted particularly for the manufacture of brown sauces and similar to improve the taste of bland food. Dried fruit including dried bananas predominated, as fresh fruit, unless locally grown, became increasingly rare. Amy McGrath, Land Girl, said they would occasionally have a consignment of oranges but never saw a banana.

Expectant mothers and young children had priority access to milk, oranges and fresh and dried eggs. Infants aged 6-16 months usually had an allowance of three eggs a week. The National Milk Scheme provided some milk at reduced price or free and with the National Vitamins Scheme thus ensured essential vitamins to those who needed them.[4] Children of school age were given milk and meals at school either free or for a small payment.[5]

Canteens had to provide hot meals for 250 employees or more. The British Restaurants, not requiring ration coupons, were available everywhere, as Nellie mentions on 20th September, 1941, for those without canteen facilities. Emergency meals were provided at Emergency Meal Centres throughout the country. The WVS set up mobile canteens and the meat pie scheme also ran in rural areas. The Ministry of Food employed expert scientists to advise on food products and methods of obtaining maximum nutritional value from them. War cookery leaflets were regularly issued to schools and WIs and to gas and electricity companies. Cooking classes were set up, including in the committee room of the Victoria Rooms, and together with posters, films, and ministry

'Food Facts' published in newspapers, the housewife was bombarded with advice and information from the 'Kitchen Front'. But the diet would today be described as mostly vegetarian though 'Vegetarians' were allowed more cheese. 'Meatless dishes' was how it was classified and a demonstration was proposed by Miss Millar of Milverton WI at their meeting on 7th January, 1941.[6] Lord Woolton, the Minister for Food, gave his name to the much mocked 'Woolton Pie' which consisted of pastry made mostly with potato flour, mixed vegetables, oatmeal, mashed potatoes, stock and grated cheese. Potatoes being a staple food, the Minister of Food had in 1943, appealed for potato recipes. Milverton WI responded by organising a competition but sadly only one recipe was forthcoming. Advertising promoted the nutritious value of chocolate bars and Rowntree described their 'Dairy Box' as 'a box of food'.

Customers had to register with certain suppliers especially for milk. But for oranges, which could be bought elsewhere, they still had to record the purchase in their Ration Book. In Milverton there were many more shops than now.

How to use the Ration Book –
- Complete the sections and Register with Grocer
- Page 2 – Coupons and points are divided into four-weekly periods numbered 1-13. This helps you to know where you are.
- Page 9 – coupons for butter, margarine and fats
- Page 11 – ration for cheese
- Page 15 – sugar and preserves
- Page 17 – tea
- Page 25 must contain names and addresses of your retailers. It is illegal to use the book without this information.
- Back page for soap

On 21st September, 1940[7] as more and more foods became rationed the Parish Council 'asked for a list of government controlled prices and goods (as on view at the Local Food Office in Wellington) to be placed on the parish notice board', but before it could be displayed 'it was

14. Food Facts.

FOOD FACTS

The Housewife's part

A YEAR ago, when our merchant seamen were fighting for their lives against the U-Boat packs, everyone at home joined in the battle by cutting down food-waste. Tens of thousands of tons were saved by the British housewife.

The need is just as great today. Lives are still at stake. Not only ships, but trains and lorries too, are wanted for the arms and reinforcements that will support our fighting men on their way to Berlin. Road transport is needed even for the foods we grow here. It's a matter of wheels as well as keels. Not a foot of space can be spared for food that is thrown away.

SAVE BREAD by allowing new bread to become quite cold before putting it into the bread bin: Using bread when it is 24 hours old, and never when it is new because you get more slices to the loaf: Using stale bread for browned breadcrumbs, rusks for children, bread puddings, sweet or savoury, for thickening soups, as breakfast cereal, or (soaked in water and squeezed out) for stuffing: By keeping it in a clean, dry bin swathed in a clean cloth: By not eating it at the same meal as potatoes.

SAVE MILK by protecting it from 'weather-waste'. Milk should be kept in the coolest spot in larder or kitchen. The floor is cooler than an upper shelf. Never place milk in an airless cupboard. Fill a basin to within 1½ inches of the top with cold water. Stand the milk bottle in the water, and having saturated a thoroughly clean flower-pot or several thicknesses of butter muslin under the cold water tap, put it over the milk bottles, resting it on the neck and touching the water. Change the water at regular intervals, every few hours in hot weather.

SAVE POTATOES by taking a little more trouble in preparation. Now that we are at the end of the season, potatoes need rather more care in peeling but peel them *thinly*. Heavy peeling wastes a quarter of the potato before you start, whenever possible don't peel them at all — this makes them more valuable as a food, and keeps the flavour too.

SAVE FAT by converting scraps of meat fat into cooking fat, and clarifying dripping so that it can be used for frying and for making pastry.

Trim the fat off the meat before cooking. Cut the scraps up small and put in a tin in a cool oven. When melted, strain off the fat carefully from the dried up bits of meat and pour into a bowl. This makes fat for pastry and puddings and can be used with half margarine for cakes.

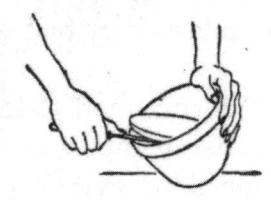

To clarify dripping, cut it up, put it in a saucepan, cover with cold water and bring to the boil. Pour into a bowl and let it get cold. Now lift off the hard white lid which has formed, scrape away any meat from the underside, and melt the fat gently, heating it till it stops bubbling. This is to remove any remaining water. If any water is left the fat won't stay fresh. Pour into a bowl and use as needed.

THIS IS WEEK 46—THE SECOND WEEK OF RATION PERIOD No. 12 (May 28th to June 24th)

THE MINISTRY OF FOOD, LONDON, W.1.   FOOD FACTS No. 205

reported that the case had been damaged and the glass smashed. It was resolved that Mr. I. Marshall be instructed to repair same.'

The County Stores sold groceries and haberdashery and it was where Nellie was registered. Sylvia Perry worked there and remembers: 'Well, one had to weigh out the cooking fat. That was in a huge great block. The margarine was also in a huge great block. The butter was in a flat, half-a-pound, which, for anybody on 48, or 24-hour's leave would get a small portion and one, one portion, one ration per person, was 2ozs. of butter. The Spam[8] was in a big tin, which you had to undo with an old-fashioned tin opener and it was lovely, because you could slice off a piece when nobody was looking if you were hungry. There were big boxes of dried apples; there were tins of these very salty biscuits, which you also had to undo with a can-opener. The WI shop would have WI jam. They also canned fruit. They made chutney. It was wonderful stuff. Also on points, you could buy tins of sausage meat from which I think people used the fat off sausages for cooking. At Christmas we were allowed so many ounces of dried fruit. Now and again you would have oranges – or were they on green books for babies?'

Tucker's Stores, almost next door, where Woodbarton now is, sold its own dairy produce delivered by pony and cart, and groceries. Mrs. Erica Tucker says that on Sundays the whole family would sit and count the coupons and points as they had to be exchanged in order to get more supplies.

People were encouraged to keep chickens. In June 1940, the WI minutes record that members were considering a suggestion from the Pig Keepers Council to join their scheme rather than organise a separate club.[9] Meanwhile, at a meeting of the parish council in 1941, there was a discussion about starting up a Pig Club[10] and also whether there should be a Food sub-Office in the village, as temporary residents had to go to Wellington or Wiveliscombe to obtain emergency rations. Wellington Rural District Council was asked if practicable to send a Food Office official once a week suggesting that 'the small shop premises in Silver

Street,[11] now rented by the WI for the sale of produce may be available any day in the week except Tuesdays and Fridays...'

Those with soft fruit were allowed extra sugar for jam-making or preserving fruit. Any spare fruit was handed over to the WVS or – in the case of Milverton – the WI who were allocated extra sugar to make jam they could sell or to go into the general distribution chain for towns and cities. Freezing food was not an option and until canning vegetables was possible via Milverton's WI, vegetables had to be preserved in other ways. On 27th May, 1941, via a request from the Somerset Farm Institute, Milverton's WI agreed that a Mrs. Chisholm speak about storing vegetables at their July meeting.

But where could they sell their produce? At a meeting at Mansell House on 23rd September, 1940 it was agreed that the room Dr. MacGaffey[12] had previously used as a laboratory (in Silver Street) would serve as a shop for the sale of surplus vegetables and fruit. Mrs. Deacon's mother, Mrs. Jenks ran the Government Fruit Preservation Scheme in Milverton, originally in the basement of Brendons in North Street. In minutes of 27th May it was agreed that they should buy a sterilizer from the previous year's balance and thus Milverton became the first Somerset WI to obtain a canning machine. Fruit juices were also made. But by 30th March, 1942, the shop was not earning enough to pay its way and so Mrs. Little at Mansell House, was approached. She offered her garage and on 25th May at the WI meeting at the 'Golden Crust Bakery' it was announced that a market stall would open once a week in Mansell House's garage, Parsonage Lane and by 29th June, at the next WI meeting at Cardscroft, Mrs. Little announced that the produce market appeared to be well worthwhile.

By the end of 1945 Milverton was chosen out of the whole county to continue with this scheme.[13] A more permanent home was found next to Thornwell and if you happened to be passing there about four p.m you might get a free cup of tea and a piece of bread with 'scum' jam for free!

One of the five bakers was Mr. Godber Ford, a former professional motorcyclist who arrived back in Britain from a trial in Germany on 1st September, 1939. A leg injury prevented him from military service and after a variety of jobs selling gasmask carriers, torches and then tinned food, he met another Milverton baker, William Mercer. Mercer taught him how to make bread by hand and slab cake in primitive premises at the back of St. Anne's Walk, where Erica Tucker's bungalow is situated. Next door was another baker, Harry Lock, who used a coal fired oven and would deliver one batch of bread by bicycle while another batch was proving. George Tucker, another baker in Sand Street, employed four men. Godber Ford eventually took over Mr. Mercer's business and shop and slowly built up a big wholesale business selling bread and a variety of cakes. He delivered bread by horse and cart. One horse having been circus trained, kept going around in circles! Eventually he bought a 1929 Ford van and was able to deliver further afield. Expanding his bakery products within six months he was providing 80-100 loaves a day, various kinds of buns, jam tarts, Queen cakes and 1lb Madeira cakes all made by hand. He also made meat pies for the Rural Meat Pie scheme run by the Ministry of Food.[14] He was eventually contracted to make bread and cakes for the British and US military[15] and various factory canteens in Taunton and Bridgwater.

Subsequently he moved to the barn behind the White Hart, and expanded to Taunton and elsewhere. His wife confirms that he was summoned to London to sign the Official Secrets Act, his secret being the amount of bread and cakes he made, which could, if leaked, identify the number of troops in his delivery area. Mr. Godber Ford left notes about his wartime experiences but without dates or any chronological order. Undoubtedly his business was greatly enhanced by his military contracts. At one time he was supplying the entire Army and Airforce Southern Command NAAFI including the large camps at Bulford, Boscombe Down and Netheravon down to Penzance. The NAAFI in Salisbury ordered 1½ tons of fruit slab cake a week, RAF at Chivenor put in a very large order of Bath Buns which were put on a passenger train from Milverton seven days a week. Named Cassanna Cake Company he eventually had three one-ton vans,[16] and filled two railway wagons but still Rossant the horse continued delivering local orders.

So successful was his business, that he bought extra shops and at one time employed 35 staff which is how he was able, one Christmas to produce 6000 mince pies and 600 Christmas cakes for the NAAFI. Just before D-Day he had an order for 600 slab cakes (at 4 lbs each) and 1000 dozen small cakes which had to be delivered to Portsmouth in 48 hours.

Interviews, with local people here during the period, suggest that Milverton did not suffer much from the restrictions of rationing. Land Girl, Amy McGrath says that she always had butter and cream, and the late Ted Perry describes how he got extra food.

'If you kept in line with the farmers, you'd say "How about a swede?" and he'd say, "Yes, help yourself." So we could go and have a swede, and also, at the time, rabbits were available… and pigeons of course, if you went out shooting. It was a normal thing for Boxing Day to pack up your sandwich and a bottle and go off with the ferret and go rabbiting … sometimes you'd get half-a-dozen.'

Rabbits were very nutritious and Basil Jennings remembers each night a 'rabbit train' started in Barnstable picking up rabbits at each of the 14 stops to Milverton before going on to London. Trains had 4ft long racks either side of the coach on which the rabbits were hung.

> Reflect when you indulge,
> It is not beautiful to bulge.
> A large, untidy corporation
> Is far from helpful to the Nation.
> Ministry of Food publication 1940

The legacy of the bland and boring wartime diet – high carbohydrate, low fat and low sugar – was a slim and fit population. Although some might have been hungry the fairness of rationing and the attention to balanced nutrition produced a generation of wartime babies who proved

Darlingest

to be bigger, stronger and healthier than ever before. But Milverton WI, as ever, saw problems ahead. The minutes of their meeting on 6th February, 1945, held in St. Michael's Rooms stated, 'That we considered the provision of school dinners would improve the cooking of the future.'

---

1. Lord Woolton – Fredrick James Marquis, 1st, 1st Earl of Woolton, CH, PC 1883-1964, was born and educated in Manchester, where he was a Research Fellow at Manchester University. But it was Liverpool where he spent most of his career as a social worker from 1906-1918 and where he eventually became a director of a Department Store. In 1940 he was appointed Minister of Food – a daunting task in wartime. The Ministry was responsible for buying and distributing supplies of food as well as devising nutritional diets for the severely rationed population.
2. Jam, marmalade, treacle and syrup all became rationed in March 1941.
3. See 'On the Fields'.
4. Bottles of condensed orange juice in a medicine bottle, were provided for young children, as was Rose Hip syrup – see 'Medicinal Herbs'. Children also could have a spoonful of cod liver oil or, better, sweet malt extract fortified with cod liver oil.
5. See 'Doubling Up – Education'.
6. To replace a talk on 'Palmistry'.
7. Meat rationed in March – tea, margarine, cooking fat and cheese in July.
8. Canned special pork and ham.
9. See 'Dig for Victory'.
10. Nellie, Post Office pig 17.11.40.
11. See below.
12. Dr. Crichton MacGaffey, MB, Ch.B Edin.B.Sc. Pathologist, Lived at St. Mildred's cottage.
13. See 'Party Now – Worry Later'.
14. The Ministry of Food gave him permits to obtain ingredients such as fats, dried fruit, sugar and jam He mostly used dried egg but sometimes managed to buy egg 'melange' – broken eggs obtained from egg packers. These went into sponges and Swiss rolls.
15. See 'Military' and 'Over Here'.
16. A van was purchased. A front wheel came off approaching Milverton and rolled away. A notice in the Post Office for a 2/6d reward lured a boy who had found it by the station.

10. ON THE FIELDS

'Up we would be 6.30 in the morning. Call in the cows – milk – take up the cans to the dairy – put the churns out on to the road to be collected, clean the dairy, get along back for breakfast.'
Milverton Land Girl, Amy McGrath

Perhaps the only good that came from the horrors of the First World War was the lesson learned from the challenge of home food production. The resulting agriculture policy – re-introduced and enacted in 1939 – without doubt became the major non-military contribution to winning the Second World War.

The British economy had long rested on 'free trade': the exporting of manufactured goods in return for imported foodstuffs and raw materials from the British Empire – the large areas of pink prominent in every school atlas. This Empire came to provide for the Mother Country. Consumers were happy, retailers were content. Successive governments let market forces rule whilst British farming declined.

That changed in 1916, when a failed harvest and the first U-boat attacks on convoys combined to jolt the government into action. The spectre of starvation at home inspired the founding of the War Agricultural Committees and the Women's Land Army – the first government-directed attempts at making modern Britain self-sufficient in food. But the U-boat menace receded. The Great War came to an end. Free Trade with the empire beckoned once again. In the 1920s, Britain returned to the *status quo ante bellum*. Both government and market forgot the nightmare of war.

Thankfully, one man didn't. In 1935, as guns and tanks began to rumble once again across Europe. Walter Elliott, Minister of Agriculture – himself the son of a Lanarkshire farmer[1] – established a committee to examine how best farming should be organised in wartime. Thanks to its findings in 1937 Elliott moved to re-introduce the County War Ag Committees chaired by local landowners and comprising representatives from the Ministry of Agriculture, scientific experts and local farmers. In those immediate pre-war years the War Ag committees made use of government grants firstly to build up stocks of lime; secondly to provide extra drainage for unused land: and in 1939 to stock up on phosphates, oil seeds, feeding stuffs and farm machinery.

Unlike Hitler's Germany which was by 1939 almost three-quarters self-sufficient in food, Britain was only producing just over a third of its requirement. Whilst the 'War Ags' got ahead of the game, in contrast Food (Defence Plans) Department – set up in the wake of recommendations from a committee chaired by William Beveridge[2] did little. However, by August 1939 the Department had secured food supplies for evacuated people. In September 1939 the Ministry of Food was created, with William Morrison as the Minister in charge of buying all food whether imported or home grown. The food rationing system was dependent on local food production; the transport to distribute it around the country and the ships bringing in essential food imports. All had to combine to make it work. The Ministry of Agriculture's initial task was to increase the production of home produced cereal crops by encouraging farmers to plough up grassland for which they were given subsidies for phosphates and lime as fertilizers. The Ministry of Food had powers to requisition food supplies at prices set by the government. With these systems and supplies in place the War Ags were on standby until after Christmas 1939. Then all livestock for slaughter had to be sold to the state via the Ministry of Food at guaranteed prices as were home produced cereals, sugar beet and other crops. As the sole purchaser, the Ministry of Food could control supplies and adjust rations when necessary. But whilst the guaranteed price policy was fair, some, especially arable farmers, certainly did better than before the war and certainly better, perhaps, when compared with prices negotiated today in super market contracts. The negative side was that it did spawn a black market. There was always a gap to be filled, because of a lack of a commodity, or a luxury food.[3] 'Spivs' as they were known could sell on 'Sugar falling off the back of a lorry'; an animal slaughtered[4] illegally and dispersed to a favoured few, or a farmer holding back some of his crop from the government allowing a racketeer to make more money. Heavy fines were imposed against those who broke the law in this way.

Early in 1940 the Ministry of Agriculture inspected and categorised all farms in order to assess their productivity and where some farms might need help. The Realm Act gave the Ministry of Agriculture authority to control and direct food production and the right to repossess farms (15,000 in all) amidst great animosity and resentment and causing great hardship.

The challenges were twofold – one dependent upon the other – producing more food, and supplying the labour to do it. Just as the landscape in Britain had undergone major changes throughout history, from the medieval three-field strip farming system, to the Enclosure Acts of the late 18th century, so now it would change again. The priority of ploughing up hitherto permanent pasture particularly affected the West Country, and other dairy producing areas. In Somerset 100,000 acres of flat land was drained. A new five-mile canal was cut and the King's Sedgemoor Drain – originally cut in 1795 – was widened and deepened. The aim was to keep livestock production going as long as possible, not just for meat, but to fertilise the soil. The ploughing up of grazing land would appear to contradict this aim, but the greater yield of cereals including barley as animal feed would be more beneficial. Cattle especially milking cows and sheep always had a priority though if there were shortages of feed stuffs, pigs and poultry might have to be slaughtered. But the resulting figures show that from 1939-1944 whilst milking cows increased by 300,000 and other cattle by 400,000, sheep numbers reduced by 6,300,000, 2,500.000 pigs and 19,200,000 less poultry.

A wet October and November preceded the first winter of the war whilst frost and snow ruined wheat which had been under sown with another crop. Yet by April 1940 the Government target of over two million acres of new arable land was reached with only eight counties failing the required acreage. Overall, from 1939 six and a half million new acres were ploughed up. But the lack of equipment was critical as tractors were few in number and expensive to purchase and maintain. This created a demand for working horses that exceeded supply. The War Ags stepped in and authorised loans enabling farmers to invest in better equipment, particularly tractors. When the Lend Lease[5] agreement with the USA came into force in the spring of 1941, tractors and other equipment such as binders, and potato harvesters, finally became available. In 1942 there were 1000 combine harvesters working in Britain.[6] By 1944, that number had grown. When the demand for war material meant that supplies of American farming machinery declined ingenious farmers managed to make their own special implements and tools.

Some land of course was commandeered for defence purposes. Farms used for firing ranges caused considerable problems for farmers and their livestock adding to the tension building up between farmers and government.

The newly ploughed land had to be carefully managed, not only in terms of husbandry but also in the matching of crop to the most suitable soil types and climate. Many farmers resented being told what to do and 'the man from the Ministry' was often seen as interfering. But, it had to be done. The War Ags cultivated a spirit of innovation by providing advice and subsidies, and offering incentives to greater production.

The demand for cereals meant arable farmers were better off. Ministry leaflets available to farmers advised on new rotations better suited to their land. For former dairy farmers who now had to grow some crops, this would have been especially useful for land now deprived of animal manure. Planting of catch crops – the adding of another quick growing crop between two main crops to increase yield could also contribute to soil nutrition. For example – corn – with a catch crop of rye grass or clover, when ploughed in would fertilise the soil ready for the next crop. The difficulty of importing sugar cane promoted a major increase in the growing of sugar beet. Potatoes – a vital part of the wartime diet – could be grown quickly in a few weeks, on a variety of poor to medium and also stored well for many months; as did other root crops including those for cattle feed.

Ministry 'interference' was clearly working. Harvests – wheat, increased by 109% from pre-war figures, barley by 115%, oats 58%, potatoes 102%, [7] sugar beet 37%, vegetables 34% and fruit 55%.

All this extra work required not only machinery but also manual labour. And farm workers were in short supply. Even those who remained behind in Reserved Occupations – like Jack Tucker[8] at Baghay had to 'do their bit' in some sort of civil defence role. Those who failed to reconcile Home Guard duties with farming sometimes faced prosecution. One such case, reported by Sadie Ward in her excellent book *War in the Countryside*, was held at Wiveliscombe Petty Sessions on March 1943. Edward Wright of Bickleigh Farm was fined £50 with 3 guineas costs 'for failure to enrol'. His plea was the long hours he worked and that 'his younger brothers should enrol first'.

The solution was to revive the Women's Land Army. Recruitment rose steadily from 17,000 in 1939 to 87,000 in 1943. After a temporary hold-up to allow for women to be drafted into munitions factories, as preparations for the invasion got underway, the WLA ultimately rose to 98,000. As in the First World War, many farmers were initially slow to employ the Land Girls, believing them not experienced or strong enough for the task, but they were eventually won over.

Milverton WI minutes of 29th April, 1940, state: 'Arising on a letter from the secretary of the county committee of the Women's Land Army, Mrs. Tucker proposed and Miss Sharland seconded, that we should ask for volunteers from members to help on the land for periods of a few hours when needed.'

There was a continual re-evaluation and movement of workforce and a conflict between the Ministries trying to achieve maximum output at any one time.

The use of Prisoners of War was considered as early as 1940 but not until July 1941, when Italians began to arrive from the Mediterranean, did some 2,400 work on the harvest. At the beginning they were kept in camps and hostels but from January 1942, with 'Good conduct' could live on the farm. There was a POW camp for Italians near Bridgwater. The War Ags supplied the POWs on request, but subject to strict regulations governing their welfare. Farmers initially paid the War Ags 40 shillings a week per prisoner rising to 48 shillings after 3 months less 21 shillings' board and lodging and an extra 6d – 1s a day direct to the prisoner in line with the Geneva Convention. By July 1943, 37,000 POWs were working on the land, 36,000 for the 1944 harvest. By now, carefully selected German POWs had joined the ranks. German and Italian POW camps were kept apart in different areas, but unlike the Italians, did not live on the farm. Mr. King, as a very small child remembers German POWs, from the Cross Keys Camp set up in 1944 at Norton Fitzwarren, working on his father's farm. They were also at Baghay Farm, where Barbara Tucker worked as a Land Girl just after the war had ended. She described an embarrassing moment during a morning ride on the trailer of a tractor driven by her future husband, who, for fun, tipped her off in front of a group of German POWs having their breakfast. They were very polite and rushed over to help her onto her feet. She remembered them as being well behaved and good mannered. Internees also joined in the land effort. In 1943, Austrian-born Mr. Brachtel of Wilscombe Wood in Milverton was released from an internment camp and allowed to work on the farm of Captain Hamilton Fleming at Spring Grove. F. W Hall from Fitzhead[8] wrote to Mrs. Brachtel, 'The wages and hours would be the statutory ones, and your husband would be under the instructions of the Farm Bailiff.'

Conscientious Objectors, Irish immigrants, other forces, Polish, Canadians and Americans, and volunteers from women's organisation also helped on the land. In fact it was almost as though they went back in history when everyone helped with the harvest – they all had the same common goal to eat!

American Forces did their bit in 1942 by cultivating over 8,000 acres of land in co-operation with the Ministry of Agriculture, who supplied seeds, tools and advice. The amount increased yearly with 50,000 tons of food produced by the British and American Forces in 1944.

Double daylight saving time, introduced over the summer months greatly assisted farm work. But the restrictive food rationing would, unlike today, have made city dwellers very aware of how food was produced and where. Not only did they take to heart the 'Dig for Victory' campaign they also volunteered at weekends, evenings and even holidays 'to lend a hand on the land' and some factories 'adopted a farm'.

Another major source of labour set up in 1941, were the Holiday Labour Camps for schoolchildren. These were placed under the Central Committee for the Ministry of Education, Ministry of Agriculture and War Ags. In May 1942 a government order provided for children of 12 or more to work no more than 4 hours in half a day on the land whenever needed – provided they missed no more than 20 school days. Even school holidays were scheduled around agriculture need. In 1942 there were 654 camps with 31,000 children increasing in 1943 to 105 camps involving 63,000 young people.[9]

But what of Milverton?

A good example of careful management and Ministry assistance was Alan Winter's father's small mixed farm in Milverton. Also a part-time postman he managed just 40 acres renting fields and paddocks around Houndsmoor; the field, now Colesmore; a field abutting Burgage and three acres in Pix Lane. He sowed clover on a six-acre field making more than enough to cover the purchase price of the field. He also kept a few pigs and 25-30 Guernsey cows. The cows were supported by growing kale, mangolds and grass also, of course producing hay. Basic slag was spread on the fields along with lime. Other feeding stuffs came from Hodges in Bridgwater. Alan remembered that new crops, such as flax were grown at Cottrells. It was pulled, bound and stacked like corn and

Darlingest

THE DAILY MAIL, Thursday, August 3, 1944.

Land Army Girls Put on Inches
A COUPON PROBLEM

By Daily Mail Reporter

BRITAIN'S Land Army girls are all outgrowing their pre-Service civilian clothes.

And it is providing a clothing coupon problem for some of them as a result of the new clothing ration demand by the Land Army authorities for 24 of the clothing coupons from land-girls with less than two years' service.

Some of the girls object that this leaves them with no coupons for a civilian outfit in which to go on leave or to evening entertainments.

The Land Army reply is that while they appreciate that the extra inches due to healthy outdoor work creates a problem, there are still 36 coupons for the Land Army girl to base her wardrobe on.

After her first month's service on the land she receives 26 coupons, and later the industrial 10.

The Land Army advises that these should be expended on warm underwear, and that for social engagements a pair of neat breeches, a Land Army shirt, stockings, and shoes are just as attractive as more feminine wear.

Their Outfit

Girls employed before July 1942 hand over only 10 coupons for replacements.

All the girls receive in their first outfit two pairs of breeches, two pairs of dungarees, two shirts, shoes, a mackintosh, and an overcoat, as well as other equipment, and there is annual replacement.

A Land Army official told me yesterday: "The young members of the Land Army nearly all develop a more robust figure while they are working on the land.

"But although they may find that their ordinary civilian clothes do not fit them, they are still better off for clothing than the average civilian girl, and they have an attractive uniform which they can be proud to wear.

"Not very many worry over changing back to ordinary clothes. They usually find that the breeches and shirts outfit is really more becoming."

Footnote.—Land Army statistics show that girls generally increase in weight and that their arms and shoulders develop in the first month of work on the land. After several months most girls have what is described as the ideal modern figure.

'Evacuees, Aid Farms'
Harvest Call

By Daily Mail Reporter

HARVEST difficulties of North-country farmers, faced with an acute labour shortage, may be somewhat lessened if an appeal for help from Southern evacuees bears fruit.

Most Northern counties report that their harvest is likely to be the best for years—if sufficient help is forthcoming to gather it in good time. Farmers are looking to evacuees to help fill the labour gap.

Captain E. Foster, chairman of Shropshire War Agricultural Committee, and labour liaison officer for Derbyshire, Cheshire, and Staffordshire, told me yesterday that it was absolutely imperative to "dilute" skilled labour with voluntary help to make the harvest a success.

Schoolchildren's "holidays on the farm" during harvesting will also somewhat help to relieve the situation. Farmers are unanimous in their praise of work done by the children, and many local educational committees have encouraged the expansion of "gather the harvest" school schemes.

Voluntary helpers are urgently requested to enrol at local War Emergency Agricultural offices as soon as possible.

In Anglesey the hay harvest is nearing completion. Crops are reported to be very satisfactory.

15. Daily Mail, *3rd August, 1944.*

collected by the Ministry. He said that Italian[10] POWs were bussed in to pull the flax. Machinery was eventually brought in to do this operated by Jack Tucker and Joe Baker. Straw went off for paper-making.

Nellie mentions the fields and farming all around her, and going to Rivers Farm in Fitzhead on 28th March, 1941 and to Wimbush Farm on the Wiveliscombe Road on 24th July, 1941. It was possible to trace a Land Girl – Amy McGrath (nee Mason) who, with the late Barbara Williams, was attached to a 75-acre small-holding owned by Mr. Jacobs at Cormiston. Jacobs had a Guernsey herd, and Amy and Barbara looked after the calves. They had two horses the big horse named Blossom, the smaller Gypsy. Amy had to plough, as well as milk the cows. She greatly enjoyed her four and a half years as a Land Girl.

'I was homesick – but we just had to get on with the job, along the way there was a few tears. I wrote home – eagerly awaited the post for letters – and so month after month went by. Living at the Farm had its good parts – we did have electric light – but only candles at bedtime – it had been lamplight at 'Olands Lodge'.[11]

Up we would be 6.30 in the morning. Call in the cows – milk – take up the cans to the dairy – put the churns out on to the road to be collected, clean the dairy, get along back for breakfast. Turn out the cows in the fields – feed and water the calves. I never used to think farming was on a schedule – but I did learn differently. All took time. We had one day a week off in our turn.

We really did see the seasons here – rain – shine. Haymaking harvest, we took it all in our stride – very much helped by local farmers – two of which had tractors, 'rich farmers'.

I did remember how lovely the spring was. We would walk in the wood, pick a few primroses – send some to Mum. One time Mr. Watson allowed me to pack some Cox's apples to send to my Mum.

Whilst the Jacobs went on holiday to 'Cumbria', we were billeted out to lovely people on the Wiveliscombe Road. A calf was born that week and I assisted Mr. Watson at that time and was very proud of myself.

At odd times if we had taken the horse and cart on the field by the road, passing convoys of Americans, would shout "Hi Land girls" and throw us out on passing – say toothpaste – soap and the odd bar of chocolate. We couldn't believe our luck.'[12]

Military words – 'fight', 'enemies', 'front' – were commonly used in propaganda or advertisements for many wartime campaigns and no more so than in the agriculture. The agricultural policy was planned and carried out with military precision and was considered perhaps the 'Fifth Line of Defence'. Without the intervention of the Ministry of Agriculture – working alongside other Ministries during the time of crisis – the people of Britain would have starved. It was an example of extreme co-operation between state and the people, those in the country and those from the cities, children and prisoners – all prepared to work on the land as peasants once did. But whilst the great achievement of the wartime agricultural policy was to feed the nation, it also forced the modernisation of British farming – a fact that was to have long term consequences.

The War Ags provided a practical framework for domestic food production that made British farming the most efficient and modern in Europe – a state of play that persisted for 30 years after the end of the War. In May 1945, just as peace was declared the Ministry of Agriculture circulated its thanks to farmers: 'You have played an essential part in achieving victory and have every right to be proud of that.'

---

1. See also 'Gone to the Country'. Elliott had a remarkable career. As a Scottish Unionist MP he served under both Ramsay MacDonald and Stanley Baldwin, first as Minister of Agriculture, then as Minister of Health. Among his achievements were the Agricultural Marketing Act which offered financial protection to British food producers unable to compete with falling prices generated by empire free trade; and the far-reaching Cancer Act, 1939 – a pre-Welfare State reform aimed at tackling cancer nationwide.
2. Beveridge is most remembered as one of the architects of the welfare state. He was a lawyer with a social conscience who was appointed director of the newly-

created Labour Exchanges by Winston Churchill while he was president of the Boards of Trade in 1908. From 1919-37 Beveridge was director of the London School of Economics. From 1937-40 he was Master of University College, Oxford. He was brought into the wartime government by Ernest Bevin, Minister of Labour. In 1942, under Ernest Brown, Minister of Health, Beveridge chaired a committee on social insurance. It was here that he wrote what became known as the Beveridge Report which outlined the National Insurance Scheme that we still have today.

3. Black market products also included cigarettes, alcohol and luxury items such as silk stockings, perfume. It became a serious problem, when American goods were being offloaded in the build up to D-Day. See Appendix 5.
4. The author was told a tale that in Hampshire, a dead pig was moved around in a coffin to avoid it being bought by the Ministry of Food.
5. Enacted in 1941 – 1945 the US provided free – food, oil, equipment to Britain, Free French, China and Russia in return they acquired overseas bases.
6. The first combine harvester seen on a farm near Milverton was 1946 and the first time a combine harvested a whole farm's output was at Baghay in 1950.
7. The public were asked to help pick the crops, but there was always the threat that the enemy would drop canisters with the Colorado beetle that could wipe out crops in weeks – the public were warned to be alert. Incendiary devices were dropped by the Luftwaffe to spoil harvests or haystacks. Alan Winter mentioned that his father noticed, when emptying the post box at Springrove, some large holes in a field containing unexploded bombs – 'the size of a 45 gallon oil drum'. The land was at Cobhay Farm then owned by Mr. Baker. Soldiers defused them and afterwards went for a drink at The George, with the defused bombs on the lorry outside.
8. Mr. Brachtel's name is not on the lists for Internees so it has not been possible to discover where he was held, or the circumstances of his release. Before the war he lived with his wife in Wimbledon, spending weekends at Springrove. Neither has it been possible to discover Mr. Hall's role in dealing with this.
9. See Nellie, 24/28.7.41 children picking blackberries at Wimbush Farm and collecting rabbits 6.8.40, and pigs 17.11.40.
10. It depends on the date. If before 1944, then Italians, but after that it would be more likely German POWs from Cross Keys.
11. Originally billeted at Olands Lodge, they were later billeted in what was the old mill by the river and railway line. They would walk across the fields to the village.
12. See 'Over Here'.

11. DIG FOR VICTORY

'The senior boys from the North Harringay School went to their gardens in Silver Street this afternoon and spent 1½ hours on their plots.' School Logs, 15.5.1942

Dig for Victory' became one of the most enduring and endearing of wartime phrases and with it some iconic publicity posters – the boot on a spade being perhaps the most famous. Set up in 1940 by The Ministry of Agriculture and Fisheries it evolved from the earlier Grow More Campaign of November 1939 calling for 500,000 allotment holders.

The primary goal of Dig for Victory was to encourage city dwellers to become less reliant on country produce – thus freeing up precious transport for other tasks. But in time rural areas also got stuck in. First off the mark in Milverton was again the WI. A meeting held just three days after war was declared considered a request from Miss Vernon, the WI Federation Secretary 'to consider how best to increase food production'. The minutes from that meeting continue: 'It was decided that the agriculture secretary should ask the members how many of them would like allotments and to endeavour to obtain ground should there be the demand.'

The scheme run by borough, parish and district councils made vast areas of land available for allotments on which, under defence regulations, pigs, chickens and rabbits could be kept.[1] Householders, large and small, were urged to convert lawns and flower beds to vegetable plots. Gardens, parks and some tree nurseries were also ploughed up –

even the moat of Windsor Castle was cultivated. Every available space was made ready for crop production.

Women were the prime target – the rationale being that growing their own food would not only help feed their families but also improve their diet. The *Somerset Gazette*, in December 1941 reported 'the allotment holder is digging for the health of her family as well as for victory'. They, along with folk lacking gardening experience, were given advice and tips on growing fruit and vegetables backed up by newspaper articles. Whilst failures were not unknown the government countered with cropping plans and the setting up of models for allotments. The response was huge, spawning many local groups who provided talks on gardening. Meanwhile the hugely popular Food Production Brains Trusts brought experts to meetings in village halls and city schools alike. Planning ahead the Ministry of Food and Dig for Victory provided information on how to preserve and to store for winter the inevitable gluts of ripening fruit and vegetables.[2] Milverton WI on 4th June, 1940, discussed applying for a speaker from the Somerset Farm Institute to give a talk on 'Wartime Vegetable Gardening'.

Such intensive use of allotments led the Government in 1942 to allocate each allotment holder 42 lbs of National Growmore Fertiliser containing 7% each of nitrogen, potash and phosphates.

Whilst the WI's initiative was not taken up, in Milverton allotments were made available by the Parish Council. Nellie mentions on 26th October, 1940, that Miss Hopkins made some land available to evacuee boys and maybe it was this land, off Silver Street, opposite the Methodist Chapel, that is mentioned in the school logs. (See below.) Evacuee Bruce Watkiss remembered that the head teacher for the evacuee children, Mr. Cann, was very interested in gardening[3] and arranged for their produce to be sold at Froggetts[4] grocery shop in Silver Street.

16. 'Victory diggers', Sunday Times, 28th September, 1943.

8th Sep and 15th 1942	Gardening lesson was held at the Silver St. plot today
22nd July, 1943	An extra gardening period was taken this afternoon to get the Silver Street plot planted.
29th July	Boys went to Silver Street garden again this week to tidy the garden and finish planting.
26th Feb	The School Rabbit Club organised a Whist Drive in the Lower School. It was well patronised and the club made a profit of £5.15s.
21st Sept, 1944	A collection of fruit and vegetables from the school garden was sent to the local allotment show in aid of the Red Cross Fund. Their sale realised £1.
17th April, 1945	Class 1 and 2 boys were taken in an extra gardening lesson from 2 p.m. – 3.45 p.m. at the Silver Street garden

Milverton residents had gardens in which to grow their own produce and that may be the reason why the WI members did not take up the offer of an allotment. Nellie's letters cease in 1942 when she returned home to London just as U-boats sank more and more shipping and rations were squeezed ever tighter. The government – aware of the threat of slow starvation – made plans for 'Siege rations' which would place an even greater burden on the rural population. People were encouraged to save their own seed, but even this did not produce what was needed and on 5th May, the WI held a ballot for seeds that had arrived from America.

As pressure mounted, the Ministry of Agriculture, Fisheries and Food reported, in 1942, that 'County Garden Produce Committees have now been set up in practically all counties in England and Wales and considerable progress has been made in establishing Village Produce Associations'. Their aim was to encourage rural areas to become self-sufficient by planning and managing their food production thereby leaving commercial supplies for towns and cities. By then, volunteers had established 50 village produce associations where no organisation had existed previously, to marshal the efforts of domestic producers. Whilst as early as 6th September, 1939, Milverton WI decided to order 5 cwt of sugar[5] producing, by October 1940, 1,726 lbs of preserves, it was not until March 1941 that they elected members to formally establish a fruit preservation centre committee which then required gas to be installed at their jam-making premises. They also formed a fruit preservation centre school, giving sessions to local women. In 1942 there must have been a glut of fruit as on 2nd June Mrs. Jenks appealed for extra helpers at the fruit preservation centre and on 6th October Mrs. Harvey announced

17 – 'Grow beans', Reynolds News, 12th April, 1942.

that almost a ton of jam had been made; an astonishing feat given the numbers of volunteers involved.

Whilst a good deal of the jam and canned food went off for general distribution excess preserves and garden produce, as described in 'Feeding the Nation' was sold locally through their produce guild.[6]

The Ministries of Agriculture and Food ultimately provided help, guidance and regulation for a diverse range of 'specialist' voluntary food producing organisations such as The Small Pig Keepers' Council; Domestic Poultry Keepers; The British Rabbit Council, and the British Goat Society.

As early as 18th November, 1940, the parish council discussed a letter from the Small Pig Keepers Council as to whether they should call a public meeting to discuss the forming of a pig club in the parish. By 24th June, 1940 the WI had received a letter from the Pig Keepers Council asking if members would like to join the Parish Council scheme rather than organise a separate club. One was set up but it appears to have been organised by women because by 1st October, the Milverton WI reported that 'arrangements for feeding and cleaning the pigs were not entirely satisfactory'. It was proposed that a sub-committee should be appointed to investigate and to appoint a man to tend the pigs if necessary.

Mrs. Deacon[7] explained that they had two pigs, and locals gave their potato and apple peelings to add to their food. All farm animals were registered, of course, and the pig club's pigs could only be slaughtered by 'farmers' wives' who were licenced to kill the pigs. Then WI members used to go and see the pig cut up and be shown how they could use the various parts of the pig – tripe, making up sausages and hams. And on 7th April, 1942, their minutes noted that a Mrs. Langdon of Wiveliscombe gave a talk on the pig club run by her institute.

The School logs report that the evacuee school children kept rabbits, and no doubt other villagers did as well. They and any members of the Domestic Rabbit Clubs could apply for an allowance of wire netting.

The eventual success of the convoy system together with Coastal Command submarine hunting played a crucial role in allowing merchant

Darlingest

ships to get through thus preventing the imposition of 'siege rations'. But much credit also goes to the inhabitants of villages like Milverton for their hard work producing food. Without rural areas bearing the brunt of home grown food production the population might have starved.

---

1. See 'Feeding the Nation'.
2. See Nellie, 12.6.41 and 'Feeding the Nation'.
3. See 'Doubling Up – Education'.
4. Not known under this name.
5. Intending to hold some back for making marmalade in January when Seville oranges are available. There is no mention that marmalade was made, and certainly imports of Sevilles would have been curtailed.
6. WI Minutes of 6th Jan. 1942 state a balance of £6 0s 1d – from which £2 each to the British Red Cross and Russian Red Cross.
7. Recorded interview about WI, June 1993 A\CMQ/2/247.

12. FOR MEDICINAL PURPOSES

"It was agreed that the money obtained by sale of nettles picked by Institute members should be paid to the Institute." Milverton WI Minutes 6th April, 1943

'Tough but fair' was how Ethel Jennings described, Milverton's Dr. Alexander. Ethel was a sickly child and remembers the care and kindness she received from Dr. Alexander, a female GP practising and living in North Street. Prior to the birth of the National Health Service in July 1948, all medical and dental treatment and medicines had to be paid for, apart from some exceptions for charitable hospitals or clinics. Schools had their own doctors, nurses[1] and dentists, and during the war years 'official' evacuee children's medical bills were reimbursed by the government. Inevitably, there was, as there had been in the First World War, added pressure to provide extra medical staff to care for war injured.

As with other commodities, importing medicines or the ingredients for them was also reduced to the absolute bare minimum.

Then, as now, nearly all medicines were derivatives from chemicals found in plants although today few are actual plants extracts. It didn't take medical authorities long to spot an opportunity to stop imported medicines with plant based, mainly wild, home grown alternatives.

The 'Collection of Native Medicinal Plants' leaflet stated that at that time 80 species of native plants were being used medicinally, ranging from amounts of 250 tons to a few hundredweight a year. Even dandelions and stinging nettles were being imported from Europe before the war! Now the rural population was exalted not only to feed itself, but to help 'heal' itself as well!

While medicinal herbs had been collected by school children from 1941 onwards it wasn't until the oft-forgotten Wild Herb Committees were set up in 1942 that collection became a priority. These committees were separate from the 'Dig for Victory' campaign.[2] They came under the umbrella of the Ministry of Supply (Vegetable Drugs Committee) with help, where needed, from The Ministry of Agriculture through the County Garden Produce Committees. The organisation was distinct, with its own funding. Its brief was to harvest indigenous medicinal plants, thus ensuring supplies of materials for use in the manufacture of essential medical preparations that would otherwise have to be imported

Miss Lewin Harris of Hamilton Road in Taunton became the secretary of the Somerset Herb Society. There were two groups of plants required, priority being given to Group 1.

GROUP 1

BELLADONNA – DEADLY NIGHTSHADE – (Atropa belladonna) the leaves and roots of this poisonous plant contain 2 alkaloids, atropine and hyoscyamine, used in some medications. Hyoscyamine continues in use today for certain gastro-intestinal problems – Atropine and HENBANE – (Hyoscyamus niger) the major primary source of hyoscyamine.

MEADOW SAFFRON CORM – (Colchicum autumnale) corms and seeds were used as a remedy for gout. It is poisonous to animals and had been widely destroyed, so supplies were very difficult to find.

DANDELION ROOTS (Taraxacum vulgaria) the roots were used as a diuretic.

FOXGLOVE LEAF AND SEED – (Digitalis purpurea) a source of digitalin, a glycoside used in the treatment of heart disease. Very important. 50 tons of leaf and two tons of seed a year from Exmoor and the Brendons. (Allerford, Exford, Dulverton and Wiveliscombe). The leaves were taken to 48-hour drying stations, maintained at a temperature of 80 degrees. 8lbs of leaf produced 1 lb dried leaf. In 1943 the Exford Station created Somerset Record of 200 lbs dried for druggists' use. A dried pound was worth 1s 6d. The foxglove became the country's sole source of digitalin.

MALE FERN – (Dryopteris filix-mas) the rhizome of which was used as a remedy for intestinal worms. 100 tons needed annually. Dried it was worth 8d a pound.

NETTLE LEAVES – (Urtica dioica) the leaves very rich in chlorophyll and used for food dyes and for medicinal purposes.

SPAGHNUM MOSS – (Sphagnum species) the absorbent properties of this moss were widely used in wound dressings during the 1914-18 war. Similar restricted use in World War II. Especially good moss comes from Exmoor.

VALERIAN ROOTS – the dried roots yield a sedative extract. 100 tons a year.

GROUP 2: Used but not as important:

Broom tops – Sparteine, used to treat irregular heart-rhythms
Burdock leaves and Burdock Root
Calamus rhizome
Centaury herb – For internal and external use as antiseptic and tonic

Coltsfoot leaves – Bronchial complaints
Couch Grass rhizome
Comfrey leaves and Comfrey root – various uses including gargles to reduce inflammation
Elder flowers
Juniper berries
Lime Tree flowers
Parsley Piert herb – various uses, also high in vitamin C
Raspberry leaves – gargles
Wormwood – digestive and kidney disorders

Also to be collected, not for medicinal drugs but needed to supplement foodstuffs or for other properties were:

ROSEHIPS – rosehip syrup, very rich in vitamin C, to make up for the lack of oranges and other citrus fruit. Somerset was required to collect each year 32 tons, or a ton for every 50 sq. miles. A teaspoonful was recommended to be added to a baby's milk

HORSE CHESTNUTS or 'conkers' – 2,000 tons gathered yearly in England, of which Somerset provided 80 tons. They yielded glucose and also two important by-products – feed stuff; and saponin glucoside which easily foams with water and was used for extinguishing oil fires.

Specific instructions were given for collecting in dry weather after the dew has dried; when to dig up rhizomes and roots; and only pick as many plants as could be dried in case of spoiling. The herbs were delivered to receiving centres organised by the group agricultural organisers of the Women's Institutes. On 6th May, 1941 Milverton's WI recorded 'that foxglove leaves would be of value if members collected them'. In Somerset the WVS collected the herbs from receiving stations and dispatched them by rail or delivered them to the companies which would process them. Some plants were artificially dried by local ladies using drying equipment set up at a number of established centres. The local Women's Institutes also tended to organise the local collection of rosehips and nettles. But in Milverton, it was Miss Ethel Jennings who volunteered in 1943 to organise the collection of rosehips paying 3d a lb.

As with so many other wartime campaigns, everyone was involved in collecting – youth organisations, general volunteers and a vast number of schoolchildren The Somerset Education Committee, with Milverton man, William Deacon, as Director, organised the county's school children, including evacuees. A press release, issued at the end of hostilities, recorded that in 1942, 57 tons of horse chestnuts, 10 tons of rose hips, 1½ tons of dried nettles, 3½ cwt. of dried foxglove leaves and 1½ cwt. of miscellaneous herbs had been collected. In that year 60 counties had taken part in the scheme with Somerset coming in the top 6 counties being 3rd for nettles, 10th for chestnuts and 12th for rose hips.

So successful was the collection of horse chestnuts by schoolchildren – no doubt competing with squirrels – that the supply outstripped demand!

By 1942 Nellie had gone back to London but her letters mention several occasions when she and her daughter Helen had delighted in picking blackberries, as we do still today. So next time you get stung by a nettle whilst leaning for a prize bunch of blackberries, see the beauty of the pink rose hips, or curse the dandelion root that refuses to budge, spare a thought for those who collected them as medicinal plants before the introduction of modern medicines.

---

1. See 'Doubling Up – Education'.
2. The *Gazette* printed an article in December 1941 'The Dig for Victory' movement could easily be called 'Dig for Vitamins'.

13. WASTE NOT WANT NOT

'Every piece of paper, every old bone, every piece of scrap metal is a potential bullet against Hitler' – Herbert Morrison, Minister of Supply[1]

At Herbert Morrison's urging, wartime Britain became a nation of hoarders. Yet more was needed. It was not asked, but expected, to save, save, save! And, 'Saving' came in a variety of forms.

The goal was to create more space on merchant and cargo ships for vital supplies. That meant cutting back on importing a wide range of commodities and devising ways of getting the public to stretch what they already had. Government-initiated campaigns encouraged people not to waste fuel. Petrol rationing meant many people sold or disabled and stored private cars for the duration and many buses were altered to work on gas. All non-essential journeys including those on trains were discouraged. Coal, essential for power, was rationed to households and hot baths were limited to a water level of no more than five inches. Housewives were advised how best to save on gas or electricity by planning meals, and discouraged from pre-heating the oven to cook just one dish.

Today the aim of recycling is to limit landfill. In 1940 – 'Salvage' was a matter of national survival.

Collection depots were manned by 'Salvage Stewards' who encouraged the sorting of waste. Sorting was taken so seriously that by 1942 those who refused to do it could be fined £2500 or even imprisoned.

In order to save paper when shopping, women took their own

paper[2] bags for food. Biscuits and eggs, for instance, were sold loose – taking them home therefore was a tricky business. Letters had to be written or typed almost edge to edge and on both sides and envelopes re-used. Nellie's correspondence is a prime example of this practice. She reused envelopes, wrote on the backs of receipts and even on tickets.[3] Lavatory paper[4] became scarce, sometimes requiring newspaper to be cut up and threaded onto string and hung for use. But even paper for this purpose was limited since the printing of books and newspapers[5] was greatly reduced.

Milverton's Parish Council, its WI and schoolchildren along with the general population, took on the challenge to collect and save. Rubber, paper, metal, bones and rags: nothing was to be wasted. Everything had another use.

On 27th May, 1940 Milverton WI reported that 'The Secretary was asked to enquire if members might help the Scouts in collecting waste paper and if the R.D.C. (Wellington Rural District Council) was collecting tins and rags.' On 4th June, in response to a letter from NFWI (National Federation of Women's Institutes) headquarters asking for help, 'Mrs. Loram and Miss Ash offered to

18. *'Thank you.'* Daily Express, 13th August, 1940.

give sacks to the Scouts in which to collect waste paper. 'The committee's suggestion that they subscribe 10s 6d was carried by vote.'

Later that month – on 24th June, 1940 – the parish council minutes state 'The chairman reported that an empty cottage in Sand Street[4] had been lent to the parish, to be used as a dump for waste paper etc., and that up to the present a considerable amount had been deposited there. On the proposition of Mr. King, seconded by Mr. Day, it was resolved that the waste paper, when sorted, be passed over to the District Council for disposal.' By August 24th, the Clerk announced that the Scouts had collected so much waste paper, that extra storage space was needed as the vacant property in Sand Street was now full. Paper continued to pile up and at the WI meeting of 27th January, 1941, Mrs. Canniford and Miss Morris heeded their Chairman's call and offered to help sort waste paper at the parish council depot. So successful was the national campaign that 60 percent of all new paper was derived from recycled salvage sources by 1942.

Concerned that current or future records of historical interest, might be destroyed in the salvage programme a 'Look Before you Throw'[6] campaign was started by the British Records Association.

No doubt Milverton households handed over discarded metal and pots and pans in 1940. However, it was only on 9th February, 1942 that St. Michael's Church Council Minute Book reports 'An opinion was expressed that the iron railings round some of the old and unattended graves would be serving a more useful purpose if they were removed and handed over to the authorities, for the purpose of war material and, at the same time, the church yard would be rendered more sightly. After a discussion it was agreed these matters had better be looked into by the Churchyard Committee – as reported on.' The railings were duly removed. As the railings in Fore Street were privately owned, there is no record of whether or not they went too and were later replaced with new. However, there continues a debate as to whether the nation's railings were ever recycled. There are no records of railings being used for munitions nor any explanation of what happened to those not melted

27. Above: Milverton School pre-1914.

28. Right: The actress Eleanor Summerfield. Her parents took over The Globe during the war whilst Eleanor worked at Hestercombe and at the Norton Fitzwarren supply Depot. She was known in the village as 'Boots' when performing, with her partner, 'Toffee' (Mrs. Frances Pryor).

29. Milverton Stores in 1930s.

30. Beattie and Lionel Hayes on their wedding day. The reception was in St. Michael's Rooms.

31. Above left: Amy McGrath, neé Mason. She was a Land Girl at Cormiston in Preston Bowyer.

32. Above right: Olive Yesford, Land Girl, (mother of Jacqye Keates) worked at Preston Farm from 1945 and was billeted with Mrs. Mearn, Preston Bowyer. Before her demob, she asked to return to Somerset as she had met Hubert Cornish – the man she was to marry. She remained in the area.

33. Right: Barbara Williams was a Land Girl who worked with Amy Mason at Cormiston. Here, she relaxes on newly cut hay.

34. Above: Private First Class John Kiacz Jnr.

35. Left: PFC John Kiacz Jnr. With truck somewhere in Germany.

36. Above: John Kiacz, 2nd row, middle with his group from 3892 Qtr. Truck company in Germany.

37. Right: Mrs. Stone with her daughter, Shirley, wearing her 'Victory' dress. Mrs. Stone lived in Turnpike and befriended some of the American soldiers and even did some of their laundry. Shirley kept in touch and it was through her that contact was made with Vincent Tuminello's son, Joe, who with Bruce, son of John Kiacz, supplied the information about their fathers' war experiences.

38. Left: Corporal Vincent 'Jim' Tuminello in photograph sent to Mrs. Stone.

39. Below: Writing on back of photograph above. He wrote this caption when back in US but date is wrong.

Milverton England
1942.

Cpl. Vincent Tuminello
3 Carlton Drive
Massapequa NY 11758

40. Vincent Tuminello in jeep.

41. Writing on back of photo sent to Mrs. Stone in 1945.

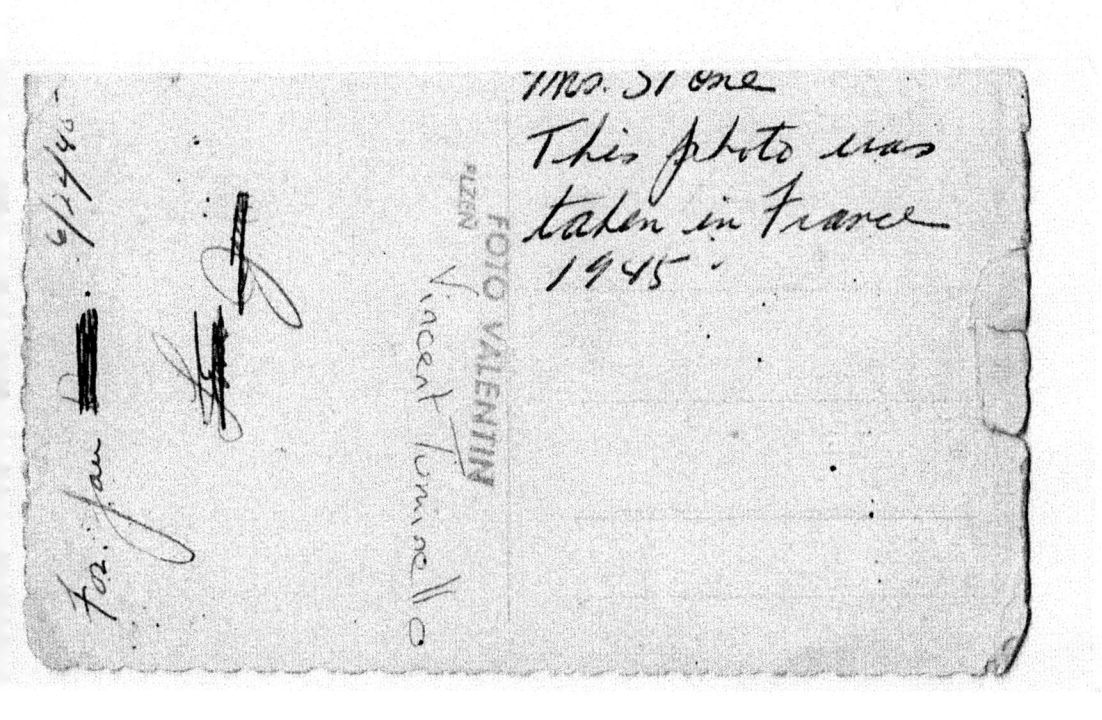

42. *Milverton Station.*

down. Whatever the truth, Milverton is fortunate in still having railings in Fore Street fronting Bank House and Mansell House.

Rags for recycling and bones to make glue, would have been kept separate, but cooked and raw leftover food was not collected for composting as it is today. Householders in towns and cities put their waste food[7] in communal galvanised bins provided by the authorities. Taken to processing depots this was sterilised by baking into a 'cake' that could with water, be reconstituted for use as animal feed. But there is no mention or recollection of 'pig swill' in communal bins in Milverton. People fed pigs and chickens with their own food scraps and Ken Burston remembered carrying heavy buckets of pig swill to Creedwell Orchard.[8]

No doubt the British and US Army had their own system of recycling waste food.

Milverton School log for 28th January, 1942 states 'that the children were invited to join the local salvage drive and responded magnificently. They collected: metal and tins 20 cwts. Paper, 9 cwts. Rubber, 3 cwts. Rags 1 cwt. batteries, 1 cwt. bones 8, ½ lbs – total 1.8 tons.'

Even BBC *Children's Hour*, organised a 'Scrap Saving' campaign and in 1943 the Children's Salvage Corps devised this song, sung to the tune of 'There'll always be an England'.

> There'll always be a dustbin,
> To Save for Victory,
> So treat it right, and let it fight
> For Home and Liberty.
> We'll win this war together
> However hard it be
> If dustbins mean as much to you
> As dustbins mean to me.

Thrift was paramount and clever government poster campaigns asked people to 'think before you spend'; told them it was 'Up to you' to 'Save for Victory' – by buying National Savings Certificates or Defence Bonds and 'Don't spend – DO lend' by saving in your bank. Buying savings stamps at the Post Office was a popular way of saving for children either at home or at school. In February 1942 a Milverton WI proposition was carried 'that for the duration of the war, saving stamps to the value of 7s 6d be presented to members' babies instead of silver spoons'. Mrs. Deacon was presented with savings stamps on 5th September, for her daughter, Lavinia.

Milverton WI on February 6th, 1940 discussed organising a War Savings Group. This was followed up on 7th May by a talk given by Mr. Price explaining the system and appealing again to members to set up a Savings Group.

But even this was not enough. How best to prise yet more money from the cash strapped population? The answer: offer prizes! Like today's Lotto, a new National Savings Scheme made emotive appeals to raise funds for specific projects with the added inducement of a prize draw.

The 'Spitfire Fund', which launched in June 1940, was first of these appeals. There is no record of the size of Milverton's contribution but the people of Taunton Borough and Rural District as a whole raised £7,801 – a Somerset record.

Next, in June 1941, came 'War Weapons Week', an appeal to fund the replacement of weapons and equipment left behind by the British Expeditionary Force in Dunkirk. In May that year, Nellie bought a 6d ticket for No. 563[9] which offered a first prize of War Savings Certificates to the value of 50% of total receipts.

Milverton WI reported on 29th May, 1941: 'That £35 of the profits on the production of plays had been invested in War Weapons Week.' This was almost half of the takings of £38.3s.4½d.

Whilst these were official National Savings incentives the organising of them was handed to local councils and the expected amount to be raised by each area was proportionate to the population. Milverton was then under the jurisdiction of the Wellington Rural District Council and Nellie's certificate of 1941 states, 'A' district for savings purposes. Nellie's little contribution should, with the others collected in Milverton

> M.R.C.
>
> DONATIONS ONLY
> This Voucher is FREE
>
> N° 563
>
> ## WAR WEAPONS WEEK 1941
> "A" District
> ### A4 Wardens' Effort
>
> This ticket is a receipt for a donation of **6d.** to the above effort and entitles holder to participate in the Free Draw for prizes as under
>
> 1st. Prize 50% OF TOTAL RECEIPTS
> 2nd. Prize 30% All prizes to be
> 3rd. Prize 15% WAR SAVING
> 4th. Prize 5%   CERTIFICATES
>
> Free draw takes place at the Wardens' Post on Saturday, May 24th. Results Sheets will be issued to Bookholders. Winners will be notified by post on Monday, May 26th. Bookholders are invited to witness the draw at A 4 Wardens' Post not later than 4 p.m.
>
> **All Books to be returned not later than Friday, May 23rd**
>
> (Featherstone Press Ltd, 555, Lea Bridge Road, E.10.)

19. *This is Nellie's receipt, with her initials, 'MRC' at the top. She used the back of this to write to her husband.*

have gone to make up Milverton's total donation but something was amiss. On 27th March, 1942, the Parish Council reported that although War Weapons week had been a success 'the question arose as to the monies invested in the banks in Taunton or elsewhere for the benefit of Milverton's share... It was brought to (our) notice ... that substantial sums which should have been credited to Milverton, were credited to the main Wellington total.'

'Warship Week' followed in 1942, by which time Nellie was back in London. The aim now was for towns and cities to raise funds to build a specific named ship. Undaunted by Milverton's landlocked rural location, the parish council on 9th February, 1942, announced 'that Warship Week would take place in Milverton on 21-28th March.' The chairman went on to say that he'd approached Wellington District Council as to the form of the necessary proceedings and wanted their views of the council before calling a public meeting. 'It was proposed to call a public meeting in the Victoria Rooms on Friday, 20th February, 1942… and the hope was expressed that the Victoria Rooms Trustees would allow this meeting to be free of charge.' As a consequence the WI, on 3rd March 'agreed to organise a social on Saturday, 28th March as requested by the Warships Week Committee'.

Mindful of the concern over the fate of their contribution to 'War Weapons Week' the matter of Milverton's share of funds had been raised at the council meeting of 27th March 'and the organising secretary, Mr. Arthur House, from Wellington, who was present, promised that all monies in banks etc., would be credited to the place nominated'.

We do not know the amounts raised by Milverton for 'War Weapons Week and for 'Warship Week'. But it is noted that the day before the above meeting, the school log for 26th March, 1942, mentioned that Mrs. Deacon presented the prizes at the Victoria Rooms. There is no indication of the amount raised by the children.

By 1943, with the build-up for D-Day beginning to get underway more funds were needed to build bombers and fighters. The parish council minutes for 22nd March, 1943 report that they would again hold a Public meeting in the Victoria Rooms on 13th April to discuss the programme for 'Wings for Victory' 12th-19th June. Milverton, we know took part, as most of an illustrated board setting donation targets, was found in the basement of Carlton House in 2004 and is now in Milverton Archives.

The WI again, at the request of the organising committee, held a social on 19th June. It was agreed that this should be fancy dress and that £5-6 be spent on band fees. On 7th April the WI announced that 'profits from this social should be invested in war bonds on behalf of the Royal National Lifeboat Institute'.

The school log for 12th June, 1943 reports that the children surpassed themselves collecting £102 when their target had been a mere £50! This was an extremely successful campaign and by the end of that financial year, 27,273 planes[10] had been built. Indeed, on 13th September, 1942 the Daily Telegraph reported that one Spitfire had been repaired nine times having six sets of new wings.

SPITFIRE NINE TIMES REPAIRED

Sir Stafford Cripps, Minister of Aircraft Production, said at a Home Counties aircraft factory yesterday that aircraft were not merely repaired once and then discarded, but went through a number of repairs.

One Spitfire was repaired nine times and had six new pairs of wings fitted. It then went back to service as good as new.

For every 100 airframes, engines, and propellers repaired in the first half of 1940, 1,080 airframes, 945 engines, and 2,207 propellers were repaired in the same period of 1942.

In addition to that, of course, a great many other items were repaired as well.

20. Spitfire Nine times repaired.

There was also a small and now forgotten 'Tanks for Attack' fund-raising appeal, followed in spring of 1944 by 'Salute the Soldier'. Again the WI was asked to organise a social event which raised £40 – used to buy a war bond on behalf of the Soldiers, Sailors and Airman's Families Association (SSAFA). Also at that meeting it was agreed to engage the RAF Dance Band to play at the dance following the fete.

The school log for 16th June, 1944 states that, 'During this savings week the children have raised a total of £274.10s after setting a target of £60.' The particular 'savings week' is not identified but it could have been 'Salute the Soldier'. On 24th May, 1944, the school log notes 'a collection was taken for the Overseas Tobacco Fund and £2.8s was forwarded'. It is strange now, to think of children raising money to buy tobacco or cigarettes albeit for troops.

Whilst Milverton folk contributed greatly to savings and organised fund raising events from the outbreak of hostilities onwards, the Mother's Union reported on 17th December, 1940 that they had to cease collecting. They had been providing stationary for the forces, but had discovered Mother's Union rules would not allow them to collect for any other organisation than their own. Some things could not be dislodged – even by war.

Darlingest

1. Herbert Morrison, Baron Morrison, 1888 – 1965, was a Labour politician and served in the Wartime coalition government becoming Minister of Supply in May 1940. From October that year, until 1945 he was Home Secretary and Minister of Home Security also serving in the War Cabinet from 1942. He became Lord President of the Council, Leader of the House of Commons in 1945 and Foreign Secretary and Deputy Leader 1951 but failed to become leader when Hugh Gaitskell took over from Clement Atlee. He retired in 1959 and became a life peer. He is the grandfather of the politician Peter Mandelson.
2. Polythene and plastic did not exist and there were no cardboard egg boxes.
3. All carefully bound with her letters at the Imperial War Museum.
4. Soft tissue lavatory paper or tissue handkerchiefs were not available in the UK until the late 1950s.
5. Ethel Jennings believes it was the first of two cottages, now demolished, that were sideways-on, next to the fire engine house. The first one was once occupied by her grandfather and the second by Mr and Mrs. Dyte.
6. Record Offices today still say to people clearing attics, 'Let us throw away, not you.'
7. Rhubarb or potato tops, tea leaves, coffee grounds, were not to be included. (Also orange and grapefruit and banana skins but as they had almost disappeared from the diet, this was not a problem.)
8. See 'Dig for Victory'.
9. This certificate with her initials survives as she used the back to write one of her letters. See Nellie, 22.4.41 and march past, 28.4.41.
10. See 'Doing Your Bit'.

14. MAKE DO AND MEND

'I'm as big as she is!' said Ethel Jennings at her delight in being able to wear her older sister's clothes.

On 28th August, 1939, just before the outbreak of war, Milverton WI suggested spending £2 to buy wool to knit blankets for evacuees 'should they be billeted in Milverton' and to make money from a 'Sale of Work'. At their meeting on 7th November, a letter, outlining 'Wartime Plans' was read out. It suggested that householders should be required to give or assist in making clothes for evacuee children. The same meeting discussed making comforts for sailors 'the majority of those present expressed willingness to make these garments'. And in June 1940 the motion was carried that 'we should apply for Miss Vernon to supply us with some wool free of charge for knitting comforts for the Royal Navy'.

But everything was about to change. Not all rags went for recycling in the 'salvage'[1] drive, as another aspect of 'saving' applied to what was worn.

On 1st June, 1941, Nellie writes of 'the shock of the clothes rationing' that had come into effect that day. Between the wars the variety of style and quality of clothes, even mass-produced, greatly increased and whilst there had been no noticeable shortage of clothes, prices rose by 72% between 1939 and 1941. Clothing manufacturers' priority was to supply uniforms and protective clothing with a depleted work force[2] so their ability to make civilian clothes was under severe pressure.

But again, the government took advantage of the situation applying the same skilful organisation and planning to clothes as it had to the production and distribution of food. To the food ration book was added a clothing book with coupons to be exchanged for new clothes.

The Board of Trade was responsible for not only securing an orderly consumption of civilian clothes but in raising the general level of public taste whilst teaching people how to make the most of limited supplies. It did this in September 1941 by introducing the 'Limitation of Supplies – Cloth and Apparel' Order.

The 'utility' scheme, with its dramatic 'two wedges' logo, ensured that all essential articles of clothing was manufactured to simple specifications, and to a good standard whilst maintaining economy of labour and materials. In other words it was a 'quality' mark. Whilst these austerity clothes restricted freedom of choice, and price fixing safeguarded the purchaser from profiteering, clever advertising and advice on maintaining and mending, enabled women to make the most of their families' clothes whilst not foregoing 'fashion'.

For most, the clothes rationing allowance was severe as every article of clothing except hats and overalls (although the latter was later incorporated into the scheme) had its coupon value.

Put simply, the policy was – one garment on, another in the wash and another ready to wear. Thus, in the first year each civilian man, woman and child was given an allowance of 66 coupons which was enough to provide each man with little more than what he stood in and reckoned to be half the amount each person would buy in a year. Victims of bombing were exempt.

Clothes for children under four years were coupon-free and for older children a lower coupon value than for adults.

Second-hand clothing was coupon free but a maximum price was imposed above which coupons had to be surrendered. 'Good as new clothes' could be bought instead of, but not as well as, new clothes.

The allowance was:

WOMAN – number of coupons	MEN
Suit or overcoat 18 coupons	A suit at 26 coupons
Woollen dress with sleeves (11)	A shirt (5)
Or	
dress other than wool (7)	A tie (1)
shoes (5)	Woollen vest and trunks (8)
stockings (2)	Socks (3)
brassiere (1)	Shoes (7)
suspender belt (1)	Handkerchiefs, each (1)
vest (3)	Pyjamas (8)
knickers (3)	Or dressing gown at (8)

By 1942 coupon allowance was reduced by 22% whilst the value changed allowing fewer coupons for clothes damaged in air-raids.

Whilst ready-made baby clothes were rationed in August 1941 expectant mothers received an extra 50 coupons for their own and baby's extra needs. Growing children had special allowances.

As a very large proportion of the population wore some kind of uniform or protective clothing – wearing 'civvies' was for off duty only.[3]

Clothes were designed to allow maximum use of fabric. Men's trousers had no turn-ups and only three pockets, whilst jackets could only be single breasted with no back vents and also just three pockets. Ladies' clothes were similarly restricted in that skirts were shorter and not over full, with just enough fabric to allow movement. Jackets again had a restricted number of pockets and buttons and were devoid of embroidery or embellishment.[4] Skirts and trousers had plain waistbands fastened with buttons or other clasps, without elastic, as did some women's underwear, the use of elastic requiring precious imported rubber being limited. These strict manufacturing rules therefore dictated the styles that became the new fashion. With padded shoulders, slim body lines, and no excess ornamentation, 1940s fashion took on an iconic shape quite different from the flowing, graceful lines of the 1930s and from the extravagant flamboyance of the New Look introduced in 1949.

With very few synthetic fabrics then, such as rayon and georgette, many clothes were made from natural wool, cotton, silk[5] or linen. Dressmaking fabrics were rationed, whilst furnishing fabrics and blackout were coupon free, though ironically blackout fabric was rationed after September 1945. Knitting wool was rationed but obtained with fewer coupons than a bought article.

The WVS set up clothing and shoe exchanges and together with the Board of Trade, the Ministry of Education and Local Education Authorities organised 'Make do and Mend' classes and exhibitions varying from humble village hall presentations to elaborate affairs in city stores. Some 50,000 such classes were regularly held and 'Mrs. Sew and Sew' appeared in advertisements, newspapers and magazines.

If you could not knit, darn or sew you would have had difficulty clothing yourself and your family. But of course in those days most women – including Nellie[6] – could sew and accepted the challenge, utilising their skills in ingenious ways. They cut down old or worn out garments to make children's clothing,[7] put on strips of different fabric to lengthen hems, cut panels from one dress to 'brighten' another. They cut down their husband's or son's civilian clothes for themselves or to fashion boys' clothing. Threadbare overcoats could be unpicked and the fabric turned inside out and made up again and, collars and cuffs were turned on men's shirts. Hand-knitted garments could be unpicked and the wool washed and knitted up again. Children's clothes did the rounds of friends and families and of course, coloured dyes were employed to transform dull colours. Sewing thread was unpicked from old garments to be re-used for hand sewing. Buttons were saved from discarded garments and added to the family heirloom 'Button box' holding as it did fancy or plain buttons from times of plenty. In an age when everyone wore hats, great ingenuity and some humour was employed in remodelling felt hats resulting in the small jaunty, cheeky little women's hats that seem to have inspired the 'fascinators' of today.

Sadly, clothes rationing impinged greatly on brides, who could, if lucky, perhaps remodel an old wedding dress. But in most cases, brides wore a smart day dress or suit and many men were married in their military uniform. Milverton's, Beattie Hayes was one who married in 1942, wearing a dress with an edge to edge coat whilst her husband wore his Somerset Light Infantry uniform.

Thus it was, on 7th January, 1941, just a few months after clothes restrictions came into force, that Milverton WI announced, 'Make and Mend' parties would commence at 2.30 p.m. on 13th January and members were urged to help.

★ *MAKE-DO AND MEND.* ★

Holiday Sun-suit

NO MATTER how you spend your holidays this August, you will want to catch all the sunshine you can. The briefer the costume you wear, at the swimming pool or in your own garden, the greater chance these active rays of the sun will have. Sun suits are not to be bought now, but you can run up for yourself the one sketched here from an old cotton frock or overall, a cotton curtain or a bedspread. The diagram is scaled to fit a 27" waist, 34" - 36" bust, 38" hip.

Make paper patterns from the diagram and cut out, allowing ½" for turnings. Allowance for hem has been made.

Dart waist of Back, in position indicated, to fit your figure. Join Top (right-hand upper diagram) to Skirt Front (below) at waistline, and join Front to Back at side seams, leaving openings for placket at left side.

Hem upper edge round back and sides up to each corner of Top.

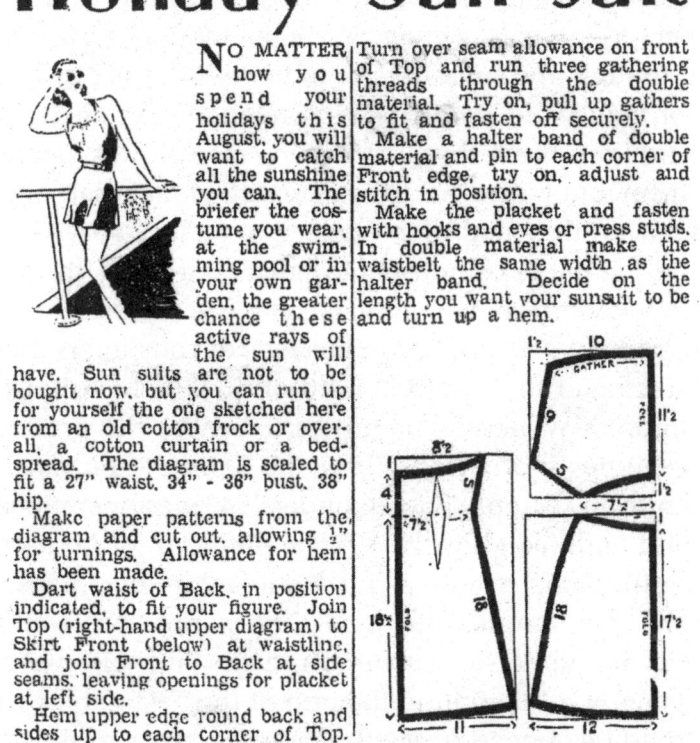

Turn over seam allowance on front of Top and run three gathering threads through the double material. Try on, pull up gathers to fit and fasten off securely.

Make a halter band of double material and pin to each corner of Front edge, try on, adjust and stitch in position.

Make the placket and fasten with hooks and eyes or press studs. In double material make the waistbelt the same width as the halter band. Decide on the length you want your sunsuit to be and turn up a hem.

21. *Sun Suit*, Sunday Sun, 23rd July, 1944.

Mrs. Deacon describes what happened. 'We took surplus clothes of our own that could be made into clothes for the children because… they only came with one dress which they were wearing. They did get a clothing allowance, like the rest of us.' But WI members wielded needles of one kind or another in diverse ways. As early as 28th October, 1940, members volunteered to teach handicrafts to soldiers recuperating at Sandhill Park. On that day also they suggested holding a 'thrift slipper-making class'. On 27th May, 1941, Miss Millar agreed to attend a class being held at Croxall to make minesweeper's gloves. On 28th October, 1941, it was announced that four jerseys had been finished and sent to the Merchant Navy. On 27th October, 1943, they held a competition for the 'best patched garment'. On 26th March, 1945 Milverton WI had sent off a number of jerseys to merchant seamen in 'unoccupied Europe'.

By 1941, though, the consequence of bombing was putting pressure on stocks of household items. Having handed over their aluminium saucepans for Lord Beaverbrook's 'Saucepans Spitfires' people needed to replace them, but with what? The shortage of materials and the need to conserve what they had plus the lack of factory space extended to even the most humble of household goods. Of these the shortage of furniture and wood from which to make it was the most serious.

The government's response to the needs of consumers on the home front was to extend the 'utility' brand of quality. In August 1942 the Board of Trade convened a committee to advise the production and design of furniture. By November 1942, the 'Domestic Furniture (Control of Manufacture and Supply [No 2]) Order 1942 was operational with an exhibition in London and distribution announced for January 1943.

Applying the same criteria as for manufacture of clothes, furniture designs were kept simple, functional, and plain – but well made. To save on metal and upholstery materials, chairs and sofas were not deep sprung. Styling was taken from the best of the past: tables with swing tops that could be opened out with storage space; simplified Windsor dining chairs; and an easy-chair that could fold out to become a single bed that owed its origin to a William Morris arts and Crafts design.

Because the scarcity of raw materials impinged on availability items were strictly rationed on a coupon basis with priority being given to:

- Those who had been bombed.
- Those setting up house for the first time either because they had a child or were expecting one; and
- Those who married just after the war, who would find difficulty in equipping a home (i.e., those married before the war would have had some furniture and household goods) and those who intended to marry three months after making an application and those requiring a bed for a growing child.

Each item of furniture was valued by units so once the need was established by the authorities the requisite units were allocated, enabling the 'buyer' to choose what they wanted. The maximum number of buying units was limited to essential items and purchasers might wait several months for delivery. By the end of 1944, however, the situation eased and those entitled to utility furniture could also obtain curtain material without coupons.

Baby furniture, was not restricted and evacuee, Mrs. Ling, described arriving back to her billet in Milverton with her newborn son to find that her hosts, the Pepperills had 'gone all the way to Bristol to get me a cot and a highchair. They knew somebody who had been bombed out. You name it I had it. I wasn't short of anything.'

One lucky newlywed Milverton couple were Ted and Sylvia Perry. They married in 1948, three years after the war ended, but at a time when wartime restrictions still applied. Ted said, 'The furniture and everything was rationed – all "utility" stuff and Sylvia reckoned the whole of our furniture, which was two armchairs, a bedroom suite and four chairs and a table and a sideboard – came to £139 and I think the mattress always went separately.'

Setting up home from scratch was difficult as other household items were scarce. Utility pottery was always available but colour and design was limited. Some items, such as jugs and teapots, could be very difficult to obtain or replace. The WI had decided on 4th March, 1940 to offer the use of their crockery and a month later, on 1st April, that their cups and saucers could be used in the local army canteen. But after a party on 16th January, for soldiers billeted in the village, '6 Institute cups had been broken and it was agreed that 1 doz. should be purchased if possible, 6 to be paid for from the party funds and 6 from WI funds'.

Refrigerators, vacuum cleaners, washing machines and other gadgets that we take for granted now were simply unavailable. This created a high value second-hand market in such items.

Even personal hygiene was subject to rationing. Soaps, household and personal items required coupons. People took their own soap with them when going away and some took their own towels to work as they too, along with bedlinen, pillows, quilts, blankets had to be purchased with clothing coupons, but at least their quality was ensured under the Utility mark.

In a world of cheap thinly veneered flat-pack furniture, 'Utility' furniture is prized today, not just for its emotional history but for its clean cut style, solid wood construction and enduring quality. The double cheese wedge utility mark can still be found on some old blankets and linens in charity shops.

22. Utility mark.

1. See 'Waste Not Want Not'.
2. See Amy McGrath 'On the Fields' and 'Doing Your Bit'.
3. On August 1944, the *Daily Mail* reported a problem with Land Army Girls' coupons. See 'On the Fields'.
4. See 2, above.
5. Highly prized was parachute silk, used to make ladies' underwear. The author's grandmother made baby clothes from lawn retrieved after soaking the blue wax covered fabric used for technical drawings.
6. On 3/8/40 Nellie writes to her husband about her sewing machine having arrived damaged.
7. The author and twin brother had very fetching rompers made from men's striped shirts.
8. This was the cost of the furniture which they could not have bought without qualifying for coupons. The mattress was not part of the bed, they needed coupons.

MILVERTON IN THE WAR

15. OVER HERE...Just a tiny bit of tin

Milverton's history spans thousands of years. Settlements have existed in this spot since the mesolithic and probably before. The Dog Tag is very contemporary in time scale terms but the fact that this Dog Tag is recent no less diminishes its worth; nor Milverton's rich archaeology.

That an ancient Roman, lost one of his coins (Emperor Constantinus II Junior — AD 321-324) but a few metres from the lost Dog Tag, nearly two thousand years earlier, is indeed amazing but not extraordinary. Like everything we find, we research but common currencies cannot tell tales. The Dog Tag, however, will have told this book a story and will leave its own mark.

Julian Dakowski, June 2016

Not heard, not seen, not expected, out of the sky and under the water early on the morning 7th December, 1941, the Japanese attacked the US Pacific Fleet anchored in Pearl Harbour in Hawaii killing 3,700 people, destroying 170 aircraft, 3 ships and damaging another 16. The next day, President Roosevelt told the American Nation, known now as his 'Infamy speech' that it was at war with Japan. Deemed as provocation, Germany and Italy supported their ally Japan and declared war on the United States four days later. Winston Churchill, half American, had months earlier been urging the United States to enter the war arena to help us 'in our darkest hours' but, clinging to its neutrality, it took the Japanese and not the Nazis to force the issue.

All this happened as Nellie was planning her return to London. In the last letter, we have, dated 9th December, she does not mention the Japanese attack on Pearl Harbour and so this is where, as far as Milverton is concerned Nellie's story ends.

Everything happened fast! On 2nd January, 1941 the Eighth Air Force Order was signed and six days later the US Forces in the British Isles was announced followed in February by the establishment in England of VIII Bomber Command. So as to accommodate the influx, first of the USAAF and then the US Army, a large infrastructure had to be set in place. In April 1942 the US and Canadians with the British devised a plan for a cross Channel invasion as early as 1943 called Operation Roundup. The UK had the code-name 'Bolero' thus the build-up of US military in Britain became Operation Bolero. Originally British troops and engineers were the first to start the preparations for new airfields or converting existing ones in strategic places along the east and south east coasts. In May 1942 some US troops were diverted to North Africa for Operation Torch in an attempt to open up a southern front from which to invade Europe. In May of 1943 at a conference in Washington Gen. Dwight D Eisenhower[1] was appointed Supreme Commander. Operation 'Roundup', he felt, was unrealistic and it was decided that a cross-channel invasion was possible in 1944 but not by the shortest route, via the beaches of Normandy – Operation Overlord. 'Roundup' was superseded and 'Bolero' ceased in 1943, though the build-up of troops and equipment continued.

But how would the US recruit the vast number of troops required? On the day Britain declared war against Germany, 3rd September, 1939, General George C. Marshall[2] became Chief of Staff responsible for organising and building up the army. He took over an American military with approximately 75,000 troops in the National Guard – many fewer in the Navy and the Air Force. Unlike the highly trained and combat ready British Territorial Army the pre-war U.S. National Guard consisted of men from poor areas, who – in return for one weekend's a month training – received a uniform, food and payment of $1 a day. Recruits did not understand that they would be fighting away from their homeland. In September 1940, The Selective Training and Service Act introduced the first peace time conscription in US history. All men between 21 and 35 had to register. Once the US entered the war, the age range was extended from 18 – 45 and eventually rose to 65. Given this broad demographic conscription it inevitably netted a large number of African-Americans. And therein lay a problem; for the US Army practised a form of segregation that confined black GIs to menial and support roles,[3] but excluded them from combat. This was abhorrent to both the British military and HM Government, who initially opposed the sending of black American troops for fear of offending the empire and commonwealth forces stationed here.

US troops began arriving in Britain in 1942. At first numbers were small. But during 1943 the pace picked up. By D-Day there were a staggering 1.6 million GIs 'over here'. They crossed the Atlantic in large passenger liners – including Cunard's Queen Mary and Queen Elizabeth. These ships could carry thousands of troops at a time and were fast enough to outrun U-boats.

Early deployments involved troops from the US Army's V Corps. As part of Operation Magnet they landed not in mainland Britain but in Northern Ireland. The idea initially was to relieve British forces who were also being harassed by the IRA. The move worked. IRA activities diminished and the GIs took over the defence of the province and set to work constructing air strips and improving naval defences.

On the mainland most combat troops disembarked at Glasgow and from there dispersed by train to wherever they were to be stationed. The United States War Department was aware that life in small rural communities might seem strange to many GIs. It therefore issued all soldiers with a booklet – of seven typescript pages on poor quality paper – entitled 'Over There'. Giving a snapshot of life in Britain, it explained that the American serviceman was a guest in Britain and should make every effort to become acquainted with British ways.

The country was roughly divided – East and West – into deployment zones. The USAAF with 649,442 personnel settled down in East Anglia. As air force units were more permanently established in bases just a few miles apart they were able to develop deeper social bonds with local people. On the western side of the country, some 667,434 US troops were mainly deployed to the north around Liverpool and Cheshire, to Wales, the Midlands, around Birmingham all the way down to Oxfordshire, Gloucestershire and to the strategically important south coast, including Dorset, Devon, Somerset and Cornwall. In the south west American support services were set up in Bristol and Taunton.

American troops were separated from the British and Canadians, training on Dartmoor and Salisbury Plain and moved around roughly every six weeks. General Marshall, concerned that all these raw recruits lacked war experience brought back troops from Italy to be in the first wave of invasion force on D-Day, followed in later waves by armies moving down from the north and elsewhere.

Censorship was extremely strict. There were no press reports of vast numbers of troops arriving and somehow they were secreted away. General Marshall insisted that the US military should maintain the same standard of living as at home. So whilst officers were often accommodated in very splendid stately homes, the men were housed in basic or prefabricated huts or in tents. But for some – coming from areas still reeling from the Great Depression – it would be better than they had previously known.

American military engineers including non-combatant US African-Americans were among the first to arrive, taking over the construction work from the British or working in the ports – especially Bristol and Liverpool – bringing in supplies. From a British point of view, with an average age of 52, many of the stevedores at the docks welcomed the young, strong fit black soldiers helping to unload American supplies.

Situated in mid-Somerset, not far from Dartmoor and Exmoor – and with easy access both to London and Glasgow – Taunton was the obvious place to become the hub in the planning of logistics for Operation 'Overlord'.

Darlingest

'The supply of our armed forces in Europe has been a remarkable achievement, involving the delivery across the ocean and over beaches and through demolished ports, and then over a war-torn countryside into France and Germany of tonnages far in excess of anything previously within the conception of man' This statement was made in the book 'United States Army in World War II – the Technical Services, the Quartermaster Corps, by William Ross and Charles Romanus. The history of the Quartermaster Corps is given in appendix 5. QM troops made up approximately 4.5% of military personnel. The supplying of Quartermaster Stores is crucial to our story, as will be revealed.

Lt. General John C.H Lee[4] commanded the Supply of Services (SOS). Having set up his Quartermaster HQ at Bristol. Lee oversaw the offloading at Liverpool and Bristol docks of a staggering number and variety of supplies from bedding and food to oil and petrol to vehicles and guns. The Quartermaster Corps had two main HQs, one in London and a larger one in Cheltenham, which also handled training.

Finally, on 12th January, 1943 the British VIII Corps – having dispersed variously to North Africa and to the 21st army Group as part of the build up to invasion – vacated Hestercombe. Two months later, in March 1943 the XIX District US Supply Services (non-Divisional) moved in. They also took over the running of the very large storage depot at Norton Fitzwarren[5] which had been under construction since 1940.

Also under XIX's umbrella was the supply of medical services – hospitals, chemicals, bomb disposal, ordnance, military police, signals and chaplains. Supplies unloaded in Liverpool went by train to Bristol and – together with those unloaded directly at Bristol – were distributed to troops along the coast or to the nearby airbase at Filton for storage at the Norton Fitzwarren Depot. Most important was the distribution of oil and petrol which was pumped through pre-war underground pipes to London and elsewhere, or put into storage tanks at Highbridge. This network was extended into a vast submarine labyrinth of pipes codenamed PLUTO – Pipeline under the Ocean[6] – that, once a foothold had been established in France, took fuel direct to the theatre of war from the Isle of Wight to Cherbourg and from Dungeness to Calais.

Food rations had to be supplied from the outset. American troops in North Africa, while under British command during Operation 'Torch', had been given British army rations and they continued to be issued to American troops in the UK until their own supplies arrived. There were some issues. Milk was in short supply and was unpasteurised, so American troops stuck to tinned or dried milk. Bread was another problem as was the supply of 'candy'. These are discussed in Appendix Five.

With so many US troops stationed in in rural areas, it was important that they should be welcomed. The US authorities were anxious for their troops to meet people, especially – as American female personnel were thin on the ground – local girls. Living and training in rural areas, out of sight of the population meant that the only time soldiers were seen was off duty. But even then they were confined, in the south-west, to 'Liberty' towns such as Exeter, Taunton, Gloucester and Bristol, where they could visit special US Red Cross organised clubs. To assist fraternisation in rural areas the British government gave grants of £30 to organisations such as the WVS to set up 'Welcome Clubs'.

The troops settled in and had established themselves socially with girlfriends by the time the bulk of US combat troops arrived. The African-American soldiers were considered well educated; had good manners and had, as with all US military personnel, considerably more money than their British counterparts. They also had access to goods not available in Britain – food and nylons – via their PX (Post Exchange). Inevitably black GIs acquired white girlfriends – a sore point with white GIs. In many towns and cities – separate black and white zones were established to keep the two groups apart. But in smaller areas local authorities designated alternative black and white leisure nights. Even so, tensions built up and major rioting erupted on at least half a dozen times – all unreported in the press. In July 1944, US MPs had to assist Bristol police in breaking up a fight involving over 400 American soldiers. At Launceston battling GIs surged back and forth across the

Tamar lasting several hours. But whilst the British police would be called to quell unrest, US troops in the UK were subject to US law – the Shepton Mallet Prison having been given over to US authorities as their penal facility.

As mentioned earlier, part of XIX Division's remit was the construction of the 67th General hospital at Musgrove Park that would take the injured after D-Day. The 801st Hospital centre was at Hestercombe House, 101st at Norton camp, and 185th at Sandhill Park.[7] Injured soldiers would be flown to the 61st Field Hospital via the Merryfield airbase, near Ilton. From there they would be transported on a continuing shuttle service by road to the Taunton hospitals.

Meanwhile, as part of the build up to D-Day, combat troops of the US First Army, began to arrive. Initially there were three US divisions – two in Devon and one in Cannington. But eventually the V Corps HQ, under the command of General Leonard T. Gerow[8] was set up at Norton Manor, near the storage depot. The combat troops and their supplies were next to each other – the former dependent upon the latter and both part of Milverton's story.

The first mention of American troops in Milverton was made by the WI at their meeting on 30th March, 1943, when two letters from the Officer Commanding the American troops in the vicinity were read. The first letter – agreeing to give a talk on America was followed by the second – apologising that the engagement would not be fulfilled as they were moving on. There were troops here in May, but who they were remains a mystery. By 31st August it was agreed that the US Army Chaplain now in the district would be asked to speak at the October meeting. But the following month, he too was moving on and it was left to Mrs. Deacon to glean the name of another chaplain. Persistence paid off as Chaplain Van der Ark[9] of the US Army gave a talk 'of outstanding interest, in which he compared the characteristics of the citizens of the United States to those of the citizens of the British Isles'.

The British Police were responsible for arranging billets for both the British and US military. Records are not available, but those who were here remember that the American officers were billeted at The Court,[10] Old Halls and at Lockyers. US army personnel were billeted at The George and White Hart, as had British soldiers before them. Basil Jennings recalled Americans being billeted in Reynolds in Fore Street. St. Michael's Rooms was their mess and he remembered seeing half-eaten chicken carcasses thrown out – which didn't go down well with the locals. American soldiers, playing darts, damaged a picture of St. George over the fireplace. As compensation, a soldier, painted the boy wearing lederhosen dancing with a girl, taken from a picture on a box of chocolates. The picture remembered by many of us, was in situ until St. Michael's Rooms was redeveloped into a private dwelling a few years ago. Lindsay Fortune, who lived at Rocklyn, on the corner of Turnpike, said that because of damage caused by American soldiers, the US Government had replaced the original wide elm floorboards downstairs with narrower oak boards. Emily Mears, writing a school project exploring the history of her home, St. Michael's House – to which Shaftesbury House School was evacuated – described an event leading to the Headmaster, Mr, Oates, suffering amnesia. The cook was off duty that night and 'Mr. Oates was cooking supper for the children'. Two drunken American soldiers threw a stone that went through a window hitting Mr. Oates. US officers apologised and compensation was awarded.[11]

Mr. Godber Ford who had been making bread and slab cake for the British NAAFI said two American officers came one day to ask, if he could supply at short notice 100 4lb (7d.) loaves[12] a day to the US Army Air Force base at Dunkerswell, on the Blackdown Hills. Unable to find other suppliers who could produce the quantities, Godber Ford took up the challenge.[13] He managed to buy a second-hand dough mixer and recruited some staff, notably from among a group of evacuated mentally deficient patients who remained with him for years. The American camp[14] purchased several trays of assorted cakes and pastries every day.[15] Once a foothold had been gained in Normandy, bread was produced by military mobile bakery units.

Apart from troops, thousands of vehicles of all sizes were imported and had to be kept somewhere. Britain became a huge car park. Milverton was full of them, as will be revealed. Fourteen year-old schoolboy Kilbourne Redwood remembers that Courtfields was completely surrounded by vehicles guarded at night by a sentry. One day he noticed a key in the ignition of a jeep. Too tempting to ignore he started it and ended up in the garden opposite. The owner was not pleased. His mother rewarded him with a beating. Kilbourne recalled that one very tall sentry was nicknamed 'Tiny'.

The Saturday night dances, already mentioned in 'Entertainment' took on a different dimension and American troops from outside areas were brought in.[16] Land Girl, Amy Mason, mentions attending them as did Sylvia Perry.

Whilst General Gerow set up his HQ at Norton Camp the first tranche of his V Corps went to Northern Ireland where, by June 1942, over 35,000 American troops were deployed in Operation 'Magnet'. On 14th July, 1942, Cos 'L' and 'B' from the 513th Quartermaster Truck Regiment – African-Americans – took up their duties at Belfast docks.

African-American soldiers were in Milverton and when I checked the details of the menu (illustration 24) it detailed the hosts as Co 'M' 513th QM Truck Regiment. This regiment was marked as being a 'Black Regiment' and is confirmed in photographs of the soldiers in Cos L and B in Belfast. This was not true in the case Co 'M', as will be revealed. Sadly, I have been unable to identify or ascertain the deployment of the black soldiers in Milverton. Certainly many black soldiers were deployed as cooks in the US army and that would have fitted well with the cooking of the meal as described on the menu. However, Co 'M' had their own cooks and they were not African-American.

Company 'M' of 513th, Quartermaster Truck Regiment did not include African-American soldiers. Activated at Fort Custer, Michigan on 27th April, 1943, it had been made up from the 'overstrength' Company 'M' of the 466th Quartermaster Truck Regiment and originally included 114 enlisted men and 1 officer. There it undertook training and on 16th May it moved to Camp Phillips, Kansas where training concentrated on motor operations. Given a special assignment to operate as a separate unit overseas it left the port of Boston on 8th October, 1943 and sailed in convoy for Cardiff. Evidently, some had been very sea sick, but by the time they sighted land at daybreak and landed at 1100 hrs, they were all deemed in excellent health. They had all disembarked on 19th October and then put on a train arriving in Milverton at 0800, where they resumed training and garrison duties including motor maintenance, convoy operations, water-proofing vehicles and amphibious operations. How and when their trucks and jeeps arrived is not mentioned in reports, but these too may have been transported by rail. One thing is clear: the Americans turned up sporadically. But Mr. Bill Stone, living in Turnpike, later spoke of one group (which we don't know) arriving early in the morning whilst it was still dark. Villagers thought they had been invaded by the enemy because American round helmets had a similar shape to those of the Germans!

General Gerow at Norton Fitzwarren now found himself commanding the biggest military force in the European theatre of war – including the GIs billeted at Milverton. As truckers, their role in D-Day was to be one of logistics and supply. But what that actually entailed once the fighting began only came to light through a chance discovery.

On 1st February, 2015, local resident and amateur archaeologist Julian Dakowski was out with his metal detector spending a pleasant hour sweeping the ploughed fields on the outskirts of Milverton. Suddenly his earphones bleeped. Just below the surface he dug out a small innocuous-looking piece of metal with embossed letters which he kept 'more out of curiosity than value'.

'I walked back from the field that day, with a hunch: could it be an identity tag – what the Americans called a "Dog Tag".[17] Was the tag's owner still alive? Was its loss remembered? Did the tag have a story to tell?

'I brushed it clean enough to be able to make out the name "JOHN" and also other letters of what seemed like a middle European surname and a load of numbers. On the Internet I found the answers: it was indeed a Dog Tag; an American one.

'The search had brought me unexpectedly to the website of a "WW2 US Medical Research Centre". The medical connection seemed odd at first until I realised of course the prime reason for carrying a dog tag, beyond giving the bearer's name and service number, was to identify the bearer's blood type in the event of casualty; something the bearer might not know nor might not be able to communicate.

'I called the MRC and the administrator Ben Major. From their website I was able to interpret the detail and confirm that it had belonged to a "John Kiacz Jnr." whose US Army Service Number was "35523857". The "T43 43" denoted two tetanus toxoid vaccinations, both in 1943. The "O" was his blood group and the "C" his religion: Catholic.

'I was told that sadly John had died in 2001. But he had been in Milverton in the war. The MRC were able to confirm his rank of PFC (Private First Class) and that he was with the 519th Ordnance (Heavy) Maintenance Company as part the 244th Engineer Combat Battalion in 1944. He had married and his wife was still alive. The fact that he had survived the war was wonderful. But did they have any children?

'Through American White Pages, I discovered his address and telephone number but when I called, it appeared to have been disconnected. Despite that, thanks to the wonders of modern technology, I could view his house on Google; even move along his road. I could almost knock on his door but what I wanted was someone to answer! Two letters later, in June 2016, an e-mail arrived from his son, Bruce, confirming his father's Service number, photographs and a combat diary. He too was in the 3892 Quartermaster Truck Company.'

After the initial contact e-mails came thick and fast between Bruce, Julian and me. Bruce was enthused and, he too, via Google, spent a happy hour driving around Milverton. He has been pivotal in providing internet links to military websites including to another soldier Vincent Tuminello, who had also recorded his wartime experiences. His name and those of others mentioned in Tuminello's chronicle, appear in John Kiacz's address book. Amongst material used by Year 6 at Milverton School, was a set of photographs, one of an American soldier in a jeep, with the name Vincent Tuminello on the reverse. Was this the same person and why were they were addressed to a Mrs. Stone in Milverton?! Who was she?

Two schoolgirls Shona and Selene Withers had innocently taken the photographs to school when in Year 6. Mrs. Stone was their great grandmother. She had lived in one of the cottages at Turnpike leading to Doltons field where both John and Vincent (known at 'Jimmy') were billeted. Vincent and a Dwight Fortier befriended Mrs. Stone. She even did some of their washing.

These soldiers of Co. 'M' 513th (later 3892 Quartermaster (Ordnance) Truck Regiment would take part in one of the greatest episodes of military history. Little Selene and Shona Withers had no idea of the importance of the photographs they took to Milverton School – the same school, where 70 years before, Nellie Clemens taught her evacuee children. But for the dog tag, safe in a Milverton field, and the photos, the story would end here.

John S. Kiacz, Jr. was born into his Hungarian family in 1922 and completed three years of high school before seeking employment to help with family expenses. Prior to the war, he worked as a warehouseman for a small refinery called Warren Refining and Chemical Company in Cleveland, Ohio. He returned to that job after his discharge and remained an employee until his retirement for health reasons at age 58.

John enlisted in the U.S. Army in November 1942. With the rank of Private, he trained as a truck driver at Fort Custer, Michigan and Camp Phillips, Kansas before he was deployed to England with the 3892 Quartermaster Truck Company. Bruce, his son, has confirmed that his father's records were lost in a fire at the National Personnel Records Center in 1973.

Vincent (Jimmy) Tuminello was born in NY, his parents having emigrated from Sicily. He too trained at Fort Custer where he was promoted to Corporal and then went to Camp Phillips, Kansas, where he became a proficient 50 calibre anti-aircraft machine gunner. He was assigned to Co. 'M' 513th Quartermaster Truck Company.

Darlingest

Company 'M', 513th Quartermaster Truck Regiment, was 'designated as 3892 QM Truck Company', in November 1943, just after they had arrived in Britain. Because John's records were destroyed we do not know if he and Vincent trained together (evidence suggests that they did not). The journey – described below – does not match the dates of letters sent by John Kiacz to his mother. Piecing together comments in letters together with post franking dates we know that in September of 1943, John wrote to his mother that he was in England – although none of the letters, of course, mention specific locations. On 3rd October, 1943 he writes: 'As usual I'm just about broke after spending a night in town and having a swell time.' He goes on to note: 'All we are doing is eating and sleeping. I don't know what we are doing up here but I guess they know what they are doing although I wish the hell they would make up their mind and put us to work on a steady job.' References to being 'Up North' could suggest that he arrived into Liverpool or Glasgow, rather than Cardiff, and remained there until he moved south. John's first Bristol APO stamp is dated 25th October, 1943. The records show that on 1st October – before leaving the US – Company 'M' had 110 enlisted men and 5 Officers but by 31st October, when they were in Milverton its strength was 122 enlisted men and 4 officers – an increase in 12 men and decrease in 1 officer. We know that there were some American troops here as early as May. We don't know who they were. They were not part of Co. 'M', 513th. But when John wrote on 17th November, 1943, 'Well, in regard to your question of the English countryside, well it's as much as you heard it was, for it is really wonderful, even more so this time of the year, although it is getting a little bit cold,' he was describing Milverton countryside in autumn. He was here, therefore, for Thanksgiving 1943. So this matches with Mrs. Stone's daughter, Shirley Davis's, comment – that Vincent and Dwight took an almost raw plum pudding to her mother to continue the cooking.

Garrison and training duties at this time involved a lot of movement both around the region and the country. It is recorded that a Sgt. Willmer on 20th November attended a Chemical Warfare school at Shrivenham,

Berks returning on 4th December whilst, on 29th November, an officer and 8 men attended V Corps Waterproofing School, which an officer and 4 enlisted men completed also on 4th December. This specialist training was in place before 12th December, when they left Milverton at 0830 in a motor convoy for a week's Amphibious Training arriving Dartmouth at 1330. That training completed, they returned to Milverton, leaving Dartmouth at 0900 on 16th December.

The 3892 Qtr. Truck Company left Milverton again on 22nd December in a motor convoy to take part in exercise 'Duck' near St. Agnes on the north Cornish Coast, and by 31st December they were living under field conditions. Christmas, therefore, was probably uncomfortable! They returned to Milverton on 7th January, 1944. On 6th January, 1944 two enlisted men – Sgt. Zantgraf and a Pfc Shelton – exchanged with British VIII Corps R.A.S.C. and went to Hull – returning on 21st January. From 6-12th February, a Lt. Parsons attended a bomb recce school at Bristol. Thereafter on 13th February the whole of 3892 company (124 men) were given leave.

From 2rd March to 18th March, 1944 there continued various exchanges of personnel with British VIII Corps in York.

Between these bouts of training, normal garrison duties would include working at the Supply Depot. Every morning the trucks loaded with troops drove down Turnpike on their short journey to Norton Fitzwarren, throwing sweets to children as they passed. Whilst they may not have had precise details of what they were going to do – 'waterproofing' training and exercise 'Duck' must have indicated that they were going to get wet!

On 18th March, 1944, the 519th[18] Heavy Maintenance Field Artillery group arrived from North Newton, Somerset. They stayed until 23rd June, 1944. John's War Record of 1944 states that he was part of 519 Ordnance (Heavy) Maintenance Company. The 3892 Truck Regiment would have been part of that but his company went off early as described to land on Omaha beach on D-Day.

A week later, at 0930, 25th March Co. 'M' 513th Qm. Truck Regiment –

now 3892 Quartermaster Truck Company left Milverton for the last time in a motor convoy arriving at their next permanent station, Montacute, at 1120.

In October 1943, 3892 Qm. Truck Company had been originally assigned to the first U.S. Army and further attached to V Corps on 2nd November, 1943. By April 1944, it had been attached to the First U.S. Infantry Division. Just prior to that, on 30th March, the Departmental Records report 'Alerted for Departure', followed by 'usual garrison duties' and 'preparing the unit for actual operations against the enemy. These would continue for the month during which, leave would continue. By then the company was made up of 129 enlisted men and 5 officers.

A month later, on 23rd April, an advance attachment of 82 men and 2 officers departed at 0830 for Marshalling Area, B-1, arriving at 1100. A few days later this group embarked at 0600 to take part in Exercise 'Fabius I' (between 1st -4th May) throughout which they were at sea. For this exercise their trucks were loaded with 350 tons of 1st Infantry Division supplies 'to be used in the invasion of Europe'.

This group then changed from Area D-1 (Poole, capacity 1800) to Area D-3 in Marshalling area. On 16th May, the remaining troops left Montacute in motor convoy at 1145 arriving at their new station at Bournemouth at 1600. By now there were 134 enlisted men with the 5 officers.

How much they knew about their role in the invasion, we can only guess, but this particular training was preparing them for Operation 'Neptune', the actual landing on the beach at Omaha. But did they know they were going in on D-Day? On 28th May, 1944 John writes: 'I hope you are feeling fine and are in the best of health. I'm feeling excellent. The weather is lovely and it sure makes a person want to relax at a nice quiet spot somewhere in the country. I'm still fooling around here with the regular duties of camp and am going to town[19] on my free evenings. This afternoon after dinner (chicken dinner at that) I will go into town to see the picture (*A Guy Named Joe*). I think that's the picture you wrote me about being so good.' His son Bruce, said: 'I suspect that was the last good dinner and a movie for a while and "regular duties" changed considerably the following week.'

Vincent noted there were four companies to a Battalion, which included a signal company, a labour company, a graves registration company – 606th[20] – who also helped load trucks and the 3892 Quartermaster Truck Company. There were 4 trucks and 8 men to a squad, the lead truck having closed doors. They carried bazookas and 50 calibre machine guns as well as white phosphorus grenades to destroy vehicles in event of capture.

John was assigned a 2 ½ ton supply truck loaded with ammunition and gasoline. His squad was attached to the 1st Division 16th Infantry. The 16th Infantry was part of General Marshall's strategy to include combat experienced soldiers in the first wave. They had returned from Italy, in November 1943 to continue training at Beaminster, near Dorchester. John and Vincent, part of Assault Group 'O' with 91 men and 4 officers left Marshalling Area D-3 by motor convoy at 1220 for Portland, where they embarked with 82 vehicles on LST[21] 286 and remained at anchor until 5th June when they moved to Weymouth harbour at 1000 hrs. The whole procedure was a highly choreographed one-way shuttle.

The 'lovely' weather didn't last. D-Day was set for 5th June, but bad weather forced a delay of 24 hours. Timing was critical, if they didn't go by 6th, they would have to wait and risk losing the advantage of surprise.[22]

General Eisenhower had prepared an undated rallying address to all 'Soldiers, Sailors and Airmen of the allied Expeditionary force, to be issued on D-Day. Those who knew the date were confined to quarters under 24-hour guard.[23]

John and Vincent eventually set sail from Weymouth at 1700 on 5th June. Meanwhile the 16th Infantry landed on Omaha beach[24] at 0345 on 6th June with General Gerow, being the first Corps commander to land on D-Day. They were in a large convoy and the report says that the 'crossing was quite uneventful' and they arrived in the prescribed call area off the coast of France at 7 p.m., some fifteen hours after the

Darlingest

first wave. A Rhine Ferry Barge was towed across the Channel. They prepared 'to debark [sic] as soon as possible'. The barge was loaded with nineteen 2½ ton trucks; nineteen 1 ton trailers: one half-ton truck, two officers and 39 men. They proceeded inland approximately half a mile under enemy artillery fire. They lost no equipment and no casualties and set up bivouac at Isigny. This means that John and Vincent had been in the area watching and listening to what was going on around them for some hours before they disembarked. Vincent's son, Joe, gives his father's account. 'Once the barge hit bottom they drove through four feet deep water to the beach.' His memories of passing the carnage of the assault waves were horrific: burning landing craft and bodies and body parts illuminated by moonlight. Navigating off the beach was yet another problem due to the extensive number of shell holes ongoing artillery and rifle fire.

The Report by Captain Abel continues, 'The remaining part of the Assault Force had to remain on the LST because the Rhine Ferry Barge was grounded before it could return, and was consequently damaged by enemy fire.' Eventually they were able to unload onto another barge but the first vehicles waded through 4½ feet of water. 'However, the barge was shifting with the tide and the 4th vehicle drove off into a water-covered bomb crater approximately 10 feet deep.' The vehicle was towed to shore. Eventually they unloaded all the stores but lost two trucks in the process.

At daybreak on D-Day+ 1, the 3892 Qm unit started to unload 'artillery weapons that had been transported. They were put to use at once. Due to the fact that our previously assigned transient area was still held by the enemy, it was compulsory that the unit move Bivouac four times in the first 24 hours. Approximately 40,000 gallons of gasoline was carried by this unit and was unloaded for immediate use.'

On 9th June, they received verbal orders reassigning them from the 1st US Infantry Division back to V Corps. They moved all the cargo to the Divisional Supply Dump and then moved to bivouac locations ready to carry on operations with V Corps. These included helping to unload supplies from barges stranded on the beach and involved 30 trucks working throughout the day and night. 'On 10th June one platoon went to assist 2nd U.S. Infantry Division, and another was despatched to transport troops (Rangers) from Isigny to the forest of Bois du Nolay.'

John and Vincent give slightly different accounts. Vincent being with the 97th Quartermaster Bn. was in what he called a 'bastard outfit' working with whatever division needed them. Initially he was, with John, attached to V Corps, 1st Division, landing with eleven trucks of which one was his. We know more trucks landed on that first phase and John was with one. Whatever – it was an amazing start to their journey, to get everything off with no casualties, which was not the case elsewhere. The official record; John and Vincent all mention bivouacking at Isigny.

The rest of John and Vincent's story and their traumatic experiences in the Battle of the Bulge are described in appendix 4. They ended up together in Pilsen, Czechoslovakia on VE Day.

We return to Milverton, where, Tom Prole said that they woke up one morning and all the Americans had gone in the night without a sound. What date this was – and which Americans he's referring to – we don't know. But undoubtedly the majority left, though, of course, there were still considerable numbers remaining to work at the storage Depot, as General Lee prepared to follow the army with his supply chain. We know that 519th Heavy Maintenance (Field Artillery) group were in Milverton just before the 3892 Qm. Truck Company left. But they too departed on 23rd June. They would have followed as a later wave of troops landing on the Normandy coast.

The hospitals of course, were then taking the burden of caring for the injured being brought back to Taunton.

According to Mrs. Frances Pryor, 'M' Co of the 513th Quartermaster Truck Regiment organised a Thanksgiving lunch for the people of Milverton in a tent near the recreation ground. But the menu gives no date. 1944 seems unlikely, as 'M' Co left Milverton in March 1944. The previous year also seems unlikely as 'M' Co were only just settling in the village and we know that they were not in the village for Christmas

Darlingest

1943 as they were away on exercise. But whenever it was held for some of the soldiers it might have been their last. Milverton had willingly accepted the invasion of both British and American troops and like all those in the United Kingdom, were grateful that they were able to play a small but vital role in welcoming and assisting those who came to fight for liberty.

---

1. General Dwight Eisenhower (1890-1868) became the 34th President of the United States, 1953-1961.
2. General Marshall became one of the most highly respected American soldiers in US history, even though he had never commanded troops in combat. He came out of retirement to become President Truman's Secretary of State. He was the architect for what is known as the Marshall Plan, 1948-1952, devised to aid reconstruction of a devastated post-war Europe with an injection of $13 billion for which he was awarded the Nobel peace Prize in 1953.
3. The USAAF remained staunchly all white except for one black fighter group. The US military only became a fully integrated force in 1947/8 under President Truman.
4. General Lee was known as one of the 'Citizen' soldiers, a martinet and unpopular with a high opinion of himself likened to Cromwell by 'Ike', General Eisenhower.
5. See 'Military Invasion'.
6. Admiral Louis Mountbatten's concept for a pipeline under the channel was devised and constructed by British scientists and engineers under the direction of Arthur Hartley chief Engineer of the Anglo-Iranian Oil Company. It became fully operational on 12th August, 1944. Along with the Mulberry Harbours, PLUTO was one of the most innovative and important engineering feats of the invasion.
7. See 'Gone to the Country'.
8. General Eisenhower, Supreme Commander of Operation Overlord, visited the thousands of troops being dispersed into the countryside around Exmoor and made a brief private visit to see General Gerow at Hestercombe. General Gerow commanded V Corps from July 1943 to the beginning of 1945, leading the first wave of troops onto Omaha Beach on D Day.
9. Chaplains came under the umbrella of the XIX SOS, working out of Hestercombe House and Norton Fitzwarren.
10. Anne Le Clere's son, Richard Spurway, remembered lines painted on a floor in a barn – for a game played by the Americans.

11. See 'Doubling Up – Education' and 'Gone to the Country'.
12. See 'Gone to the Country'.
13. Mr. Godber Ford did not say whether the bread he produced for the US was a National Loaf, or whether he had access to extra white flour for US consumption. See also 'Feeding the Nation'.
14. Camp not identified.
15. His wife said he knew the date of D-Day but this is unlikely as those who did were confined to quarters. He wrote that he realised that NAAFI orders were decreasing after the invasion of France and eventually his contract would cease.
16. See 'Raising a Laugh – Entertainment'.
17. Military 'dog tags' consist of two identifying discs, varying from one military service to another. Their purpose is to enable one to be left as identification of a serviceman and the other, in the case of a death, to be returned to the next of kin with his belongings. Losing one's dog tag was a minor disciplinary offence – possibly two days confined to base. Losing one in the theatre of war was more serious, for if found by the enemy it could be used fraudulently. Identity was everything.
18. John's War Record of 1944 states that he was part of 519 Ordnance (Heavy) Maintenance Company. The 3892 Truck Regiment would have been part of that but his company went off early as described to land on Omaha beach on D-Day.
19. Bournemouth.
20. 606th Graves Registration Company was an African-American company – See Appendix 4.
21. Tank Landing ships and there is a US naval film showing the loading of the vehicles, all completed in three hours.
22. A bad weather forecast gave General Eisenhower a nail-biting decision as to whether to abort and wait a month for the next good tides and better weather. In the event, all those loaded on ships and landing craft had to wait a day.
23. Young Private Sam Levitas a clerk-typist at Hestercombe, HQ of XIX Supply Services had seen General Montgomery's address to British Forces, showing the date for invasion as 5th June. See booklet 'Hestercombe at War'.
24. Omaha is the codename given to a five mile (eight km) stretch of beach that lies east of the Douve River estuary on the Normandy coast. It was one of D-Day's five invasion sites and provided the link between US and British forces landing respectively on the adjacent Utah and Gold beaches. The first wave comprised two divisions – the 1st and 29th. The former – also known as the 'Big Red One' after its distinctive shoulder flash – was a crack outfit; but the 29th was untested in battle. Planners believed they would be facing a motley group of Russian POWs co-opted into Wehrmacht service and 'volunteers' from various occupied countries. They were wrong. A few days before the landings, veterans

from the 352nd infantry division had been moved into forward positions. The Germans had also constructed multiple lines of mined beach obstacles. The result: landing craft and amphibious tanks could not get ashore. GIs jumped into deep water under withering fire, crawled 300 yds to a shingle bank and were quickly pinned down. Access inland was through five heavily defended gaps in bluffs that overlooked the beach. As the situation deteriorated, nine companies of US Rangers were diverted from another landing site and scaled the bluff at Omaha's eastern end. This breach in the German line allowed a unit of engineers to assault one of the other gaps using a Bangalore torpedo – a long steel tube packed with explosive. As GIs poured through, the German line fragmented. By late afternoon American forces had pushed a mile and a half inland. But many pockets of resistance remained. And when supply trucks began landing in the evening the beach was still under artillery fire. The assault cost the Americans some 5,000 casualties. The German defenders lost around 1,200.

16. PARTY TODAY, WORRY TOMORROW

'Well. We've been in the thick of it here you know.'
'Oh really – you've been in the thick of it?'
'Yes, a bomber came over and dropped a bomb on a hayrick.'

Reported conversation between Londoner, Mr. Rooksby visiting his evacuated wife and baby daughter, and their host [1]

At 02:41 on the morning of 7th May, 1945, in the French city of Reims, General Alfred Jodl, Chief-of-Staff of the German Armed Forces High Command, unconditionally surrendered all German forces to the Allies. Late at night on 8th May, three representatives of the German military forces signed the definitive text of unconditional surrender at Karlshorst, Berlin.

Earlier that day, speaking from 10 Downing Street, Prime Minister, Winston Churchill announced victory in Europe. 'We may allow ourselves a brief period of rejoicing; but let us not forget for a moment the toil and efforts that lie ahead.'

Despite this veiled reminder that Britain was still at war against Japan, there was no stopping spontaneous celebrations with street parties and massed crowds in London. The government immediately declared 8th and 9th May, 1945, a public holiday and Milverton school records that the school closed for those two days.

Evidently Milverton's party spirit was typically modest. For on 25th

May the parish council convened a 'special meeting at the Council School Milverton for the purpose of considering the payment of small expenses incurred in connection with V-E Day celebrations, 8th May, 1945'. Those present were Mr. A. G. F. King, Chairman, Rev. W. F. Glover, Messrs. E. C. Kick, W. G. Andrews, T. Baker, E. Redwood and H. Buller, Clerk. 'On the proposition of Mr. Kick, seconded by Mr. Baker it was unanimously resolved that a letter of appreciation and thanks be sent to Mr. J. Thomas of Milverton Court and his men for labour and the supply of fuel for the bonfire and celebrations held at Milverton Court. In accordance with the Ministry of Health Circular 80/45 of 30th April, 1945, it was proposed by Mr. Kick seconded by Mr. Redwood that three small amounts be paid to the following persons being expenses incurred in connection with V-E Day Celebrations, 5s. to the Portreeve[2] of Milverton for the cost of a telegram to H.M. the King, 5s. to the Town Crier of Milverton for announcing the Victory Celebrations, bonfire etc and 10s. to Mr. Cyril Edmonds, member of the Home Guard for getting together a firing squad for salute also supplying and fitting loud speaker for the King's speech and various other duties: It was unanimously resolved that a cheque be drawn on the council's account for £1 to cover these expenses.

On the proposition of Mr. Glover, seconded by Mr. Baker, it was resolved that a public meeting be called at the Victoria Rooms, Milverton on Monday, 4th June at 8 p.m. under the direction of the parish council and in co-operation with the Portreeve of Milverton for the purpose of deciding what form, if any, celebrations should take, on the occasion of a second[3] and final termination of hostilities.

The meeting had been well attended and a committee[4] was formed to carry out 'necessary arrangements and suggestions as to collecting funds for sports and teas for children and elderly people and various other purposes'.

On 5th June, the WI – that had done so much for Milverton's war effort – held its first meeting after VE Day at which those present sang the national anthem and Mrs. Glover read a patriotic thought for the month. Twenty members decided to celebrate with an outing by train to Weston-Super-Mare and have lunch at the British Restaurant.

As early as 22nd September, 1944, Ernest Bevin, the Minister of Labour and National service announced the demobilisation plans for those serving in the forces. Except for a few key positions where some were released early for post-war reconstruction, men and women in the forces were to be released according to their service number which that which reflected their age and months of service. But they were going to have to wait.

Six weeks later, on 18th June the slow release of 4.5 million service personnel began. After the initial joy of victory, there was now growing undercurrents of despair. Those men and women who had been demobbed returned to civilian life looking for work. Men came home to meet children they had never seen and enter into family life against a backdrop of continued austerity. It was a difficult time to adjust to 'civvy' street. Men were issued with a 'demob' suit, which – although of good quality – did not always fit. Homes too were in short supply, and, most important, so were the jobs.

It began dawning on women that they may have to give up their jobs to returning men. Having experienced an independent life earning their own money, many married women would once again have to return to home and hearth. Meanwhile on 19th April, 1945, the *Daily Mirror* reported that all married women in the armed forces with at least six months service could leave subject to operational need.

But whilst some were looking forward to picking up the threads of a normal life, some were worried. Two months earlier on 13th April the *Daily Mirror* had printed a headline 'Spinsters are afraid of peace … Spinsters who were taken out of their peace-time jobs by the Ministry of Labour and sent to war work – sometimes in other towns away from their homes – are beginning to fear the future. While wives and sweethearts are shouting for joy on Victory Day, thousands of scared spinsters will be trying to hide their faces.' It then reported letters from worried single women who feared they would not get their old jobs back. The article contacted employees about this problem. One said, 'If an older woman, aged thirty-eight to forty-eight, has taken care of her appearance and is cheerful and efficient, I would employ her. Older women are an asset in the retail trade if they look bright and cheerful.' Another retail employer commented, 'I have always found the public liked young pretty assistants. This was proved pre-war by the amount of commission young women earned when compared with commissions earned by older, staid assistants. If I am free to choose… I will certainly give preference to young live-wires with pretty faces and groomed hair.' The report ended, 'There will be many "war casualties" among older women who were sent to war.' It saw a problem ahead, as the Ministry of Labour had no special scheme for placing older women in employment. The *Mirror* hoped, however, that 'the Control of Engagement Order',[5] might help, as employers could only get labour through the exchanges and may not be able to only employ young women.

The WI meanwhile – incorrigible as ever – carried on in party mode. It announced, at its meeting on 25th June, that the Welcome Home Fund Committee has asked them to organise the 'Hoopla' at their fete on August Bank Holiday. Then on 27th August the WI announced that the Milverton Peace Celebration Committee had asked them, together with the wives of men serving on the committee, to arrange a tea on 15th September, for the children. At that meeting also, the Milverton Welcome Home Committee asked them to organise a working party for the Xmas Bazaar. By their meeting on 25th September, everything was going well with these plans, but it is worth noting that austerity was still biting and the tea hostess announced that she had no tea for their October meeting. Fortunately, Mrs. Deacon offered to give some.

Perhaps taking their cue from the WI, other local bodies continued organising celebrations throughout the summer and autumn.

The school reported that in July, Miss W. Mills had been recalled to London by Hornsey Authorities and Miss D. Jacoby by West Ham Authorities. On 27th July the newly introduced 11+ examination results announced that Margaret Lockyer, Joan Arthur, and Doreen Down would be going to Bishop Fox's School and Tom Cotterell to Huish's Grammar School. Evacuee Joan Leach from West Ham had passed the Joint Board Metropolitan Examination[6] and was going to Plaistow High School.

By this time nearly all evacuee children had returned home and those that had no home to go to became the responsibility of the County Council who supervised both their welfare and education.

Eventually, the war with Japan came to an end and V-J Day was celebrated on 2nd September. The School logs note – 'As the official Victory over Japan days came during the school summer holidays, the two days were granted on 3rd and 4th September.' Then on 5th November, 'the school remained closed as an extra "Victory" holiday.'

In the wake of final victory, celebrations were quickly harnessed to the reconstruction effort. On 15th September, Prime Minister, Clement Attlee, opened London's Thanksgiving Savings Week in Trafalgar Square. He asked the public to see victory as a beginning and to save all they could for the tasks of peace. He quoted a message from the King, 'We are now free to start on the tremendous task of reconstruction.' The target for Thanksgiving week was £125m. Included in the final total would have been £80 collected by the children at Milverton School. They had set a target of £50 which they had far exceeded.

The WI announced at a meeting on 6th November that the Milverton Thanksgiving Week Committee had asked them to organise a social on 10th November to raise funds. As there was no time to discuss this at a meeting they had gone ahead and booked the RAF Band. A month later at the AGM it was agreed that there should be a party on 26th January and that the 67 MU RAF band be engaged and if not available the Norton Convalescent Depot Band. On 1st January, 1946 a Lt. Cdr. Hayward showed part of a film of the bombing of London, but as the apparatus (presumably projector) broke down the Commander finished with a talk on the West Indies. The WI life continued as normal.

Thanks to the slow pace of demobilization the official victory celebrations only finally took place on 8th June, 1946 – ten months after final victory – when many more of the soldiers had returned. All

Darlingest

children were given a certificate from George VI: 'Today, as we celebrate victory, I send this personal message to you and all other boys and girls at school. For you have shared in the hardships and dangers of a total war and you have shared no less in the triumph of the allied Nations.

'I know you will always feel proud to belong to a country which was capable of such supreme effort; proud too, of parents and elder brothers and sisters who by their courage, endurance and enterprise brought victory. May these qualities be yours as you grow up and join in the common effort to establish among the nations of the world unity and peace.'

The *Somerset Gazette* recorded Taunton's celebrations on 14th June. There was a church service attended by the Mayor and other dignitaries and a march past of the Somerset Light Infantry ending with dancing in Vivary Park.

But whilst fear and danger may have gone – there was nothing but hard work ahead for all – including Milverton.

---

1. See 'Gone to the Country'.
2. Portreeve is an ancient name for the head official (mayor) of a market town. The Portreeve was elected by, and then chaired, meetings of the Court Leet. Courts Leet date from Anglo-Saxon times. They were part of a system introduced by the kings for managing their kingdom and for collecting everything due to the Crown. For administrative purposes England was divided into districts known by various names including 'Leets' and 'Hundreds' each under the control of a Baron or Lord. Trusted lords could be granted an additional right to deal with quality of life and criminal issues in their district through the establishment of a Court Leet. Courts Leet were maintained in Norman times and their role was formally defined in the Magna Carta. Law and order was maintained through the system of frankpledge. Free men declared an oath of loyalty to the King and pledged to be responsible for the behaviour of peasants in their hundred. They reported on this to meetings of the Court Leet. This was known as the 'View of Frankpledge' (i.e. roll-call of the pledges of the freemen). The Court Leet was also responsible for managing the market and for controlling standards of trade, food, drink and agriculture. They could try minor misdemeanours in their Hundred but serious crimes would be sent to the King's Justices. The

Court Leet was responsible for appointing several officials including an Ale Taster and the Town Crier.

The Milverton Court Leet has existed since Saxon times although, in common with all such Courts in England, its role has steadily diminished from the fourteenth century as other systems of administration evolved. By 1945 its role was largely ceremonial. It continues to meet today to maintain the ancient tradition – and they still taste ale!

In March 1945, the Portreeve was Frederick L. Jones, and the Town Crier – William King. The present Portreeve in 2016 is Lindsay Fortune, and Martyn Lee, Town Crier. (Lindsay Fortune)

3. Victory in the Far East.
4. This may have been what the WI refer to as Milverton Peace Celebrations Committee.
5. The Control of Engagement Order – effective for a year from October 1947 – ring fenced some essential industries, including mining and agriculture. Except for some exemptions it covered all men between 18-50 and women 18-40. Unemployed workers after this date would be allotted work through Labour Exchanges and with discretion, officials were empowered to divert some workers from un-reproductive jobs. It did not prevent workers from changing their jobs but they would have to go via the Labour Exchanges where they would be directed to essential work.
6. London 11+ exam rather than that set for Somerset children.

17. SILVER LININGS AND DARK CLOUDS

'From Stettin in the Baltic to Trieste in the Adriatic, an iron curtain has descended across the Continent.'

Winston Churchill

The only legislation dealing with post-war reform passed by the Coalition government, was the 1944 Education Act.[1] In 1945 R.A Butler[2] Minister of Education circulated a message 'We in the educational world are fortunate in having our new objective clear before us. The end of hostilities in Europe does not solve all our troubles or allow us to rest on our oars. It does, however, enable us to concentrate together more fully on the task which has absorbed an increasing amount of or attention during the later stages of the war – the construction of an educational system really worthy of our nation.

Whilst work on the legislation for the Education Act had been ongoing during the war years others in government had also been planning for the future.

'The Shape of things to come' was the title of a talk given to the Milverton WI on 4th November, 1941 at the Congregational schoolroom. Mr. Harris, the speaker, discussed the post-war planning of village homes and described many labour saving devices. For Milverton women still coping with a meagre electricity supply, candle light and outside lavatories, all this must have seemed a dream. But it was going to be many years before their dreams actually came true.

It is not surprising therefore, just two months later, at a debate on 6th January, 1942 the WI defeated the motion put forward – 'That the old fashioned home was more comfortable than the modern one'. Ever optimists – they held onto their dreams.

As early as 1942, William Beveridge[3] a Liberal Economist – eager to tackle what he described as the five "Giant Evils" in society: squalor, ignorance, want, idleness, and disease – chaired a committee that published a report on Social Insurance and allied services. It was the nucleus of the modern welfare state and was, of course, popular with the public. It proposed expanding National Insurance and laid the foundation for the National Health Service.

On 25th January, 1944, some five months before D-Day, Milverton WI announced that it would apply for ten tickets to attend a conference and exhibition on post-war planning of the countryside exhibition to be held in Taunton on 10th February.

A year later the end of war was in sight, and in January 1945 the WI was able to have its meetings once more in St. Michael's Rooms. But the WI's work was not done. Rationing would continue for some years and so would the Jam Preservation Society. The Society's premises, at Brendons a private residence in North Street, was no longer suitable. On 9th March they announced that two former Home Guard Huts had been procured with a long term loan of £50 from the SFWI.[4] and were placed alongside Thornwell by Jubilee Gardens. It was at the end of this meeting, they debated yet again 'That there should be equal pay for equal work'.[5]

Hard on the heels of the fall of Nazi Germany, came Britain's first general election in ten years. Winston Churchill had become Prime Minister in May 1940 and had led the nation to victory. But in July 1945 he faced defeat at the ballot box. The returning soldiers and the population at large wanted a new beginning and decided that a Labour government would provide it. Churchill's reputation however, as one of the world's greatest leaders remained unscathed.

The Coalition government had been aware of the problems likely to be faced in peacetime. Post-war austerity, the lack of housing, continuing rationing and lack of jobs cast giant shadows over the initial mood of joy. It was going to be some years before a British Prime Minister could tell the public that they'd 'never had it so good'.[7] But in some areas rapid progress was made. As early as 1942 the Coalition government discussed the problem of having to provide some 500,000 houses quickly at the end of hostilities. Between 1945 and 1950 1.2 million homes had been constructed of which 156,623 were the neat and clever module-designed 'pre-fab' houses.

The soldiers and evacuees had gone and Milverton, as elsewhere, settled down to welcome home their young men and women and mourn those who would never return. Difficult times were ahead and there was to be no lightening of the burden of producing food for the nation. Prisoners of War continued to work on the land awaiting repatriation, in some cases not leaving until 1947/8. And in a gesture of appreciation to the troops of the Dominion, the National Farmers' Union offered to host Dominion and overseas Prisoners of War waiting, perhaps six months before there was a ship available to take them home. No fewer than two men were to be allotted to each farm where they could work if they chose to do so.

The Women's Land Army was not stood down until 1950, and of course, some food rationing continued, until as late as 1954.

It would take until 1948 to set up the NHS, but to do so would require more trained staff. Expecting to be part of this were the young women, who had shown their worth and achieved much during the war. But university places for women were few compared with those for men.[8] But even before D-Day, the *Daily Telegraph* printed a letter from medical students in Cardiff on 27th March, 1944, complaining about the shortage of student places to train new doctors and the large number of women 'clamouring to become doctors'. Their argument being that the cost of training was the same for men as women, but women would not always be full-time doctors, whereas men would. 'It would be a bad investment.'

They were ahead of the times – 'We are not diehard anti-feminists.

We simply feel that... the people need more doctors to make an efficient new Health Service and that the woman doctor is not the quickest and, in fact, is the least economical medium to achieve the necessary numbers.'

Recruitment for doctors in the NHS today continues to be critical. Women doctors have throughout its existence played a major role in the NHS as today whether full or part time.

Whilst 1947 produced a huge 'baby boom', 60,000 applications for divorce were processed. 'Make do and Mend' might have devoured their pre-war clothes and many returning in uniform had no civilian clothes to wear. Clothes rationing continued until March 1950 even though, by then, Christian Dior, had, in 1947 produced his 'New Look' designs of tight waists and very full, long skirts. Glamour was what was being promoted, but how to achieve it?

The wedding of Princess – later Queen – Elizabeth to Prince Philip – was the first time elaborate embroidery and bead work was allowed, as displayed in her wedding dress. Then, a century after the Great Exhibition of 1851, the Festival of Britain in 1951 drew together from across the world the modern and futuristic designs in homes, in technology and science. With British innovative skills and the new workings of the welfare state British people moved forward to a better world than they had ever known. But was that true? Whilst Britain and Europe were adjusting to peace and reconstruction, dark clouds loomed from the Soviet Union. It had been gobbling up eastern and central European countries not unnoticed by Churchill who just nine months out of office on 7th March, 1946 at Westminster College, Fulton, Missouri in the presence of President Truman, warned of dark clouds coming from the Soviet Union: 'From Stettin in the Baltic to Trieste in the Adriatic, an iron curtain has descended across the Continent.' The consequence for Britain, Europe and the West was to prove very serious and difficult for the following 40 or more years.[9]

Milverton though, was a long way from these dark clouds, or was it? In July 1953, during the Cold War the Royal Observation Corps post at Chelston (Wellington) was moved to a site N of East Nynehead on

Oak Road. In April 1958 it was made into an underground monitoring post to watch and locate nuclear bursts and watch for nuclear fall-out and measure radiation. It remained in use in 1975 – marked on the 1995 map as 'reservoir covered'.[10]

Dark clouds or silver linings, Mr. Godber Ford changed tack. He sold the bakery and moved to a different kind of manufacture. At first his workforce made winceyette nightgowns and underwear for county council nursing homes and hospitals. Later they produced own brand of similar goods for Debenhams and Woolworths. His widow, Mrs. Sally Godber Ford said that her husband was extremely proud of his workforce throughout the war. They never flinched about hard work and, if a late order came in, they would just work on into the evening to get it done.

It is very difficult to imagine what would happen now if we were in the same position. Milverton people had no alternative but to accept strangers into their homes. Life had to go on as normally as possible. Our story would not have been told but for Mrs. Vickery. Not long widowed and caring for an elderly mother descending into dementia, she took in Nellie, her daughter and Miss Rattenbury with good grace and kindness. This attitude and dedication to the war effort shown by her and so many Milverton people, and the gratitude of the evacuees and others who found themselves here is still appreciated by those who return to visit many years later. The purpose of this book is to recognise those who lived here then and to offer thanks from those who enjoy life here now.

---

1. The 1944 Education Act provided free secondary education for all via a selection process to Grammar Schools, Secondary Modern or Technical Schools. Whilst successful, the system led to some children feeling stigmatised and in 1965 was superseded by the non-selective comprehensive system.
2. Robert Austen Butler, known as 'Rab' a Conservative in the Coalition Government became Minister of Education in 1941; Chancellor of the Exchequer

1951; Home Secretary 1957-62 and Foreign Secretary, 1963-64. He failed to become Leader of the Conservative Party.
3. See 'On the Fields'.
4. Somerset Federation of Women's Institutes.
5. See 'Doing Your Bit'.
6. In July 1957 Conservative PM Harold MacMillan made an upbeat speech to a Tory rally in Bedford marking 25 years of service of the local MP, in which he said: 'You will see a state of prosperity such as we have never had in my lifetime – nor indeed in the history of this country. Indeed let us be frank about it – most of our people have never had it so good.'
7. Though it was going to be some years before factories would be turning out affordable modern day appliances such as washing machines and refrigerators.
8. The irony was that the 1944 Education Act produced many more young women qualified to go to university in the 1950s who could not do so because there were so few places available and colleges remained single sex. It wasn't until the massive building of new universities in the 1960s that women and more young men could get a university place.
9. With threat of expansion of Communism there had, since 1948, been serious discussions about reconvening the Home Guard to act as a Home Defence Force where the police, unarmed, could not handle British Communist insurrection as well as to guard vulnerable strategic sites and defend against possible Soviet invasion. Winston Churchill, again Prime Minister in 1951 promoted the importance of this force and eventually The Home Guard Act 1951 was passed on 6th December, and enrolment commenced on 2nd April, 1952 though only 23,288 of the 170.000 needed, enlisted with a further 20,000 enrolled on a Reserve role in case of emergency. It was expensive to set up and run, especially as it had full-time officers. By 1955 it had been reformed to just having a Reserve Roll but even that was not enough and it was disbanded in July 1957. The Home Service Force, 1982-93 was established at the height of the Cold War, recruitment was open to ex-servicemen not able to join the Territorial Army. Their role would be to guard strategic points. It started to disband in 1992 as part of the peace process.
10. PRN 44674 – information on line Somerset Heritage Centre.

Darlingest

When Mr. Cann, the Head teacher for the North Harringay school children left, he wrote this poem for Ethel Jennings who lived next door in Sand Street. She had a cat of which he was fond. Ethel, in her early 90s, recited it to me and it makes a fitting end to this book.

>We once knew a cat
>>that lived next door
>With eyes of amber
>>and four white paws.
>She was sometimes a saint
>>and sometimes a sinner
>But she loved us most
>>when we'd rabbit for dinner.
>
>When back to old London
>>we go once more,
>We shall often think
>>of the cat next door
>And all the kind people
>>who gladdened our stay
>in Milverton village,
>>down Somerset way.

Appendix One: IN MEMORIAM
Devised by Clive Perry

BAILEY	HAROLD 35 10.7.1944	LANCE SERGEANT 4th Bn. Somerset Light Infantry – Banneville La Campagne War Cemetery. Killed during the battle for Caen.
CORNISH	ARTHUR ROBERT 31 3.8.1944	SERGEANT 5th Royal Tank Regiment – St Charles de Percy War Cemetery. During the afternoon of 3rd August the German 326th Division counter attacked and fierce fighting took place around Aunay sur Odon, where both the Queens Infantry and 5 RTR suffered heavy casualties. The 5th RTR was attacked by several Tiger Panther and Panzer Mk IV tanks and both 'A' and 'B' squadrons were nearly annihilated. (5 RTR war diary.)
FENTON	GEORGE GEOFFREY Unknown DOB 26.5.1944	LIEUTENANT COLONEL 85th Mountain Regiment Royal Artillery – Sangro River War Cemetery Italy. Officer commanding 3 batteries of 75mm pack howitzers. Carried on mules led by African Basuto tribe muleteers.

LING	THOMAS JOSEPH 33 04.04.1944	CORPORAL 2/7th Bn. Middlesex Regiment Cassino Memorial. The memorial is situated in the Cassino Cemetery with the names of those with no known grave. Husband of Daisy Harriet Ling of Milverton.
MAUNDERS	THOMAS VICTOR 20 14.07.1942	PILOT OFFICER Royal Air Force Milverton St Michaels Churchyard. Son of Charles and Hilda Maunders of Milverton. Co-pilot of Vickers Wellington mark IV, Z1341, call sign QT-L of 142 Squadron RAF Grimsby. On bombing mission to Duisberg lost engine power in bad weather and crashed in forced landing at Scole Road, Diss Norfolk. Only the rear gunner survived from a crew of five.
POOLE	ANTHONY ALBERT 31 12.07.1944	PRIVATE 4th Bn. Somerset Light Infantry – St Manvieu war cemetery, Cheux. Killed during the battle for Caen.
PERRY	PERCIVAL EDWARD 27 16.02.1942	ACTING STOKER PETTY OFFICER (Stoker on memorial) Royal Navy HMS *Sultan* (Singapore) Plymouth Naval Memorial . Unknown grave on land. At sea in convoy to Hong Kong to join MTB flotilla when the colony surrendered to Japanese so diverted

		to Singapore. Last seen the night before the surrender but not at muster the following morning at 6 a.m.
ROWEN	HERBERT 32 08.06.1944	PRIVATE 1st Bn. West Yorkshire Regiment . Imphal war cemetery. Killed in the last few days of the battle for Imphal.
SHARLAND	CECIL 25 15.06.1941	SERGEANT Royal Artillary – Milverton, St Michaels Churchyard.
WINTER	DOUGLAS 26 10.12.1941	MARINE Royal Navy HMS *Prince of Wales*. The wreck of HMS *Prince of Wales* lies upside down at a depth of 223 feet near Kuantan in the South China Sea. Sunk by Japanese 'Nell ' and 'Betty' bombers while supposedly out of range of land based aircraft.

Appendix Two: MILVERTON CIVIL DEFENCE including FIRST AID 1938–1945

ANDREWS	Mrs. M. C.	5/39
BEDFORD	Miss B. M.	12/41
BURTON	Mrs. E. M.	7/41
CHAPMAN	Miss E. M.	5/39
CORNISH	F. J.	5/39
DAY	Mrs. E. M.	10/41
DEACON	Mrs. W. J.	5/39
DYTE	Mrs. L.	5/39
ENGLAND	Mrs. A. H.	5/39
ENGLAND	Miss R.	9/40
FEARON	Mrs. O. C.	1/42
FENTON	Mrs. H. M.	3/41
FLOAT	Mrs. M.	7/41
FREMANTLE	Mrs. L.	5/39
HARDING	Miss B.	8/43
JACKSON	H.	9/39
JAMES	Mrs. D. E.	9/39
JENKS	G. A.	9/40
LAWRENCE	Miss O. M.	5/39
LEE	E.	5/39
LOGAN	Col. R. H.	7/39
MAUNDERS	A.T.	5/39
MILLER	Mrs. F. K.	5/39
MOBERLEY-BELL	E. E.	5/39
MORRIS	Miss M. B.	5/39

NURCOMBE	S. T.	5/39
NURCOMBE	Mrs. W. M.	5/39
PALFREY	Miss K. M.	1/42
PALMER	Mrs. G. N.	5/39
POPE	Miss C. F.	5/39
POTTER	Mrs. A. M.	8/43
PROCTER	Mrs. A. M.	3/41
RAFFILE	A. E.	6/39
SHARLAND	Miss P. E. R.	5/39
SINDERY	Mrs. L. A.	10/41
SMITH	Mrs. A. S.	7/41
SPURWAY	Mrs. O. R.	5/39
TREMBATH	Mrs. M.	5/39
TUCKER	E. G.	6/44
VICKERY	Mrs. F. E.	5/39
WESTON	Mrs. A.	5/39
WILLIAMS	Miss H. M.	5/39
WINTER	Mrs. C.	5/39

C/CD 1/5/2

RESCUE PARTY

BAKER T.	Warden	7/38
BENDING H. J.	Dep. Div. Warden	7/38
BUCKINGHAM D. G.	Warden	7/40
BENDING D. J.	Messenger	3/41
CHAPMAN E.	Warden	7/38
CHILCOTT A. L.	Warden	7/38-11.41
CRIDLAND G	Warden	11/38
CRIDLAND H	Messenger	4/41-10/42
HARVEY C. E.	Warden	7/38

Darlingest

HOLCOMBE C. C.	Messenger	8/42
KICK E. C.	Warden	11/40
LARWOOD D. C.	Warden	8/42-4/43
MAUNDERS C. V.	Warden	7/38
PALMER W. H.	Warden	11/38
PERRY E. W.	Warden	3/41
QUICK W.	Warden	7/38
REDWOOD A.	Warden	11/38
SEDGBEER H.	Deputy Head Warden	11/38
SHATTOCK R. G.	Warden	10/41
TUCKER A. C.	Messenger	3/44
WIMBUSH A.	Div. Warden	7/38

C/CD 1/5/1

Appendix Three: THE 2ND BATTALION, THE MIDDLESEX REGIMENT – BRITISH EXPEDITIONARY FORCE (B.E.F.)

The 3rd Division, of the BEF known sometimes as the 'Iron Division', was originally commanded by Maj. General B. l. Montgomery,[1] included the 1st, 2nd and 7th Battalions of Middlesex Regiment. They comprised of an HQ; an HQ Company plus four Machine Gun Companies all equipped with 12 Vickers .303 machine guns. It would have numbered 740 all ranks at full strength armed with 175 pistols, 559 rifles and 18 light machine guns. By 10th May, 1940 (see below) the Division was Lt. Gen. AF Brooke (Later Lord Alanbrooke) took command.[2]

Mobilised in early September 1939 and except for a small advanced party, the Battalion left Gosport for Southampton, where they sailed on S.S. *Maid of Orleans* disembarking at Cherbourg on 30th September. Companies 'A' and 'C' were attached to 9th Infantry Brigade. The Division was moved into Belgium to help stabilise the border which was suffering incursions from German aircraft abusing Belgian neutrality. In early December, HRH King George VI visited the troops and Christmas was peaceful. The turn of the year, however, brought severe frosts that made digging impossible. It was so cold that anti-freeze did not work bringing most transport to a halt. Throughout February and March the Battalion continued with training exercises or practising driving in convoys at night. The B.E.F.'s task was to hold the eastern end of the Maginot Line at Sedan along the Belgian frontier. The Battalion was, therefore, kept busy strengthening the line with as many fixed gun positions as possible.

The Battalion logs tell the story:

1940. MIDDLESEX REGIMENT LOGS: – FEB. 1940 WO 73 (NA)

GONDECOURT –	Capt. E Bazalgette *BEF
Belgium	listed amongst officers (*annotated lst
Feb 1940	reinforcement)
30th March	'Jumboland' invaded France
17.3.40	Capt. Bazalgette Leave in UK to 26.3.40
31.3.40	Capt. Bazalgette back from leave

10th May brought heavier than usual enemy air activity. The worsening situation was confirmed by a BBC news announcement at 7 a.m., that Holland had been invaded by the enemy and that the Belgian King, Leopold, had responded by appealing to the British and French governments for help. Immediately the Battalion prepared to move, ready for instructions. They proceeded to Louvain[4] in an attempt to stem the enemy advance and have time for a firm line to be in place to hold back the enemy. The 2nd Bn. Middlesex Regiment Diary describes how they drove through the night and crossed the Belgian border at 1710 hours on 11th May. It was noted that there was no enemy aircraft disturbance and that the population's reaction was indifferent to their presence. Their worries mounted when they saw the large numbers of Belgian soldiers and refugees moving west and blocking roads. Heavy bombing attacks were made on their positions but they sustained no casualties. RAF fighters saw off the enemy.

12th May	'C' Company in depth position in area EIKENBOECHE, covering L flank. The quiet of the night, earlier on, now continues. BNHQ established in 3 hours 1 mile west of Louvain.
13th May	Lt. Col. B.G. Horrocks* MC joined Bn from England and assumed command. He was due to assume command on 20th May but hearing the 'news' on 10th May had left for France at once and

	hitch-hiked up. Having passed through a number of higher formation H.Qs he had a far wider and clearer appreciation of the situation than anyone in the forward area.
LOUVAIN3 15th May	Reports were received that the French had suffered a major disaster in the area of CHARLEROI and the BEF were to withdraw.
DENDERLEUW 18th May	0800 Several cases of arrows being dug in the turf to point out our positions were discovered. This was a constant fifth column practice that had been recurring ever since the beginning of operations.
SYNGHEM 20th May	A strong point is being prepared in area WARCOING. All civilians will be turned out of the area now. Invalids will be allowed to stay, but a report made. All spies will be shot.
PETIT LANNOY 21st	A quiet day on the whole. Orders were made to make use of local food resources (supplies had been cut off). Cattle, pigs and poultry were plentiful. A corporal of 'B' Coy – having been ordered to obtain a cow for his Coy – went off into the fields and shot seven! During lst light the enemy attempted to bring up some mortars along a road close to the units in the WARCOING area. One section of 'B' Coy observed this and engaged and knocked out 4 mortar positions.
WATRELOOS 24th May	Heavy fire. Lt. Col. Horrocks4 watched operation from the church tower and while there was told he was needed at Div. HQ. At Div. H.Q. the Div. Commander Maj-Gen. B.L. Montgomery told him

26th May	that the enemy had broken through to Belgium and that the 2nd Middx were to extend so as to take over the position at present held by 1/7th Middx. Lt.Col Horrocks summoned to Div. HQ where he learnt that the BEF were cut off from its bases and in company with the French Army were, except for a small stretch of coastline, surrounded. Hence it had been decided to withdraw to the coast in stages.
ZUYDSCHOOTE 28th May	0700 In the early morning 3 Div Rescue parties appeared to take over the defence of the canal line – the following message was received from Maj. E. Bazalgette, command of 'C' Company. 'Belgian officer informs me King of Belgians has signed separate Armistice with Germany. Shall I blow bridge on my front?' Answer despatched. 'Yes.' This officer later took charge of a battery of Belgian 75 mm Field Guns, complete with horse transport – but no personnel. This was not, however, used.
ZUYDSCHOOTE 28th May	The owner of the farm in which Bn HQ was sited apparently bred fighting cocks and about a doz. of these were kept in sep. coops. The lighter side of war was produced by freeing the lot together amongst a lot of hens. Most cocks appeared terrified of the opposite sex. Ultimately a number of fights took place, but coaxing was continually interrupted by a number of enemy aircraft bombing POPERINGHE.
EIKHOEK 29th May	Lt. Col. Horrocks visited 'C' Coy which had been the canal bank into reserve, about 5370 and explained to all ranks the following embarkation to England.

FURNES 29th	'C' Coy FURNES and to the North, both in support of 7th Guards Bde. French tanks belonging to 2 D.L.M. were being abandoned and their crews did not appear at all willing to take any action. C & D Coys considerably hindered in completion of position by enemy sniping.

On 31st May, at 2030 hours the final withdrawal orders were received. The Battalion closed its HQ. The diary continues that, 'just after midnight, the enemy began systematically to shell the approaches to the beaches; the beaches themselves and the temporary embarkation piers'. Organised embarkation was impossible and it became 'every man for himself'.

1st June	Enemy started to shell beaches and all touch with Coys and platoons was lost. From then onwards the struggle of the evacuation resolved itself into individual exploits and incidents. Capt. Beach and 33 other ranks are missing and it is doubtful anything will ever be known of their fate. Capt. Willoughby was with him about 4 a.m. organising parties of 'C' Coy to wade out to boats, but Capt Beach went on down the beach at about 0900 hrs armed with a rifle and a bandolier of ammunition slung around his shoulder firing at every Germany aircraft in sight. It was reported that still later he was known to have got a party of men on to a boat, but some shells landed close by, causing a number of casualties, and he ordered only unwounded off the boat, loaded it with wounded and then left the boat himself. It is feared he eventually boarded a boat which received a direct hit from a dive-bombing attack.

Darlingest

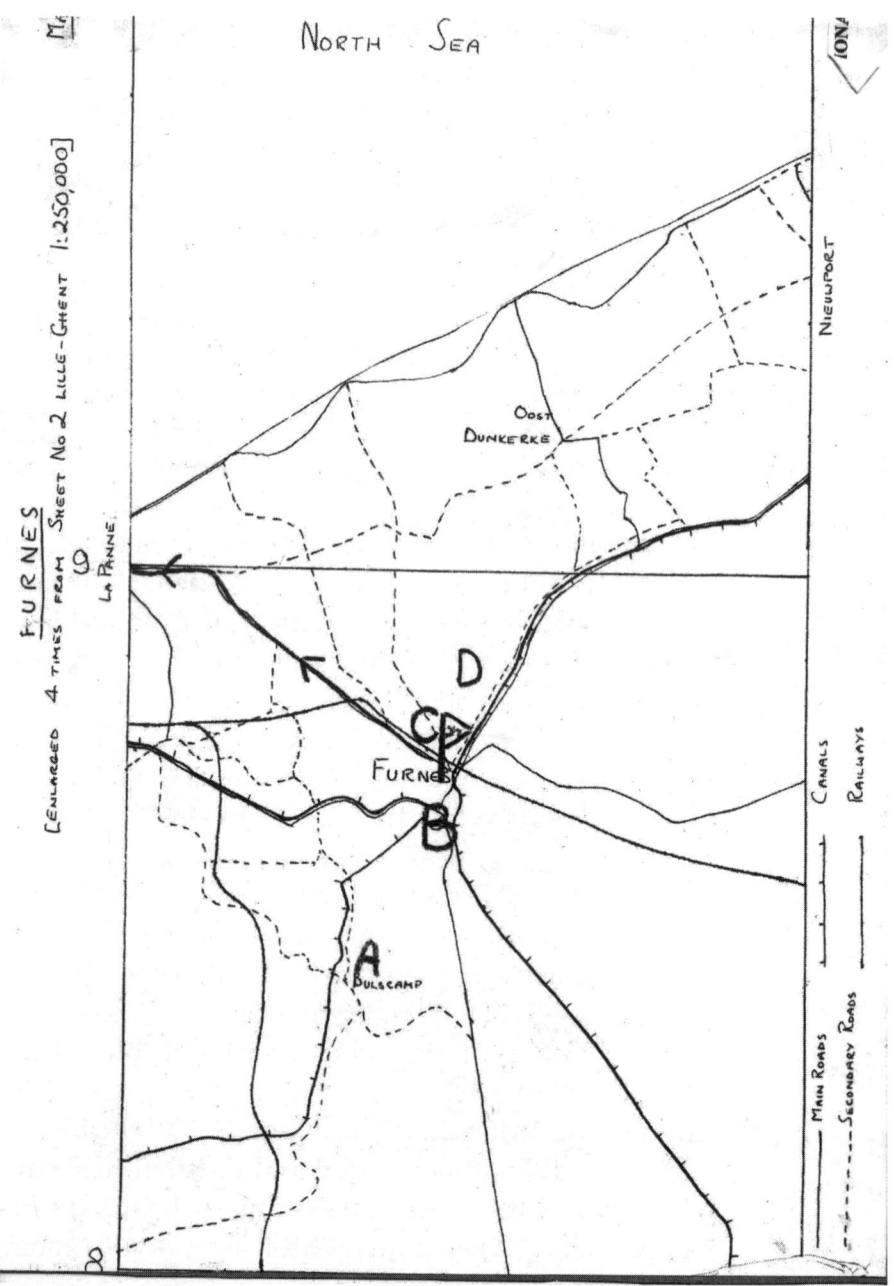

23. Map of Furnes, showing position of 'C' Coy. and its proximity to the beaches at Dunkirk.

One report by the Company Commander, described a man who was intent on taking back 1000 cigarettes he'd packed in biscuit tins! As it grew lighter, a witness reported his delight at seeing a group of Middlesex men – 'marching in good order under Major Reid and Capt. Bazalgette'. How and on which ship 'C' Company got back is not recorded, but the Battalion suffered 18 dead and 54 taken prisoner.

---

1. Maj. Gen. B.L. Montgomery then Divisional Commander – 'Monty' (1st Viscount Montgomery of Alamein, KG, GCB, DSO, PC, 1887-1986). As Field Marshal, he was to command the 8th Army at the battle of El Alamein and to lead it as it moved to Sicily and up the coast of Italy. In 1944, under the command of General Dwight Eisenhower he conducted the D-Day invasion of June 6th, 1944 and led the British and Canadian 21st Army group across Europe finally receiving the surrender of the German northern armies on 4th May, 1945.
2. Alan Francis Brooke (1st Viscount Alanbrooke, KG, GCB, OM, GCVO, DSO & Bar (1883 –1963) was Chief of the Imperial General Staff, during the Second World War, and was promoted to Field Marshal in 1944. He was the foremost military advisor to Winston Churchill, and went on to co-ordinate the British military role in the Allies' victory in 1945. He was forthright and not above criticism of Churchill as his diaries reveal.
3. The German forces were expected from the east and north-east side of Louvain, coming in from Diest and Tirlemont. The Belgian and British Forces in Herent were ordered to defend the line of the canal Louvain-Malines which was build up in the wintertime of 1939-1940 as a line of defence with blockhouses (bunkers) and trenches. Herent village was a bulwark with bunkers everywhere in the hope that it could be defended even as an island behind a German advance. In fact the order to withdraw came very soon and the village Herent was not used for combat. (Dr.Luc Vanderweyer, National Archives of Belgium)
4. Col. Brian Horrocks 'Jorrocks' (Later Lieutenant General Sir Brian Gwynne Horrocks, KCB, KBE, DSO, MC, 1895 – 1985) took command. In the 1950-60s he was to become a prominent television personality presenting a series of programmes about the major battles of World War II.)

Information online at WW2 Talk forum – 2nd Bn. Middlesex Regiment in the BEF.
Logs – WO73 – National Archives.

Appendix Four – 3892 QTR. TRUCK COMPANY AND THE BATTLE OF THE BULGE

Chapter 15 describes in detail the experiences of 3892 Qtr. Truck Company running up to D-Day; D-Day itself and to 10th June. For those wishing to know what happened next…

John Kiacz's diary continues:

> On 25 July we moved about ½ mile SW of Balleroy. On 3 August we moved to Torigny-Sur-Vire, and on 12 August moved to Annebecq.
>
> On 17 August we moved to Germain de Tellevende for 3 days from where we moved to Sees.
>
> On 28 August we moved to Gif and 2 days later we moved to St Denis, just outside of Paris.
>
> On 31 August we moved one mile W of Frenonville (sic) for 2 more days and then to Montgobert for another 2 days.
>
> On 4 September we moved 1 mile S of Rozy and on the 6th of September to 1 mile SE of Tournes.
>
> On September 10th we left France and moved 1 mile SE of Palisuel, Belgium.
>
> On 11 September we moved to Bastogne which later became a stronghold of the enemy forces on their noted breakthrough of December 18, 1944.
>
> On 15 September we again moved to a new country and bivouacked ½ mile N of Goedingen, Luxembourg.
>
> On the 4th of October we moved back into Belgium and bivouacked 1½ miles SW of Bullingen.
>
> The 21st of November saw us move into the woods about 2

miles SE of Eupen where we made our homes for the winter.

It was in these woods that during the enemy breakthrough we were alerted and moved into the city of Eupen to defend it. Parties were organized to search all the houses for paratroopers that had been dropped behind our lines. Positions were set up and it was close to our area that the enemy was stopped at the Eupen-Malmedy road. '

The Eupen-Malmedy region was an area of intense activity leading to the Battle of the Bulge (16th December, 1944 – 25th January, 1945) – so named because of the inward bulge it made in the American front line – was a last ditch German offensive through the Ardennes Forest in Belgium. The aim was to split British and American forces by seizing the port of Antwerp. Planned in total secrecy, the Germans launched a massive surprise attack on 16th December involving some 400,000 men, 1,200 tanks, and 4,000 heavy guns. Since D-Day the Allies had become over reliant on air superiority to keep German forces on the defensive. But poor weather had grounded British and American aircraft. The initial assault nearly overwhelmed Allied units on the ground. The Germans sowed further confusion by infiltrating English speaking troops dressed in American uniforms behind Allied lines. But stubborn American resistance around Eisenborn Ridge at the northern end of the 'bulge' and around the village of Bastogne to the south derailed the Germans' schedule. In sub-zero temperatures GIs of the famed 101st Airborne Division held out against fierce attacks even after Bastogne was surrounded. On 22nd December, the Germans presented an ultimatum: surrender or be annihilated by heavy artillery. Brigadier-General Anthony C. MacCauliffe the ranking officer on the ground gave a terse reply: 'Nuts!' The German colour party had no idea what this meant. An American corporal who spoke German translated it as 'Du kannst zum Teufel gehen!' ('You can go to the Devil!') On reflection the German officer commanding General von Luettwitz decided to spare Bastogne and press on with his prime objectives. In early January the weather broke and Allied air attacks soon put paid to the German advance. Ultimately they lost between 67,000 – 125,000 men killed, wounded or missing. But the price of Allied victory was high. The Americans sustained 89,000 casualties including 19,000 killed. The Bulge turned out to be the largest and bloodiest battle fought by US forces in World War Two.

John does not report on his experiences between September and November, nor mentions the dramas of December, as he was assigned elsewhere. But his son, Bruce re-reading his father's letters, says that on 14th December he was away from his company 'billeted "inside"' (e.g. a building vs. tent). However the letter is postmarked with the APO of the 3892nd and also has a 3892 return address. On 31st January he writes, 'I am still with the same TD outfit living in the same place' but the return address is now HQ Co, 23 TD GP.Bruce comments, 'This sounds more like a real outfit – like the 23rd Tank Destroyer Group[1] – which would have an HQ company.' Letters of 27th February and 12th March also have return addresses of the 23rd TD GP, but he writes next to the date 'Belgium' and also mentions that he is driving a Jeep, not a truck. So, where do we place him in December? Bruce remembers his father saying that somewhere between Eupen and Bastogne his truck was cut off from the American lines and he spent a week in the woods avoiding German patrols. When he realized he was stranded, he burned his truck and took what little supplies he had along with a frozen tarp for protection from the weather. Scared and cold, he was trying to untie a knot in a rope that was attached to the tarp. Frustrated, he used his teeth to pull at the frozen knot, and promptly yanked out his two front teeth. For the rest of his life he wore a silver bridge with porcelain teeth to replace those left in the Belgian woods. Bruce continues, 'Was he with his unit during the breakthrough (unlikely based on the Journal entries)? Was he driving a truck on his initial detached service with the 23rd TD? If the story about getting separated and "behind the lines" is accurate, was this during December with the 3892nd or some later winter date with the 23rd TD?' We can't verify this because, as mentioned, John's records were destroyed. But Bruce thinks that if he was driving a Jeep it was to ferry officers about.

Vincent, however, did make a record of his experiences on these dreadful days. Joe, his son, says, 'I do know from talking to Dad what happened as he related those stories from that period many times, except one. That one was difficult and he only spoke of it once. For the sake of the story I will now refer to him as Corporal Tuminello.

'Sometime On the night of 16th December or the morning of the 17th non-coms like Corporal Tuminello (sergeants, corporals, short for non-commissioned officer) were assembled in a hut trying to figure out what was going on as not an officer was to be found. (They probably were called to assemble somewhere else for a briefing, I don't know.) Suddenly they heard the sound of a buzz bomb circling down and then a huge blast which sent the heavy wooden door of their hut flying shut with such a force that anyone standing in its way might have been killed. It was in that period when non-coms were trying to figure out what to do that Lt Parsons' tattered driver shows up reporting that Lt. Parsons left him with a Jeep outside of Bullingen. While waiting for Parsons to return, he spotted infantry soldiers approaching which he soon recognized as being German. Slowly sliding down in the seat he crawled away like a snake for over 300 yards. Looking back he saw the Jeep now ablaze surrounded by Germans.

'Until they finally received orders to transport infantry, nobody knew what was up. Riding in the cab with Tuminello was a lieutenant (from possibly the 29th division if I remember correctly). Their conversation went like this. The lieutenant remarks he does not really know where he is going or what his objective is, they are moving and he has practically no ammunition. Corporal Tuminello gave the lieutenant several magazines of his ammunition and the Bazooka which was kept behind the seat saying, "You are going to need this more than I do." They never saw each other again.

'Sometime between the 19th and 23rd events took place that no one wanted to record especially since the likelihood of being captured was real. I do know that Captain Abel was ordered to destroy all his vehicles at one point, an order which he disobeyed and which caused him to be relieved of command after the action was over. This, despite the fact that the 3892's trucks were repeatedly pressed into badly needed duty.

'One of the reasons why there were so few trucks was that on 17th December, some had been diverted to evacuate the 44th Evacuation Hospital, just a few miles from Eupen. They managed to remove 175 patients in the wards. This hospital had been involved in dealing with the remains of the 'Malmedy Massacre' of 17th December in which 84 American POWs were brutally treated and shot by the Kampfgruppe Peiper (part of the 1st SS Panzer Division) at the crossroads by Bangrez and Malmedy. This massacre was classified as a war crime and was tried as such. Whilst Vincent was not in the area at that time the 606th Graves Registration[2] Company had to later deal with the gruesome task of handling the frozen bodies of those killed. Joe Tuminello says, 'Some of the men from the 3892 did take part in the retrieval of the bodies of those massacred at Malmedy as related to me in 1994 by one of the other men from the unit who was from Chicago.'

Joe's account of his Dad's story continues – 'On 17th December German paratroopers did land near by their encampment near Eupen which had received enemy artillery fire and bombing by aircraft. Now they were living in foxholes, with rags wrapped around their boots to stay warm in the extreme cold and snow due to the lack of winter boots. Four 50 calibre machine guns were removed from the trucks, mounted on tripods and placed one at each of the corners of their bivouac area. Corporal Tuminello, who was 28 years old at the time, and an 18-year-old soldier named Private Perry from Texas, manned one.[3] (The story that follows, I only ever heard once, and it pained him so much to tell me I could never ask again. My mother made him tell me. I don't know why.)

Lying in wait in for a possible attack, Corporal Tuminello and Private Perry fight off the bitter cold. Rags are wrapped thick around their leggings and army shoes. While the troops in Paris were well equipped for winter, things like overshoes never got to this new front line. A group of about 30 German Paratroopers were spotted walking directly towards them. Corporal Tuminello held his fire. When the first man was but a few yards way he opened up. The Germans had walked right into their well concealed gun emplacement. A fifty calibre machine gun fires about 600 rounds a minute. They fired for a about minute. Private Perry feeding the belt, Tuminello sweeping the gun back and forth, trees being used for cover by the enemy were cut in half. The furious sound of gun fire from the 50 calibre and the seemingly feeble return fire from the enemy alerted the entire Encampment. When the firing ceased all that could heard were the moans of the dying. A patrol was hastily assembled to reconnoitre the machine gun outpost on the perimeter. Medics were called and they soon discovered that some of the dead German paratroops were mere young boys.'

This story is poignant and it could be what John Kiacz was referring to one Thanksgiving when, for the first and only time he spoke to the family gathered about him and asked for their forgiveness. His son, said that his father described being in a wood where they knew there were a lot of German soldiers. He heard noises and fired his weapon. The next day he was told that they had shot children!

In researching this book I contacted the Belgian National Archives to check this account. Dr. Luc Vanderweyer told me that it was not true – at least they were not Belgian children. Bruce Kiacz thinks that his father was out on patrol, and not part of this incident. He might have said 'we' shot them rather than 'he himself'. But obviously he was burdened by this event for the rest of his life.

On 18th December, Vincent and his group (not John) were ordered to Stavelot to clear a petrol store. Of the 52 trucks assigned, only two squads – his, and Corporal Broadwater's – comprising just eight trucks – arrived. They were greeted by Captain Wilson of the 606th Graves Registration group, which was, as mentioned earlier, an African-American company who loaded the trucks. It took them three trips. When they returned to base they were ordered back to their company. Vincent intended to return to evacuate Captain Wilson and his men. Corporal Broadwater's squad did not want to go, but Vincent insisted. They managed the evacuation but roads were blocked and being swept for mines. They were ordered to report to Lt. Colonel Koosa at 97th Battalion Command Post, who asked why so few trucks had got through.

Joe recalls, 'The chaos continued, there were burned-out vehicles everywhere and yet they found themselves hauling soldiers, gas and ammunition from areas being over-run. Added to the uncertainty was the fact that Germans were masquerading as Americans. As Tuminello would proudly tell Joe DiMaggio when he met him in Remo's barber shop in San Francisco long after the war ended…"Hey Joe, if someone didn't know who you were in the Ardennes, he got it!" GI's were constantly testing each other to be sure they were the genuine article.

'And that's what happened when the American pilot was shot down strafing a train he picked as a target of opportunity. Being hit by AA fire he was told by his wingman to climb to 5000 feet and bail out, which he did. Upon landing he made his way to a barn where he was hidden by an old Belgian woman. When she saw American trucks lumbering down the road she ran out shouting "American Aviator, American Aviator…". That's when the trucks stopped and Cpl. Tuminello asked the sergeant from the 606th what he wanted to do, as he was top ranking man. The Sarge said "You're the combat man, you go in and see who he is, we will cover you". When Tuminello entered the barn, carbine at the ready, the pilot leapt from hiding and said "boy am I glad to see you…" But Tuminello took no chances. "Keep those hands up….now who does Joe DiMaggio play for?" After further questioning the pilot was soon recognized as American and was taken to transport that got him back to his unit. He was such a nice fellow from the Midwest that Tuminello wished he could have stayed in contact with.

'During the weeks of this engagement they did road block duty as well. Cpl Tuminello was stopping traffic seemingly by himself with his carbine when he stopped a Jeep with a colonel, a driver and two aides in it. Upon giving the proper password the colonel said. "If we were Jerries you'd be dead corporal." "That's true colonel," he replied, "but take a look to your left." There the colonel saw the muzzle of a 50 calibre machine gun trained on him. "Oh and by the way, colonel, there's another one just around the bend waiting for you." The colonel's eyebrows raised and he then gave a salute to the Corporal and said, "Carry on soldier!"

'One night during the Bulge the muffled call of a soldier's name could be heard in the frigid still night air. "Corporal Tuminello, Corporal Tuminello"…before he could answer Sergeant Rinaldi came to his foxhole, grabbed him by the arm and said…"Don't answer, they want you to take out another patrol…let someone else do it this time." Night Patrols were now truly risky business with the possibility of being shot by friend or foe. Tensions were high and all sentries were placed in pairs back to back.

'Crossing the Rhine and entering Germany they saw German soldiers who had deserted their units hung from lamp posts by the retreating SS. They were also surprised to see that some German civilians had newly placed photos of relatives in American uniforms on their walls. However there was the ever present fear of booby traps and snipers.

'Once in Czechoslovakia they liberated several concentration camps. In the 1990s a Holocaust survivor group awarded dad and some other men a medal for participation in this action. I do not know how they found him, but they did.'

We pick up John's diary again on 28th February, 1945. 'We left Eupen and moved to Hofen, Germany. In Hofen we occupied houses, or facsimiles thereof, for the first time since invading the continent. It was a very welcome change for all after eight months of living in tents, under trucks, and crudely constructed cabins.

'On 10th March we left Hofen and arrived at Satzvey where we were billeted in a bank and a cafe. March 23rd we moved to Sinzig and stayed for three days. On the 26th we moved to Neuwied. One week later, on 30th March, 1945, we moved to Wetzlar where we occupied a German Army Camp where there were numerous cases of foodstuffs, barrels of wine and beer, all of which were "liberated" by us. Our stay here was very short and the next morning we moved to Allendorf where we were billeted in a camp the Germans used to house slave labourers.

On the 2nd April we moved to Brundenson.⁴ Germany where on the 2nd day we were alerted for a possible breakthrough by enemy troops. There were 10,000 SS Troops located about 4 kilometers away from us. A platoon of medium tanks moved into the rear of our CP where they set up positions and opened fire on the enemy. Two days later the SS Troops including one SS General surrendered to our forces in the area. On April 10, we moved to Uder, Germany for 2 days and on 12 April we moved to Allmenhausen. 3 days later we moved to Grossjena, Germany. On the 30th of April we moved to Pressath, Germany and then on the day before VE day we moved to Pilsen, Czechoslovakia.'

Joe Tuminello, reading John Kiacz's synopsis says that after John Kiacz rejoined the 3892 in March 1945 their 'experiences are parallel'. It is likely that they were together in Pilsen on VE Day. His son has said 'I hope Dad is not cross with me, wherever he is, for telling you his horribly tragic story. Yes they were the enemy. As he said it was kill or be killed. After the war ended they were just people. He liked people. It was a heavy burden for a truck driver from Brooklyn.'

John Kiasc returned to his warehouse job. He died in 2001 aged 83 and is buried in the Ohio Western Reserve National Cemetery, but, his son believes he suffered from PTSD from his experiences.

John's older brother, Steve C. Kiacz, also played his part. Having enlisted first, he joined the Army Air Force as a bombardier attached to the 398th Bomb Group, 601st Squadron, flying B-17's from Nuthampstead, Hertfordshire. Unlike John, Steve, who as an officer, remained with the U.S. Air Force for his entire life until he retired and passed away in 2011.

Vincent Tuminello relived his experiences aboard a Liberty Boat in San Francisco Bay, celebrating the 60th anniversary of VE day in 2005. His son Joe writes ' But he did not forget Milverton. In June 1994 on a cruise from New York to Southampton and Cherbourg aboard the QE2 to celebrate 50th anniversary of D-Day landings, he took time to return to Milverton. He met with Bill Stone and his daughter Shirley. He also told how he visited 'an attic above a carriage house located behind a Pub'⁵ where Tuminello was billeted with seven other men and met a resident who had been a boy aged ten at the time. The man, then in his 60s remembered 'how children were given rides in Jeeps when seen walking along the roads and given candies. This unknown resident said, "When our troops were here they never did that but you Yanks could use a Jeep as your personal car." ' His friend Dwight Fortier sent regular food parcels to Mrs. Stone. In the mid-1970s, Mrs, Stone's widowed daughter and two sons visited him in the US where Vincent, 'Jim', joined them. Even later she met Vincent again when he'd moved to California to be with his son. He died on 30th March, 2005 and is buried in the Sonoma Brooklyn Veterans' Cemetery, California. Joe adds that, 'After his death in the late 1980s the son of Private Perry would take the time to write Tuminello informing him of his father's passing and noting that he said many times, if it were not for Cpl. Tuminello "I would not have made it."

'Vincent Tuminello received five bronze campaign stars one each for the major battles he was in. They are Normandy invasion, Argentan Felice Gap, Ardennes, crossing the Rhine and I think the battle for Germany would be the last. For emptying the gas dump under enemy fire and evacuating Captain Wilson and his men the entire 3892 was awarded the meritorious service medal, a unit citation, even though only 8 trucks and 16 men were involved in the actual action. I believe it was under the recommendation of Lt. Colonel Koosa. He also received the Indian arrowhead for being part of the first assault on Omaha beach June 6-7.'

As for John's medals, Bruce says 'Back in 1987, Dad applied for the service ribbons he was entitled to (don't know if he ever originally received them or they were lost). The list included:

Good Conduct Medal
European-African-Middle Eastern Campaign Medal
WWII Victory Medal
Army of Occupation Medal with German Clasp
Driver and Mechanics Badge with Driver "W" Bar
Marksman Badge w/Rifle and Carbine

Darlingest

Final note on the list is the following remark "A Silver Service Star is awarded in lieu of five Bronze Service Stars. We are unable to verify entitlement to any additional awards from available records" – which makes sense since his records were lost in the 1973 fire at the National Archives and Records Administration.

So this is the story of two non-combatant soldiers who landed on Omaha beach on the first day of the greatest invasion force ever, and who then ended up in the thick of one of the nastiest battles involving American troops. They were truck drivers working out of the Norton Fitzwarren Supply Depot where they commuted daily from their billets in Milverton.

---

1. John Kiacz was, as described above, attached to the 23rd Tank Destroyer Group Unit. It had been activated at Camp Hood, Texas, on 12th June, 1943, and attached to XXIII Corps on 18th February, 1944. They sailed from Boston on 11th October, 1944, and arrived in England on 18th October, 1944. And a few days later shipped to France, landing on 21st October, 1944. The unit moved into Belgium on 26th November, 1944, and then into Germany on 10th March, 1945. The dates seem to match John's detached service and location.
2. But what of the African American soldiers? Whilst it is sad that it has not been possible to properly account for the deployment of these soldiers in Milverton – the role of African-American soldiers in WW2 should not be underplayed. Some African-American soldiers became part of the "red ball express" responsible for getting supplies from the beaches and moving them nearer to the front lines. While technically not combat units they would have driven through fire and witnessed at first hand the horrors of war. The 606th QM Graves Registration Company, too had a tough job to do under dangerous circumstances as recalled by Vincent Tuminello and his group. They had the very unpleasant and distressing task of recovering the frozen bodies of their comrades killed in the Melmedy massacre. Later, once a foothold had been established black vehicle maintenance groups were able to repair vehicles in situ rather than in the UK.
3. Corporal Tuminello's son, Joe, writes, 'To Corporal Tuminello, many of the men in his company were boys.' Remember they called him "Pops". 10 years is a big difference in age to an 18-year-old. This is significant because when one thinks about it the German paratroopers who were possibly 15 years old, and we consider children too young for war, were closer to Private Perry's age than

his. Joe continues – 'I met the crew of LST 286 at a reunion. They took Vincent and John to Omaha beach. Amongst them were sailors like Seaman Don Hunt who had just turned 16 at the time of the invasion. He was a big fellow who had lied about his age to enlist.' Joe then says, but I don't think this is relevant as it is obvious – 'When one gets up in age that tragic waste of life becomes apparent. Unfortunately it was what had to be done at the time. John Kiacz's son should not worry that his dad shot at "children" in the Eupen woods.'

When 'M' Coy 513th Quartermaster Truck Regiment was set up the list of personnel includes Sam Horowitz. Joe Tuminello says that he 'was busted from master sergeant to private. He had been the company cook. Tuminello said it was because Horowitz was Jewish. Horowitz was from Tuminello's neighbourhood before the war. They did not know each other then. At the beginning of the battle Horowitz was on guard duty on a road by himself with only a carbine and did make a tank halt! Yes, it was American. Horowitz also captured a German soldier who he really wanted to kill for obvious reasons but did not. Horowitz and Tuminello were best friends during and after the war. As was Sgt. Jimmy Rinaldi, who was a bear size of a man from New Jersey. While stateside during training then Pvt. Rinaldi tore the shirt off a mess sergeant who was trying to force him to eat some food he did not like. Highly respected by the men and capable instead of being punished he was promoted to Sergeant shortly after the incident. Someone in command thought they might need a man like this in charge where they were going.

4. It has not been possible to locate Brundenson. It might have been the name of a house or estate.
5. This could be the 'Skittle alley' above The George which is where some of the Middlesex Regiment had been billeted, John Kiacz does not mention living in such a place.

Appendix Five – US QUARTERMASTER CORPS

As described in Chapter 15 – many of the American soldiers based in Milverton and the surrounding area – worked out of the Storage Depot at Norton Fitzwarren. It seems fitting to give a brief history of the Quartermaster Corps and its extraordinary achievement in supplying its vast military forces overseas. Whilst, Vincent Tuminello and John Kiacz transported gasoline, ammunition and occasionally food ration packs as well as a variety of other items, it is the supply of food that is relevant to Milverton's story. The Quartermaster Corps was just part of those deployed in SOS (Supply of Services) for which the depot at Norton Fitzwarren was integral. The official history – from which I draw this information – took 16 years to complete, is in 4 volumes, the fourth of which can be read on-line –

UNITED STATES ARMY IN WORLD WAR II
The Technical Services
THE QUARTERMASTER CORPS:
OPERATIONS IN THE WAR
AGAINST GERMANY
by William F. Ross and Charles F. Romanus

The Quartermaster Department was set up in 1775 as a logistical supply service for the army. During the Civil War it supplied clothing, animals and equipment and by 1862, its duties extended to looking after the dead and war graves. As early as 1903 it began using motorised transportation. In 1912, when it became the Quartermaster Corps, it added to its list, the supply of sustenance – food rations. When the US entered the First World War the corps had, for the first time, to supply its military forces overseas. It took on the role of handling ports and unloading supplies in order to better control the distribution of supplies. It also provided laundry and bathing facilities. The experience gained was invaluable when it came to planning for Operation 'Overlord'.

By then QMC's main function was to supply food and clothing and other supplies, but not ammunition. As before, it was also responsible for laundry, bathing and burial facilities and added the supply of parachutes and their maintenance to its list. And – applicable to John Kiascz and Vincent Tuminello's experience – Norton Fitzwarren depot also handled chemicals for waterproofing and training.

Chapter 15 also mentioned that there were two HQs. The main one, though numerically smaller, was based in London. It comprised 72 officers, 86 enlisted men and 124 British civilians. The other HQ was based in Cheltenham with 84 officers, 320 enlisted men and 69 British civilians. All in all, by at the end of 1943 there was a total Quartermaster strength of 30,000 which rose by June 1944 to 72,000. The proportion of Quartermaster to military personnel was around 4.5 per cent.

There were also two main zones where supplies were unloaded. Zone I – including the ports of Barry, Bristol and London which could unload 20 US ships a month or Liverpool and Zone II – able to handle 35 US ships a month. Storage depots all over the country were utilised including vacated warehouses, in particular breweries and tobacco stores, where demand for the products had dwindled.

At that time, telephone lines were limited, and no computers or mobile phones, so communication between the London and Cheltenham HQs – some 90 miles apart – relied on couriers and the frequent exchange off staff carrying messages back and forth. However difficult this system was it was also seen to be a useful training exercise for communicating later on when in the war zone.

The organisation was therefore massive and complex and relied on close co-operation between the British and American military. The Americans were able to select the sites and use British ports, roads and railways for transhipment of supplies.[1] U.S. procurement had to follow an agreed format but Ross and Romanus state that 'British were always willing to make exceptions for occasional small emergency purchases'.

In order to avoid unnecessary construction, depots were to be set up on existing sites where possible and services supplied as near as possible to troop concentrations. Laundry and bread baking were to be provided locally by the British, if resources allowed.

Stores would be located near the areas with the highest troop concentration with two general central stock holding areas, one in Northern Ireland and the other in the Midlands. Ross and Romanus also state that 'The depots were to maintain 100,000 men' with a 30-day supply. In order to comply, it was therefore necessary for Quartermaster personnel, supporting staff and supplies to be in place at least two weeks before the arrival of combat troops.

When American troops joined Operation 'Torch' in North Africa they were under British command. Accordingly they ate British rations – as did some American troops in Britain before their own ration supplies were available. Whilst balanced nutritionally there were some items that the Americans were not used to or disliked. The British agreed compromises on some supplies – bread was one of the items in contention. Until American baking facilities were in place the British government agreed not only to bake but also to supply bread. The report states 'They produced one type of bread only: the national wheat meal loaf. This was a graham[2] type of bread of very high nutritional value. It had been developed to permit the fullest use of local grains.' The US Army – perhaps reluctantly – forwent its supplies of white flour to save on shipping space and accepted the national loaf. Controlling supplies of bread flour to be used by British bakers for US bread would be a problem, so it was agreed that white flour be handed to the British government to be mixed with ordinary flour, whilst the Ministry of Food agreed to supply white flour for bread to be supplied to American forces outside the UK.

Because the Americans disliked the bread, and ate so little, their diet was compromised. The answer was to remove the oats and barley included in the British flour mix. Meanwhile, US Quartermaster scientists came up with a formula with added fat and sugar that made a more palatable loaf. What part Mr. Godber Ford played in all this, we don't know. But by late 1943, when John Kiazc and Vincent Tuminello arrived in Milverton, there were a considerable number of American bakeries in the UK. American bakers were brought over here with their own men but they used local equipment and also trained up local staff.

Mrs. Stone's daughter, Shirley Davies, remembers how American troops tossed sweets to children as they drove off to the depot. The children had a meagre weekly allowance as sweets were severely rationed in Britain and prized impromptu gifts. But American 'Candy' sold through post exchanges was causing a headache for suppliers. Once again, to reduce shipping loads, the British offered to supply locally produced candy if the Americans reduced the allowance to match, but not exceed the British. This would mean just two chocolate bars and one pack of chewing gum or candy roll per week. This did not go down well and the American authorities asked for an increase of three more bars per week. Negotiations began between the British and the QM, the suppliers, who were prepared to import the difference. This was never resolved, but the problem 'went away' once the American troops were in France and out of British jurisdiction.

Such was the goodwill between the American and British that American GIs joined British Tommies in 'Dig for Victory' gardening activities. On 11th August, 1942 an Agricultural Branch was established to liaise with the Ministry of Agriculture to provide seed and equipment. Produce was consumed locally or sold on to NAAFI and any profits awarded to funds for troops. The turnover of troops made precise accounting impossible because sometimes American troops harvested crops planted by British troops, but nearly 8,000 acres was planted in 1942, and 15,000 in 1943. As air force personnel tended to be more static, they were able to produce more food. Ross and Romanus in their report state that 'The Eighth Air Force was particularly active in this work and continued it during 1944, after the bulk of the ground forces had departed for the Continent. In that year the product of combined British and American military agriculture was estimated at 50,000 ship tons.'

Once a foothold was gained in France, mobile bakeries were set up; gasoline went through PLUTO and other supplies were being delivered direct by sea to harbours in France. General Lee moved his HQ and Supply Services to France continuing to supply the needs of the American Army.

But, of course, Europe was just one war zone where American soldiers had to be supplied. The US Quartermaster Corps (and the British), were supplying its forces in other areas, including the Far East. It was a tremendous undertaking, requiring careful forward planning. Even after VE Day, they had a role to play. The official history states that 'By the spring of 1945 the Quartermaster organization in the European theater was feeding and clothing and otherwise providing necessities and comforts to more than seven and one-half million people, the largest human support operation by a single organization in all history to that time.'

---

1. Pilfering from stores being unloaded became a problem – sometimes organised to supply the Black market. It was dealt with firmly by the American and British authorities.
2. Graham bread was a wholemeal bread with a high protein content devised in the US by vegetarian Presbyterian Minister Sylvester Graham in 1829.

SOURCES

PART ONE
Extracts of Nellie Clemens' letters IWM207231.
© Linda Yerrill

PART TWO
General Information used throughout book -
   Milverton Parish Council Minute Books
   Milverton W.I. Record Books
   Milverton school logs
   Recorded interviews in 2004 with
   Mr. Ken Burston
   Mrs. Deacon,
   Mrs. Beattie Hayes,
   Mrs. Ling
   Mr. and Mrs. Ted Perry
   Mrs. Scott
   Mrs. Taylor
   Amy McGrath, Land Girl
   Pre-War Voting Register
   Kelly's Directory for Milverton 1939
   68 contemporary newspapers loaned in 2004/5
   Microfische newspapers Somerset Heritage Centre
   On-line information

Additional information relevant to each chapter:

Chapter One – Preparing for the Worst

Darlingest

Newspapers, ARP/First Aid List – Somerset Heritage Centre
Chapter Two – 'Sup Up and Clear the Cellars – War Declared
Wartime and civil defence leaflets from Imperial War Museum and Somerset Record Education material. *British Home Defences, 1940-45* by Bernard Lowry, Published, Osprey Publishing 2004

Chapter Three – Defending Milverton – Home Guard
The Home Guard, S. P. Mackenzie, OUP 1996
Somerset at War, Mac Hawkins, Hawk Editions 1996
The Somerset Home Guard, Jeffrey Wilson,
British Home Defences – Bernard Lowry, as above
David Hunt, conversations and earlier research for *Hestercombe At War*, 2007

Chapter Four – Doing Your Bit
Eve in Overalls by Arthur Wauters, IWM 2001
Observer Corps information – 'Decoys' see below Chapter 5.

Chapter Five – Military Invasion
The wartime logs of 2nd Bn. The Middlesex Regiment, W073 – National Archives W0166/4460,
Green Howards W0 166/4313/4314//4315/4316/4460/4190 NA
BEF material in appendix from various on-line sites including WW2 Talk Forum
The logs, where available of 2nd Bn. Cheshires, NA
Decoy information, SHER 44685, SHER 44535, Army Supply Depot, SHER 44543, Castlemans Hill, SHER 44684 'Somerset and Defence of the Bristol Channel' – Dawson/Hunt/Webster

Chapter Six – Gone to the Country – Evacuation
Somerset At War, Sadie Ward, as above,
County of Somerset, Government Evacuation Scheme C/CD1/6/1
County of Somerset Evacuation Scheme, Functions of the County Council,

C/CD/1/6/4 and C/CD 1 /6/5 Somerset Heritage Records
Letters and memories written by evacuees, Bruce Watkiss,
Letter to Shirley Adam from Patricia Bishopp

Chapter Seven – Doubling Up – Education
Milverton school logs
Emily Mears – Shaftesbury House School

Chapter Eight – Raising a Laugh – Entertainment
Radio Times typescript article, *Workers' Playtime*, BBC Archives
Front and first page of a *Workers' Playtime* script, from Courtaulds, Yorks – BBC Archives

Chapter Nine – Feeding the Nation
Civilian Supplies in Wartime Britain – Monica Felton, IWM 2003
Written memories provided by Mr. Godber Ford

Chapter Ten – On the Fields
War in the Countryside, Sadie Ward
The Women's Land Army 1939-1950 – Bob Powell and Nigel Westacott, Sutton Publishing, 1997
Rotations, Bulletin No. 85 Ministry of Agriculture, 1944
Interview with Land Girl, Amy McGrath
Information from local people

Chapter Eleven – Dig for Victory
Newspapers
War in the Countryside, Sadie Ward

Chapter Twelve – For Medicinal Purposes
Letter from Secretary Garden Produce Central Committee, Ministry of Agriculture and Fisheries, 17th July, 1942, INF9/1130 Somerset Heritage Centre

Chapter Thirteen – Waste Not Want Not
War in the Countryside, Sadie Ward

Chapter Fourteen – Make Do and Mend
Wartime House, 1939-45, Mike Brown & Carol Harris, Sutton Publishing, 2000
Make Do and Mend, facsimile of publication by HMSO, 1943, IWM

Chapter Fifteen – Just a Bit of Tin – Over Here
History of Milverton, Frank Farley and Don Ekless – The Milverton & Fitzhead Society, 1986.
Hestercombe at War, 2007
Department of the Army, US Army Records, QMC0-38920.3
Unit History 3892 Quartermaster Truck company, provided by Joe Tuminello
'Over Here' lecture, Derek Smith

Chapter Seventeen – Silver Linings and Dark Clouds – Post War
PRN 44674 – ROC at Somerset Heritage Centre

THOSE NAMED IN BOOK – by first mention only

ACKLAND, Mr and Mrs, Chapter 4
ACLAND, Admiral, Part 1
ALEXANDER, Dr., Introduction
AMY, Dennis, Helen Amy biography
ANDERSON, Capt. Chapter 5
ANDREWS, Bill, Chapter 6
ANDREWS, Miss Mary, Chapter 6
ANDREWS, Miss, Part 1
ARNOLD, Rita, Chapter 7
ARTHUR Joan, Chapter 16
ASH, Miss, Chapter, 13
BAKER, Joe, Chapter 10
BAKER, Mr. T. C. M, Chapter 1
BEDFORD, Mrs. Part 1,
BEVIN, Ernest, Chapter 4
BISHOPP, Pat, Chapter 6
BLACKMAN, Dr. Byram, Milverton 1939
BLACKMORE, Shelagh and Bev, Introduction
BOND, Dr. Barbara, Chapter 5
BOND, Mr. and Mrs, Chapter 6
BRACHTEL, Hans, Chapter 10
BRETT, Mike and Jane, Introduction
BROADMEAD, Mrs. Part 1
BROOKMAN, B. J. Chapter 1
BROWN, Ernest, Chapter 6
BULLER, Mr. H., Chapter 1
BUNDY, Vicky, Chapter 5
BURSTON, Ken, Chapter 2
BURSTON, Mr, W. E, Chapter 1
BURSTON, Mrs. Chapter 2

BUSH, Lt. Col. W. E., Chapter 5
BUTLER, Frank, Chapter 6
BUTLER, Miss, Chapter 7
CANN, Mr., Part 1
CANNIFORD, Mrs, Chapter 13
CASLEY, Mr. and Mrs. Chapter 6
CHAPMAN, Miss, Chapter 4
CLARKE, Jack, Chapter 8
CLEMENS, Helen, Introduction
CLEMENS, Wilfred, Biography
CLEMENTS, Miss, Chapter 7
COOPER, Mr. Chapter 6
CORNABY, Miss, Chapter 6
COTTERELL, Tom, Chapter 16
COTTON, Billy, Chapter 8
CRIDLANDS, George, Chapter 5
DAKOWSKI, Julian, Introduction
DAVIES, Mrs. Shirley, Chapter 15
DAVIS, Lavinia, Introduction
DAY, Mr. Chapter 13
DEACON, Mrs. Part 1
DEACON, Mr. Part 1
DOWN, Doreen, Chapter 16
EDMONDS, Michael, Chapter 7
EDMONDS, Mr. Cyril, Chapter 16
ELLIS, Mr. Part 1
FLEMING, Capt. Hamilton, Chapter 10
FORGAN Mrs. Nicola, Chapter 5
FORTUNE, Lindsay, Introduction
FOURACRE, John, Chapter 5
GARSIDE, Jack, Chapter 5
GIBBONS, Keith, Introduction

GIBSON, Mr. Chapter 15
GLOVER, Mr. W. F, Chapter 1
GLOVER, Mrs. Chapter 16
GODBER FORD, Mr. Chapter 9
GODBER FORD, Mrs. Sally, Chapter 17
GODBERT, Geoffrey, Introduction
GOLDSMITH, Bridget, Introduction
GOULD, Muriel, Chapter 7
GRANT, Mrs., Part 1
GRAY, Mrs. Gill, Introduction
GREEDY, Tom, Chapter 2
GREEN, Ernie, Chapter 5
GREENHOW, Chris, Introduction
GREGORY, Mrs. Chapter 4
HALL, Mr. F. W., Chapter 10
HANCOCK, Mrs. Chapter 4
HARDCRAFT, Miss, Chapter 7
HARRIS, Mr. C., Chapter 1
HAYES, Albert, Chapter 4
HAYES, Beattie, Chapter 4
HINCKS, Miss, Chapter 4
HOARE, Mr. Part 1
HOPKINS, Miss, Chapter 11
HORNER, Bill, Introduction
HOUSE, Mr. Arthur, chapter 13
HUNT, David, Introduction
HUTCHINS, Bob, Introduction
JACOBs, Mr and Mrs, Chapter 4
JENKINS, Emma and Russell, Introduction
JENKS, Mrs., Chapter 2
JENNINGS, Basil, Chapter 15
JENNINGS, Ethel, Chapter 5
JEWELL, Mr., Chapter 2
JONES, Laurence, Chapter 7
JONES, Mr. Part 1
KEATES, Jacquie, Chapter 4
KIACZ, Bruce, Chapter 15
KIACZ, John, Chapter 15
KIACZ, Steve, Chapter, 15
KICK, Mr. E. C., Chapter 1
KING, Mr. A. G. T., Chapter 1
LAMB, Mr. Chapter 7
LE CLERE, Mrs. Ann, Chapter 15
LEACH, Joan, Chapter, 16
LEE, Ernest, Chapter 2
LING, Mrs. Daisy, Chapter 5
LITTLE, Mrs. Chapter 9
LLOYD-FOX, Mrs. Chapter 6
LOCKYER, Margaret, Chapter 16
LORAM, Cyril, Chapter 3
LORAM, Mrs. Chapter 13
MACGAFFEY, Dr. Milverton 1939
MAJOR, Ben, Chapter 15
MANN, Chris, Introduction
MARSHALL, General G., Chapter 15
MAUNDERS, Ralph, Chapter 5
MAUNDERS, Thomas, Chapter 5
MAY, Kenneth, Chapter 7
MAY, Kenneth, Part 1
MAYNARD, The Rev. Part 1
McGILL, Margaret (née Loram), Chapter 3
MCGRATH, Mrs. Amy, Introduction
MCMAHON, Tony, Introduction
MEAD, Mr. and Mrs. Chapter 6
MEARS, Emily, Chapter 6
MILLAR, Miss, Chapter 14
MILLS, Miss, Chapter 6
MILLS, Miss, Part 1
MOBERLEY BELL, Lt. Col. C.V. Chapter 1
MOON, Wenda, Chapter 8
MORRIS Mr, Emlyn, Part 1
MORRISON, Herbert, Chapter 13
MUFFETT, Capt. Eric, Part 1
NUTT, Royston, Chapter 7
OATES, Mr. Chapter 15
PALMER, Rev. Part 1
PEPPERILL, Mr. and Mrs. Chapter 6

PERRY, Cyril, Chapter 4
PERRY, Percy, Chapter 4
PERRY, Sylvia, Chapter 5
PERRY, Ted, Chapter 2
PICKLES, Wilfred, Chapter 8,
PIPER, Mr. and Mrs., Chapter 6
PITT, William, Chapter 3
PLAICE, Gerald, Part 1
PRICE, Mr. Chapter 13
PRYOR, Mrs. Frances (Vera Dick), Chapter 8
PUGSLEY, Rear Admiral A. F. Pugsley, Chapter 5
RATTENBURY, Miss, Part 1
REDWOOD, Kilbourne, Chapter 15
REDWOOD, Miss, Chapter 7
REDWOOD, Mr. E., Chapter 1
ROCKETT, Betty and Joyce, Chapter 8
SCOTT, Mrs. Chapter 7
SCOTT, Mrs. Yvonne, Chapter 3
SCOTT, Mrs. Yvonne, Chapter 6
SHAPLAND, Mr, Chapter 3
SIMPSON, Mrs. Marjorie (née Sumpter), Chapter 6
SPILLER, Mrs. Part 1
SPILLER, Mrs. Part 1
SPURWAY, Richard, Chapter 15
STOCK, Brenda, Chapter 7
STONE, Mr. and Mrs. Bill, Chapter 15
STRICKLAND, Mr. Chapter 6
SUMMERFIELD, Eleanor, Chapter 8
TAYLOR, Mrs. Diane (née Rooksby), Chapter 6
THOMAS, Mr, J. Chapter 16
TOTTERDELL, Mr. and Mrs. Chapter 6
TUCKER, Barbara, Chapter 10
TUCKER, Herbert, Chapter 5
TUCKER, Jack, Chapter 5
TUCKER, Mrs. Erica, Chapter 9
TUMINELLO, Joe, Chapter 15
TUMINELLO, Vincent (Jim), Chapter 15
VAN DEN ARK (Chaplain), Chapter 15
VERNON, Miss, Chapter 6
VICKERY, Joan, Part 1
VICKERY, Miss Gertrude, Part 1,
VICKERY, Mrs. Part 1
WARD, Eva, Chapter 7
WARREN, Mr., Part 1
WATKISS, Bruce, Chapter 5
WATSON, Dr. David, Introduction
WATSON, Mr. Chapter 10
WICKHAM, Mrs. Chapter 4
WIGHT-BOYCOTT, Michael, Introduction
WILLIAMS, Barbara, Introduction
WILSON, Capt. Chapter 15
WIMBUSH, Mr., Part 1
WINTER, Alan, Chapter 5
WITHERS, Solene and Shona, Chapter 15
WOOD (née, BUCKLAND), Barbara, Chapter 6
WOODLAND, Jane, Chapter 4
WOOLTON, Lord, Chapter 9
WRIGHT, Edward, Chapter 10
WYATT, 'Squeaker', Mr. Chapter 3
YERRILL, Linda Nellie Clemens Biography
YESFORD, Olive, Chapter 4